Mastering
Exchange Traded
Equity Derivatives

market editions

Mastering Exchange Traded Equity Derivatives

A step-by-step guide to the markets, applications and risks

DAVID FORD

FINANCIAL TIMES
PITMAN PUBLISHING

FINANCIAL TIMES
MANAGEMENT
LONDON · SAN FRANCISCO
KUALA LUMPUR · JOHANNESBURG

*Financial Times Management delivers the knowledge,
skills and understanding that enable students,
managers and organisations to achieve their ambitions,
whatever their needs, wherever they are.*

London Office:
128 Long Acre, London WC2E 9AN
Tel: +44 (0)171 447 2000
Fax: +44 (0)171 240 5771
Website: www.ftmanagement.com

A Division of Financial Times Professional Limited

First published in Great Britain 1997

© Pearson Professional Limited 1997

The right of David Ford to be identified as author
of this work has been asserted by him in accordance
with the Copyright, Designs, and Patents Act 1988.

ISBN 0 273 61974 8

British Library Cataloguing in Publication Data
A CIP catalogue record for this book can be obtained from the British Library.

All rights reserved; no part of this publication may be reproduced, stored
in a retrieval system, or transmitted in any form or by any means, electronic,
mechanical, photocopying, recording, or otherwise without either the prior
written permission of the Publishers or a licence permitting restricted copying
in the United Kingdom issued by the Copyright Licensing Agency Ltd,
90 Tottenham Court Road, London W1P 0LP. This book may not be lent,
resold, hired out or otherwise disposed of by way of trade in any form
of binding or cover other than that in which it is published, without the
prior consent of the Publishers.

10 9 8 7 6 5 4 3 2

Typeset by Pantek Arts, Maidstone, Kent.
Printed and bound in Great Britain by Bell and Bain Ltd, Glasgow.

The Publishers' policy is to use paper manufactured from sustainable forests.

About the Author

David Ford is a professionally qualified and experienced training consultant. After serving ten years in the Army, seeing active service in the Falklands campaign, he joined the London Stock Exchange in 1987. He was responsible for the regulation of trading on the London Traded Options Market, and also for training and development of Exchange staff and trainee traders. He organized and lectured on traded options to both market professionals and private investors on behalf of the London Traded Options Market, Chicago Mercantile Exchange (Europe), The City University Business School and the London Stock Exchange.

CONTENTS

Introduction	ix
Acknowledgements	xiii

1 The Market Place – Background and History — 1

History of futures and options	2
London Traded Options Market (LTOM)	4
Merger of LTOM and LIFFE	6
How OMLX came to London	7

2 Market Structure — 13

Introduction	14
London International Financial Futures and Options Exchange (LIFFE)	15
London Securities and Derivatives Exchange (OMLX)	20
Regulation of the industry	22
Compliance – *Mark Satterthwaite, ED&F Mann Ltd*	28
The Securities and Futures Authority – *David Jones, SFA*	36

3 Trading and Clearing — 41

Introduction	42
Open outcry versus screen-based trading –	
Andrew Reierson, financial journalist	52
FT-SE 100 futures trading	57
OMLX	70
Product development – *Julian Perrins, OMLX*	75
Marketing and promotional support –	
Tony Hawes, Equity Products, LIFFE	82
Clearing and settlement –	
Jacqueline Totley, Monument Derivatives Ltd	88

Contents

4 Basic Characteristics of Options and Futures — 99

Introduction — 100
Traded options — 100
What is a futures contract? — 106
Option pricing — 110
Basic trades — 126
Futures trades — 149
Flex options — 152
Index traded options — 156

5 Uses and Benefits of Index and Equity Derivatives — 165

Introduction — 166
Risk — 166
Portfolio protection — 168
Asset allocation — 173
Performance enhancement — 176
Anticipatory hedging — 180
Cash flow management – buy write — 181

6 Important Guidelines — 185

Check list for fund managers — 186
Corporate events — 189
Trading rules/guidelines — 192
Taxation of options for private investors — 194
The regulation and taxation of futures and options in
   UK funds — 195
Barings — 203

Appendices — 209

1 Derivative instruments: risk disclosure statement — 211
2 IMRO notice to members – the use of index derivatives
   for efficient portfolio management — 217
3 The Inland Revenue Statement of Practice SP14/91 — 220
4 LIFFE index and equity futures and options — 226
5 Contract specifications — 228

Glossary — 229

Index — 235

INTRODUCTION

The recent publicity given to a small number of derivative trades has meant that derivatives have rarely been out of the media's attention for long. Unfortunately, the majority of media attention has been for the wrong reasons, for while a small number of derivative trades have gone wrong, with disastrous consequences, the vast majority of derivative users undoubtably achieve their desired results – whether that is hedging, portfolio enhancement, speculation or arbitrage. The incorrect use of derivatives, whether through inadequate management controls or insufficient understanding of the instruments, can lead to highly expensive and damaging losses – Orange County and Barings Bank to name but two.

While all forms of financial instruments carry some degree or other of risk, the media coverage given to derivative losses in the past does tend to indicate that the risks with derivatives are out of all proportion to the rewards on offer. While this may appear so to the person in the street with little or no knowledge of derivatives, it is obvious from the large and increasing number of financial institutions and individuals in the derivative markets that this is not the case. If the risks did outweigh the rewards, no one in their right mind would be willing to use the markets.

Given that the risks do not outweigh the advantages and rewards, what are derivatives, and how and why are they used by large institutions and individual investors alike?

First, derivatives are financial instruments that obtain their price and therefore their value from another financial instrument, the underlying security. Thus the price of a futures contract on the German Government Bond derives its price and value from the spot price of the corresponding German Government Bond. In addition, the term **derivative** is a catch-all phrase that includes such financial instruments as swaps, options, futures, forwards and warrants on such underlying securities as interest rates and foreign exchange rates, equities and various indices, to name just a few.

Introduction

Not only are derivatives available on a wide and ever-increasing range of underlying securities, they can be traded on either recognized investment exchanges, under their rules and regulations, or off-exchange, i.e. directly between institutions such as banks and security houses. These off-exchange trades are known as **over-the-counter (OTC) trades**. Such a "mix and match" form of investment can and does lead to a number of incorrect stories and ideas.

So what are derivatives? how are they traded? who uses them? and for what purpose are they used? These are just some of the questions this book attempts to answer by looking at just one specific area of derivatives – index and equity futures and options.

While futures and options are not suitable for every investor they can be tailored to suit most users' risk profiles. They can be used to enhance the returns of either an existing individual holding or portfolio, or used to adjust the purchase or sale price of a future transaction. They can be used as a form of insurance – hedging – again for either an individual holding or an entire portfolio to counter an adverse price movement. Finally, and possibly the most common form of their use by private investors is for speculative purposes – taking a geared view on the direction of price movements.

Index and equity futures and options are far more commonly used than most people think, the main users being pension and unit trust fund managers. They are used to either enhance the returns of a portfolio or an individual position, or to insure the portfolio's value against an adverse price movement in the underlying securities.

A thorough understanding of and an ability to use futures and options should be a prerequisite for all professional and private investors alike. Knowing how futures and options work, both in theory and practice, is not enough for serious investors: they should also have an understanding of how the instruments are traded, the flow of information to and from the market and the surveillance systems in the market place. Armed with this information and understanding, the investor will appreciate the need for timely and precise information and decision-making.

This book is divided into six chapters, taking the reader from the history and background of index and equity futures and options, through the different markets, their organization and management structures, to their different methods of trading, the basics of futures and options and on to their uses both inside and outside of portfolio management for private and professional investors alike. A number of the topics are explained in greater detail, giving an in-depth look at the workings of various sections of the market, by market practitioners. Regulation of the market is explained from the point of view of both the Securities and Futures Authority (SFA) and a Compliance Officer responsible for the regulation of a member firm of LIFFE. Other topics covered by market professionals include product development, settlement, marketing and a comparison of open outcry trading versus screen-based trading.

This book is not mathematical, and uses as little jargon as possible for a number of reasons. First, there are already a considerable number of in-depth mathematical-jargon-riddled books available on the subject and secondly, and possibly more importantly, when trying to acquire basic knowledge and experience, maths is the last thing an investor or a student needs to get bogged down in.

The subject of derivatives is one of the most dynamic of all investment areas and is constantly changing. It is therefore necessary for all those involved in finance and investment to keep abreast of the changes and developments within the derivative markets. The *Financial Times* not only publishes the prices of a large number of derivatives traded around the world, but also has a regular column covering developments within the derivatives markets.

ACKNOWLEDGEMENTS

I would like to acknowledge and thank all those people who have helped and contributed their time, articles and support to this book. In particular I would like to thank:

    Julian Perrins – OMLX

    Tony Hawes – LIFFE

    David Jones – SFA

    Andrew Reierson – financial journalist

    Mark Satterthwaite – ED&F Mann Ltd

    Jackie Totley – Monument Derivatives Ltd

for their contributions and help.

In addition, I would like to thank the following organizations for allowing various articles to be reproduced:

    London International Financial Futures and Options Exchange

    Investment Management Regulatory Organization Ltd

    The Inland Revenue.

I would finally like to thank all those at Pitman Publishing involved with this book for their patience and encouragement.

■ ■ ■

'To many, derivatives are a recent addition to the investment world, dreamt up by "rocket scientists", extremely complicated and extremely dangerous to their financial health. Nothing could be further from the truth.'

The Market Place – Background and History

History of futures and options

London Traded Options Market (LTOM)

Merger of LTOM and LIFFE

How OMLX came to London

History of futures and options

To most investors, both private and professional, derivatives are recent additions to the investment world, dreamt up by "rocket scientists," extremely complicated and extremely dangerous to their financial health. However, as we shall see, nothing could be further from the truth.

Far from being new additions to the investment world, references to options being taken out on olive presses in ancient Greek times have been found in history books. References have also been found to option trading in Spanish metals, particularly silver, in Roman documents. In the early 1600s an advanced and sophisticated rice exchange was established in the Japanese port of Osaka which was known as the Dojima Rice Market and is often called the first organized futures exchange. It was officially recognized by the Japanese Imperial Government in 1730.

The first centralized commodities market in Britain was founded in the 1560s in the Royal Exchange (later to become the first home of the London International Financial Futures Exchange). Unfortunately the Royal Exchange was destroyed by the Great Fire of London in 1666, although trading continued in the various coffee houses that were springing up in the City of London at the time. Eventually each coffee house started to specialize in one particular product: the London Commodity Exchange in the Virginian and Baltic coffee houses: the London Metal Exchange in Jerusalem and the London Stock Exchange in Jonathans. At the same time there was an options market in Holland at the Amsterdam Trade Centre based on tulips. Unfortunately the speculative use of these options brought about the collapse of the Dutch economy.

> **The first centralized commodities market in Britain was founded in the 1560s in the Royal Exchange**

Organized futures markets as we know them today really developed in the last century, primarily in the US, when the Chicago Board of Trade (CBOT) was established in 1848. At that time Chicago was not only at the center of the railroads; it was also an important port on the great lakes and close to the midwest farmlands. With Chicago being such an important center for agricultural markets the CBOT was established to provide farmers with a central market place to guarantee the prices for their livestock and grain.

These early futures contracts were known as "to-arrive contracts" which allowed farmers and agricultural buyers to specify the delivery details of a commodity. While they may have been introduced by the farmers and the agricultural merchants to manage the fluctuation in farming due to weather and supply and demand, they soon began to be used for speculative purposes, and the one thing the speculators brought to the markets was liquidity.

Jumping forward to the 1960s, Chicago Mercantile Exchange (CME), which had grown out of the Chicago Butter and Egg Board of the late 1890s, introduced the pork bellies futures contract. The contract is based on frozen slabs of uncured, unsliced bacon, and has become one of the world's most successful futures contracts. With the demise of the Bretton Woods Agreement in 1972, which until then had limited the fluctuation of the US dollar and other major currencies, a need was identified for financial futures contracts (more recently the terminal within the European Exchange Rate Mechanism has given financial futures a further boost). In response to this need for financial futures, the CME established the International Monetary Market (IMM) as a division of the CME to trade financial futures. With the introduction of financial futures and options, the derivatives markets started their rapid expansion. This expansion, which in some markets and products borders on an explosion, continues today as new products, trading methods and exchanges are introduced the world over. In part the expansion has been the result of increased sophistication among all types of investors, the advent of personal computers and the globalization of financial markets with improved communications.

Of all the developments since the introduction of futures and options, the most significant step forward of all was in 1973 when the Chicago Board Options Exchange (CBOE) introduced standardized contracts and a Clearing House. Until the introduction of the standard contract, each trade was separately negotiated between the two parties concerned; details such as the quantity and price of the underlying instrument; the exercise price of the options or futures contract and the expiry date. However, the standardized contract detailed exactly what and how much was being traded, the duration of the contract and the quality of the underlying instrument and could not be varied by the traders. There are many advantages to standardized contracts including the fact that they allow dealings to be centralized and speed up the process of trading.

> Once a trade has taken place and has been cleared and registered, the Clearing House steps in, breaking the link between the buyer and seller, ultimately becoming the counterparty to the trades itself.

The Clearing House was introduced to serve as the ultimate counterparty to all trades, allowing contracts to be opened and closed with different counterparties. Once a trade has taken place and has been cleared and registered, the Clearing House steps in, breaking the link between the buyer and seller, ultimately becoming the counterparty to the trades itself. This means that the buyer has bought from the Clearing House and the seller has sold to the Clearing House. The introduction of exchange-traded contracts provided the investor with three major benefits:

1. Ease of trading
A central market place means that contracts may be more easily traded and liquidity concentrated in one place. This is a significant advantage compared to when they could only be traded over the counter and buyers and sellers had to be individually matched.

2. Secondary market
The establishment of a secondary market allows buyers and sellers to trade out of their positions at a profit, or at least at a reduced loss, without having to trade with their original counterparty. The original counterparty, knowing their position, may not be prepared to trade at a fair price.

3. Counterparty risk
The introduction of a Clearing House ensures that investors are not exposed to counterparty credit risk and should anyone, be it a market professional or a private investor, default on their contractual obligation, the Clearing House will ensure that all users of the market are safeguarded against any loss.

London Traded Options Market (LTOM)

In 1978, after much opposition from some of the City of London's old establishment, the London Stock Exchange introduced the London Traded Options Market (LTOM) to trade UK equity options. In 1978 LTOM became one of only two options markets outside the US. Today, virtually every European country has its own futures and options market with many more planning to introduce their own in the near future. Much of the early opposition was unjust and ill-informed, especially after the success of the CBOE in the US. (Unfortunately most of the present-day criticism of derivatives is just as ill-informed as in 1978.) The market got off to a relatively slow start, due to a number of factors including: a new market with a new product; the small number of stocks with options available on them; a lack of training and education and a lack of commitment by the London Stock Exchange. It has been suggested in more recent years, that the only reason the Exchange listed traded options in the first place was to keep control over UK equity products and to stop any other exchange from taking the lead.

When opened, LTOM initially traded only call options on just ten stocks. It was not until 1981 that put options were introduced and even then not on all the option stocks available. The market grew steadily as both knowledge and experience spread, and by March 1982 over a million contracts had changed hands, which in money terms represented over £200 million. This growth was also helped by the steady rise in the stock market. Put options, first introduced in May 1981, were finally introduced on all stocks two years later in 1983.

In the same year it was recognized that the then market indices (FT All Share and the FT-SE 30), being updated only at the end of the each trading day, were not suitable for the trading of futures and options contracts and so the London Stock Exchange, in conjunction with the *Financial Times*, started work on a new index. This was to become the FT-SE 100 (known as the Footsie) and was introduced in January 1984. New futures and options contracts were introduced to LTOM (options), and the London International Financial Futures Exchange (futures), markets, with the introduction of the FT-SE 100 Index. Being updated on a minute-by-minute basis, the FT-SE 100 allows investors to take advantage of movements in the market as a whole and thereby manage market or non-specific risk as opposed to stock-specific risk with individual stock options.

During 1987 more option contracts were traded on LTOM in a single year than in all the previous nine years combined. Unfortunately the crash of October 1987 hit investors' confidence

> **During 1987 more option contracts were traded on LTOM in a single year than in all the previous nine years combined.**

hard, not just in traded options but in the stock market in general, and volumes suffered accordingly. While the UK was not the only market to suffer as a result of the crash, recovery in the UK stock market, and hence traded options, has taken longer than in other markets like the US or the Netherlands. Nevertheless, further equity contracts have been introduced, as interest in the options market has grown.

Merger of LTOM and LIFFE

In 1990 it was announced that LTOM and the London International Financial Futures Exchange (LIFFE) would merge into a single futures and options market.

LIFFE (pronounced "life") was established in 1982 to trade futures and options on financial products, the need for which had been brought about by the ever-increasing volatility in the foreign exchange markets. This volatility was in response to the collapse, in 1972, of the Bretton Woods Agreement on exchange rates and more recently the turmoil within Europe and the ERM. Since its opening, when it initially traded only two futures contracts, LIFFE has managed to develop into the largest and most actively traded futures and options market in Europe and the third largest in the world.

The merger between LIFFE and LTOM, with the new market being known as the London International Financial Futures and Options Exchange (LIFFE), easily consolidated LIFFE's position in European and world rankings. The new market has proved to be so successful that in 1992 it had to move to larger and more up-to-date premises at Cannon Bridge, with a purpose-built trading floor of over 31,000 square feet in total. The market now trades over 17 fixed-interest and money market futures and options (which represents the most comprehensive range of financial futures and options traded on a single exchange, in the world), as well as 72 equity options and four FT-SE index contracts. These contracts fall into three categories:

- Short-term interest rates
- Long- and medium-term Government Bonds
- Index and equity products

Short-term interest rates

- Three-month Sterling + ^
- Three-month Eurodollar + ^
- Three-month Euromark + ^
- Three-month EuroSwiss + ^
- Three-month Eurolira +
- Three-month ECU +

Long- and medium-term Government Bonds

- Long Gilt + ^
- German Government Bond (Bund) + ^
- Italian Government Bond +
- Japanese Government Bond + ^

Index and equity products

- FT-SE 100 + ^ #
- FT-SE 250 +
- Individual Equity Options ^

Key
+ Futures

^ Options

Flex option

Since the merger LIFFE has continued to expand and develop the equity side of the exchange, introducing new contracts, an auto-quote system, which automatically displays the options' theoretical fair value, the introduction option prices on to CEEFAX and a range of new educational materials.

How OMLX came to London

While LIFFE is the best-known equity and index derivatives exchange in London, it is by no means the only one. The second and much smaller London index and equity derivatives exchange, in terms of area but not importance, is OMLX: the London Securities and Derivatives Exchange. OMLX was initially established as OM London (OML) in December 1989 as a wholly owned subsidiary of the Swedish option market, OM Stockholm (OMS), which was itself established in 1985. The introduction of a Turnover Tax on equities and bonds by the Swedish Treasury resulted in as much as 40 percent of Swedish stock and bond trading going overseas to London. When it was announced that a similar tax was to be introduced on derivative trading, OM Stockholm decided to learn from the example of the equity market and set up a marketplace for Swedish derivatives in London. The result of this innovative response to the Turnover Tax was the creation of OM London. Although the products traded on OML were based on the shares of Swedish companies, because the exchange was offshore to Swedish investors they were exempt from the Turnover Tax.

In order to facilitate the trading of the same instrument in two separate locations, an electronic link was established between London and Stockholm, enabling both orders and price information to be relayed from one to the other. Initially OML was the identical twin of OM Stockholm, with its product range, rule book and procedures all being brought over from Sweden and adopted *en masse* in London. In addition, most members of staff were Swedish, having gained their experience of the market in Stockholm. The success of the exchange has attracted a number of international trading companies. At the end of the first year just over half the members were Nordic-owned or -based, but by 1994 just under a quarter of the exchange's 99 members fell into this category.

In 1991 OML and OM Stockholm introduced "CLICK" trading, a screen-based, computerized trading system. The exchange is the only derivatives exchange in London, to date, to have a fully automated trading system, which means there is no need for a trading floor as such, as the traders remain in their own offices, linked to the exchange by a telephone line and computer. However, the main advantages of the system are that the prices displayed are firm dealing prices and not indicative ones as with an open outcry system and also a short response time when introducing new products and services.

In late 1990 the Swedish government realized that its Turnover Tax, designed to raise additional funds, was having the opposite effect and driving investment business overseas, so in 1991 the tax was halved and completely abolished in 1992. This meant that the main reason for the existence of OML had disappeared.

While the abolishment of the Turnover Tax could have resulted in closure of OML, it was decided to turn the exchange into an international derivatives exchange based in London. This has resulted in the introduction of new products and the forging of new alliances. Unfortunately, not all of the new products have been as successful as the exchange would have liked, but OMLX has not been deterred and continues to be a forward-looking and an innovative exchange.

While the US has played a leading role in the development and organization of futures and options markets, it should not be forgotten that London is also a world financial centre for derivative trading. In total, London has five futures and options exchanges and markets. Not only is there LIFFE and OMLX but the list includes the London Commodity Exchange (LCE) trading contracts on "softs," i.e. sugar, potatoes and other agricultural products; a freight index, the London International Petroleum Exchange (IPE) dealing in crude oil and associated products and the London Metal Exchange dealing in forwards and options on a range of base metals. Together the five exchanges and markets provide facilities for trading over 60 different contracts, the most diverse outside of the United States, in addition to the 72 equity traded options available on LIFFE and the 24 futures and option contracts on the OMLX.

The reasons for the success of the different derivative markets around the world are many and varied. However, one of the main reasons must surely be that, apart from acting as any other market place and bringing people, in this case investors, together in order to trade they allow for the effective management of risk. The users of the markets fall into three distinct groups: hedgers, speculators and arbitrageurs.

1. Hedgers

For one reason or another, hedges are unwilling to accept risk, and transfer it to speculators, who are willing and able to assume it.

2. Speculators

In return for accepting risk, the speculators are looking for high returns.

3. Arbitrageurs

Arbitrageurs are trying to buy and sell the same instrument on two different markets, taking advantage of pricing anomalies in order to lock in a risk-free profit.

While it is the exchange that brings the three groups of users together, it is not the role of the exchange to establish market prices or trade any of the contracts traded on the market, that is the role of the market traders. The role of the exchange is to act as a centralized, structured and coordinated location for the conduct of investment business. In addition it will set and enforce trading and conduct of business rules as well as collecting and disseminating trading information.

> *'The role of the exchange is to act as a centralized, structured and coordinated location for the conduct of investment business.'*

Market Structure

Introduction

London International Financial Futures and Options Exchange (LIFFE)

London Securities and Derivatives Exchange (OMLX)

Regulation of the industry

Compliance – Mark Satterthwaite, ED&F Mann Ltd

The Securities and Futures Authority – David Jones, SFA

Introduction

Until recently the accepted structure for derivative exchanges was based around the open outcry trading system used by the well-established US exchanges. This system includes a separate Clearing House and also means that there are a number of interested parties in the structure of the market place in general. First, there is the exchange itself. The role of the exchange is to act as a centralized, structured and coordinated location for the conduct of investment business.

In addition, it will set and enforce trading and conduct of business rules on its members as well as collecting and disseminating trading information. The exchange is normally owned by its members who are also the traders on the market. They are governed by a board of directors elected by the exchange's membership and administered by executive staff on behalf of the members. The exchange is not usually a profit-making organization and in the event of a profit being made will redistribute it among the member firms in proportion to the amount of business conducted during the year.

> **The exchange is not usually a profit-making organization and in the event of a profit being made will redistribute it among the member firms in proportion to the amount of business conducted during the year.**

The second interested party is the Clearing House which works with and alongside the exchange to register all trades, as well as being responsible for the exercise and assignments of the exchange's contracts, while at the same time facilitating payments from the various traders and investors.

Third on the list are the investors and traders who use the market and its products. They can be classified into three groups depending on their use of the products: speculators who are willing and able to assume risk and therefore increase their potential returns if they are proved right; hedgers who, for whatever reason, are risk averse and are trying to reduce their exposure to it; and finally arbitrageurs who try to take advantage of anomalies in the pricing of two identical instruments, sometimes traded on separate exchanges, to lock in a risk-free profit.

Overseeing the three groups mentioned so far is a regulatory body. In the UK this involves two separate bodies, the Securities and

Investment Board (SIB) and the Securities and Futures Authority (SFA). The SIB is responsible for the exchange and its functions as a Recognized Investment Exchange and the SFA looks after the traders and the investors.

London International Financial Futures and Options Exchange (LIFFE)

Introduction

The London International Financial Futures and Options Exchange is a conventionally organized exchange, run along the lines already described in Chapter 1. It is run and managed by LIFFE Administration and Management, an unlimited company which, in itself, is a wholly owned subsidiary of LIFFE (Holdings) plc, the group holding company. LIFFE (Holdings) plc is in turn owned by its members, the firms who, in one way or another, trade on the market floor or have an interest in the exchange.

The membership is made up of approximately 200 of the world's leading banks and securities houses, consisting of UK 30 percent, US 21 percent, European (ex UK) 23 percent, Japanese 21 percent and others 5 percent.

> **Definition**
>
> *The exchange operates on a "seat" system, with each "seat" being the equivalent of a share in the holding company, entitling the holder to one or more market traders on the market floor. Any organization or individual wishing to trade on the market floor of LIFFE must hold a seat or share in LIFFE (Holdings) plc or, alternatively they may become an associated member of the exchange by leasing the trading rights associated with a seat from a holder who does not wish to trade on the market floor.*

The seats on LIFFE are constantly being bought or sold at a cost of several hundred thousand pounds, the actual price depending very heavily on the prevailing trading volumes on the market. However, unlike shares in a company, to hold a seat, or lease the trading rights of a seat for LIFFE, an individual or a company must not only have the necessary funds to purchase the seat, but they must also meet certain other qualifications. These are:

- a sound business reputation;
- the experience and qualification of their trader(s) must be relevant and sufficient;
- ability to meet the financial requirements of the board of LIFFE;
- as a member, to comply with the rules of the appropriate regulatory body.

If, for whatever reason, any member is unable to satisfy any of the criteria at any time, their membership could, and indeed would, be withdrawn.

While all owners of a seat are exchange members, they are not necessarily members of the Clearing House. Those exchange members who are not also members of the Clearing House must have an agreement with a Clearing House member in order to have their trades cleared and registered.

Trading permits

Attached to each seat is a trading permit. The permit allows the holder one trader on the market at any one time in the contracts that the permit relates to. There are at present five types or classes of permits, each allowing the holder to trade off a different range of products. The seats and permits are "A", "B", "C", "D" and "E" shares.

"A" shares

An "A" share entitles the member firm or holder to register up to three qualified traders. However, only one of these traders is allowed to trade at any one time. The "A" share covers all financial futures as well as the FT-SE 100 and 250 futures contracts traded on LIFFE. Holders of "A" shares are Futures Members.

"B" shares

"B" shareholders are able to register up to two qualified traders, but again only one is allowed to trade on the market at any one time. "B" shares cover financial options, that is, options whose underlying security is a financial future.

"C" shares

Holders of a "C" share can register any number of qualified traders, but they can only trade in a limited number of futures contracts.

"D" shares

"D" shareholders are for equity option traders. Again, the organization must register their qualified traders and they are only permitted to trade in the 72 equity options and two FT-SE 100 Index option contracts.

"E" shares

Due to the success of LIFFE and its products, there has been increased pressure, not just on the traders but also on the resources of LIFFE. To help overcome this and to help finance future expansion, LIFFE have issued "E" shares which allow organizations to register any number of qualified traders but restricts their trading to a nominated number of products.

Board of directors

LIFFE is managed, or as it refers to it, governed, by a board of directors drawn from, and elected by, market participants. This does not mean to say that the directors must work directly on the market floor, but that they and/or their organizations must hold seats and be directly involved with futures and/or options. The normal length of service for a director is three years, although they can serve for longer if successfully re-elected. On an annual basis a chairman and deputy chairman are elected by the board.

The operations and development of LIFFE are looked after by a number of committees which are all practitioner-based. This ensures that all new systems and products developed for the market meet with the end-users' approval before any costly mistakes are made. Each committee reports in turn to the main board. The committees are made up of the following:

1. Membership and rules committee. Setting and reviewing membership criteria and rules.
2. Floor committee. Responsible for advising on the physical layout of the market floor together with trade-related facilities. It will also review floor-trading procedures.

3. Automated trading committee. Supports and advises on the exchange's Automated Pit Trading (APT).
4. Equity markets committee. Specializing in the equity and index markets.
5. Default committee. Responsible for the actions taken should a member firm default on its financial commitments.

Market regulation

Under the UK Financial Services Act, LIFFE, as a Recognized Investment Exchange (RIE), is required to maintain an orderly and fair market. To achieve this, LIFFE has introduced a multi-level system to monitor and supervise member firms and their trading activities on the market.

> **Definition**
>
> *Trading on the market floor is regulated by exchange officials known as **"pit observers."** Their role is to oversee trading in order to ensure compliance with the rules and regulations of the exchange and to communicate trade price information to price reporters who enter the details into the exchange systems.*

Their duties for the contracts they are in charge of include:
- ensuring an orderly market;
- calling trading halts;
- calling a fast market;
- monitoring attendance of market makers;
- accepting and trading Public Limit Orders.

Pit observers have the right and the powers to fine traders for minor breaches of the rules and regulations.

Market supervision

While the first line of regulation is the responsibility of the pit observers, it is not only their job to supervise the trading activities of the member firms on the market, the main responsibility also lies with the Market Supervision Department (MSD). The main aim of

MSD is to prevent incidents arising by monitoring and consulting with member firms. To achieve this MSD works closely with other departments within the exchange as well as SIB, SFA and LCH and is organized into three units: Compliance and Audit; Market Surveillance and Trading Surveillance.

Compliance and Audit

The Compliance and Audit team is responsible for detailed visits to member firms' offices. In particular they will look at how the firm conducts the day-to-day administration of its business, control and procedures.

Market Surveillance

The Market Surveillance unit is responsible for the integrity of both the market and the individual contracts. It achieves this by routine maintenance and event-specific actions. The routine maintenance includes the daily calculation of open interest, setting margin levels in conjunction with the London Clearing House (LCH), monitoring the price movements in the underlying securities and assets; and establishing the Exchange Delivery Settlement Price (EDSP).

For event-specific activities, the unit will respond to corporate events for equity-based products, reviews, on a by-member and a by-contract basis, all trading and monitors intraday volatility for margin purposes.

Trading Surveillance

The Trading Surveillance team is responsible for the trading integrity of the market and will help member firms and individual traders with interpreting the rules and regulations of the market. It will also identify and deal with any suspected abuse of the market whether identified by pit observers, other market users or the team itself. All trading pits on the market are subject to audio and video surveillance to help cut down and prevent trading disputes and abuse of trading rules. This, together with the recording of all telephone lines to the market, provides the Market Surveillance team with a comprehensive range of information with which to conduct any investigation.

Reports on any investigations conducted by the Market Surveillance team are submitted to a panel of senior practitioners who have the power to punish misconduct if and when identified.

London Securities and Derivatives Exchange (OMLX)

Introduction

OMLX is London's first, and to date, only derivatives exchange operating a fully computerized electronic trading system. Its real-time electronic link with OM Stockholm was the first example of two exchanges linking both their products and trading systems, which when combined produces the fourth largest derivatives exchange in Europe. OMLX is also unique in that it operates with an integrated trading and clearing system.

OMLX is part of the OM Group which is a publicly listed company in Stockholm, Sweden and is therefore not a member/committee driven exchange in the way LIFFE and the majority of other exchanges are. It is a profit-motivated company with shareholders and a board of directors accountable to them. This system does mean that it can react quickly to market demands and developments without having to enter into what can be lengthy and long drawn-out committee procedures.

Membership

There are just two types or categories of membership of OMLX: General Clearing Members (GCMs) and Exchange Members (EMs).

General Clearing Members have the right to clear all their own trading accounts, all their customers' trading accounts and trades conducted by other exchange members.

Exchange Members on the other hand have the right to clear all their own accounts trades, and the trading accounts of their clients.

The difference between the two categories of membership is that Exchange Members are only allowed to clear trades for themselves and their clients, whereas General Clearing Members are allowed to clear trades for any member as long as an agreement is in place between the two parties and the exchange.

Financial requirements

In recognition of the different responsibilities of the two categories of exchange membership, each has financial requirements to reflect the varying degrees of financial risk likely to be incurred by themselves or the exchange.

General Clearing Members must be able to demonstrate and maintain minimum net current assets of £2 million and have a minimum issued and fully paid-up share capital of £1 million. To be an Exchange Member, they must demonstrate and maintain a minimum net current asset value of £1 million with a minimum issued and fully paid-up share capital of £500,000. However, where an Exchange Member has an agreement with a General Clearing Member OMLX waives both the minimum net current asset requirement and the minimum issued and fully paid-up share capital. This acknowledges the fact that the Exchange Member will not maintain any positions directly with the exchange. The General Clearing Member is required to ensure that the Exchange Member has the financial backing to meet any possible requirements as it, the GCM, will be responsible for the Exchange Member's positions.

Apart from the financial requirements, there are no other membership costs involved with membership of OMLX in the way of either initial membership or annual fees. OMLX makes its revenue from levying transaction or clearing fees. These fees are calculated as a percentage of the premium and have a fixed minimum and maximum rate. Market makers are charged a separate and lower fee than brokers in recognition of their increased commitments.

However, for those members who use the electronic "CLICK" trading system, there is a connection fee for access to the trading network, OMnet, in addition to a licence fee for using the CLICK software.

OMLX member firms are allowed to have any number of traders accessing the system to trade, with no restrictions other than that all traders must be qualified and authorized by the SFA, or the appropriate overseas body.

Management structure

With OMLX being part of the publicly quoted company OM Group, which itself is managed by a board of directors, so OMLX has its own board of directors made up of six of the top managers from within the exchange. The OMLX board is in turn advised by the Market Advisory Board made up of senior market practitioners.

While OMLX does not have the same structure or number of member committees that LIFFE has, it is a customer-driven exchange and is responsive to its members' needs. In response to its members' needs, OMLX has a number of forums to address topics of importance to its members. These forums include a market-making forum, a technology forum and a clearing forum, all designed to address matters of importance and interest to the market practitioners.

Market regulation

Even with OMLX being a computerized electronic exchange, there is still a need for market supervision. To this end, OMLX maintains a fair and orderly market and encourages high standards of integrity and dealing.

Exchange market staff are divided into two groups. The first are responsible for monitoring the dealing screens of the different contracts. Their role is very similar to that of the pit observers on LIFFE.

The second group of exchange staff are responsible for helping member firms with any dealing queries that may arise with the CLICK dealing system.

In addition to the market "floor" staff, OMLX also has its equivalent of LIFFE's MSD, who also visit the member firms themselves to monitor their in-house management procedures and regulations. If, for whatever reason, any discrepancies are found, they have the power to suspend the membership of the exchange of the firm where such discrepancies may be discovered.

Regulation of the industry

Introduction

In 1984, a report on investor protection by Professor Gower (the Gower Report) recommended self-regulation for the industry and ultimately led to the 1986 Financial Services Act. The report recommended the establishment of a register for investment advisors, categorized by the type of business, an insurance scheme to protect investors' money and approval of all advertising and promotional material.

Securities and Investment Board (SIB)

The powers of the FSA have been delegated by the government and the Treasury to a number of agencies, the first and main body is the **Securities and Investment Board (SIB)**. The board or governing

2 · Market Structure

body of the SIB is appointed jointly by the Treasury and the Governor of the Bank of England. The SIB in turn has delegated some of its powers to four Self-Regulatory Organizations (SROs) and to Recognized Investment Exchanges (RE) as illustrated in Figure 2.1.

The four SROs which cover all aspects of investment within the UK are:

- **The Securities and Futures Authority (SFA).** Firms involved in the securities industry, futures and options.
- **The Investment Management Regulatory Organization (IMRO).** Firms whose main business is fund management, i.e. pension funds, investment trusts and unit trusts.
- **The Financial Intermediaries, Managers and Brokers Regulatory Association (FIMBRA).** Independent intermediaries giving advice on, and arranging deals in, unit trusts and life assurance.
- **The Life Assurance and Unit Trust Regulation Organization (LAUTRO).** Firms marketing life assurance and unit trusts.

At present FIMBRA and LAUTRO are in the process of being replaced by a new combined SRO known as the **Personal Investment Authority (PIA)**. The PIA will be responsible for the areas covered previously by both FIMBRA and LAUTRO, i.e.

FSA Power delegation

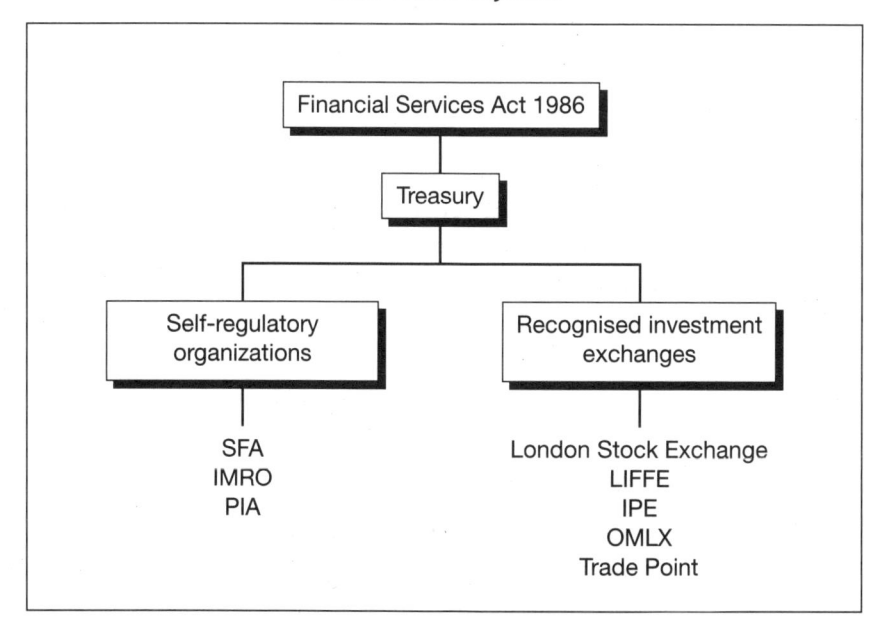

Fig 2.1

```
              Financial Services Act 1986
                          |
                       Treasury
                          |
           ---------------------------------
           |                               |
   Self-regulatory              Recognised investment
   organizations                     exchanges
           |                               |
         SFA                     London Stock Exchange
         IMRO                            LIFFE
         PIA                              IPE
                                         OMLX
                                      Trade Point
```

advising on and arranging deals for private investors in unit trusts and life assurance.

The SIB has the authority and the powers to refuse the recognition of an SRO if the SIB feels there is an overlap of interests (i.e. LAUTRO and FIMBRA). An SRO is only allowed to oversee business in respect of the type of business for which it is recognized. Consequently the SROs' members can only conduct the type of investment business that the SRO is recognized for. If a firm wishes to conduct a number of different types of investment businesses, covered by more than one SRO, it must join the appropriate SRO(s).

The SIB works on a system incorporating a three-tier structure. Its rule book makes provision for:

- Ten general principals, written by the SIB but applicable to all SROs.
- Approximately 40 core rules, written by the SIB in consultation with the SROs. They are also applicable to all SROs.
- Detailed rules and codes of practice written by and for each individual SRO.

All SROs are required by the FSA and the SIB to have in place rules and procedures which cover the following areas:

- members to be fit and proper;
- admission, expulsion and discipline;
- safeguards for investors;
- monitoring and enforcement of rules;
- investigating complaints;
- promotion and maintenance of standards.

Securities and Futures Authority (SFA)

The SRO responsible for authorizing firms which conduct business in equity and index futures and options is the Securities and Futures Authority (SFA). The SFA was formed in 1991 when the Securities Association and the Association of Futures Brokers and Dealers merged.

Under the SFA's conduct of business rule, all SFA-registered firms must deal with clients' orders as soon as reasonably practical and may not delay the execution of the order, unless it believes the delay is in the best interest of the client.

When dealing, the firm must ensure it transacts all client business at the best price available in the market. This requirement is also covered by the London Stock Exchange rules on "best execution".

Where an investor relies on the firm to give investment advice (advisory service), or deal on behalf of an investor (discretionary service), a firm may not recommend or deal for an investor if the deal could be regarded as too frequent. This is to stop the firm dealing just to earn commission for itself. This type of dealing is known as "churning."

Each firm must have adequate internal procedures to ensure members of staff do not breach any SIB, SFA or FSA (Financial Services Act) rules and regulations. To oversee this requirement, each firm must have a nominated manager responsible for compliance matters and in most firms there is a dedicated Compliance Officer. It is their responsibility to inspect company and client records for irregularities.

The core of the FSA is Section Three which says that anyone carrying on investment business in the UK must be either authorized to do so or exempt. Under the act investment business is defined as:

- dealing in investments on behalf of others;
- arranging deals in investments on behalf of others;
- managing investments such as pension funds and discretionary accounts;
- giving advice on investments;
- setting up and running collective investment plans.

The act works by requiring any firm or person conducting investment business to be authorized by the appropriate regulatory body. Authorization is dependent on two main conditions:

The person must be *fit and proper*. The act does not define "fit and proper," but it is generally taken to mean the person must be solvent and with no criminal record.

The company must have *capital adequacy*. This is designed to prevent a company with inadequate capital backing from using money belonging to clients to support the company.

Any person or firm giving investment advice who is not authorized to do so has committed a criminal offence and, if convicted, faces a maximum sentence of two years' imprisonment, an unlimited fine or both. Not only does the individual who gave unauthorized investment advice face conviction, but any contract entered into by the investor is unenforceable.

Recognized Professional Bodies (RPB)

Certain individuals, while allowed to conduct investment business, are not regulated by any of the self-regulatory bodies. This group of people belong to Recognized Professional Bodies (RPB). This allows professional people such as accountants and solicitors to give investment advice to their clients.

The FSA recognizes that these groups of professionals maintain a high degree of professional integrity under their own regulatory bodies. Under the FSA each RPB must limit the amount of investment business their members undertake. Other exemptions to being a member of an SRO include:

- the Bank of England;
- Lloyds of London Insurance market and its agents;
- representatives of one company (life insurance and unit trust companies);
- some listed money market institutions which are regulated by the Bank of England;
- recognized Investment Exchanges.

Recognized Investment Exchanges

All investment markets in the UK are authorized under the FSA as either Recognized Investment Exchanges (RIE), or alternatively, foreign or international exchanges can be recognized as a Designated Investment Exchange (DIE).

> **Definition**
>
> A **Recognized Investment Exchange** is a company or organization that provides a structured and coordinated market place where investment business is conducted. The exchange must ensure there are adequate means for the establishment and dissemination of investment prices, supervising market activities and have provision for dealing with complaints and illegal market activities.

A DIE, while not under direct control of the SIB, is acknowledged as being regulated in an appropriate manner by its domestic regulator.

Membership of an investment exchange does not grant the right of an individual, or a firm to conduct investment business, that right can only be granted by an SRO or the SIB. Membership of a RIE allows the individual or firm to conduct investment business on that exchange once authorized by an SRO or the SIB.

Investments

Under the FSA financial investment is defined as any right, asset or interest within the following groups:

- stocks and shares in the share capital of a company, excluding building societies;
- debentures and loan stock;
- government, local authority or public authority securities including foreign countries and organizations;
- warrants;
- certificate conferring the right to convert, acquire or dispose of a security;
- units in a collective investment scheme (unit and investment trusts);
- options to acquire or dispose of investments;
- futures contracts on anything for investment purposes;
- contracts for difference (FT-SE 100 Index futures and options);
- long-term insurance contracts.

The act also lays down *conduct of business* rules on a firm's relationship with its clients: whose interests should be put before those of the company. One of the key areas of the FSA is the treatment of client assets. Client assets must be "ring fenced" and kept totally separate, not only from those of the firm itself, but also from other clients. In this way, if the firm or another client was ever to be in default, the assets of the client are safe and cannot be used to support it, the company or a client.

> **Definition**
>
> **Client money** *is separated into two categories – "**client free money**" and "**client settlement money.**" Client free money is money held by the firm for short periods awaiting investment and must be kept separate from the firm's money and from other client's money. Client settlement money is money received from a client for the settlement of a specific transaction and in this instant is pooled with other client settlement money awaiting transfer to the market.*

Risk disclosure statement

A requirement of the SFA in its regulation of the futures and options markets is its risk disclosure statement. The letter sets out the risk associated with different aspects of options trading and must be read, signed and returned to a broker before he can:

- recommend a trade;
- arrange or execute a trade whether it was his recommendation or not;
- act as discretionary manager.

A copy of a risk disclosure statement is shown in Appendix 1.

Compliance

Mark Satterthwaite, ED&F Mann Ltd

The role of the compliance officer is often thought of as that of the market policeman, ensuring that the traders and administration staff abide by the rules and regulations laid down by both the firm, the Securities and Futures Authority (SFA) and the Securities and Investment Board (SIB). Mark Satterthwaite, MSI (DIP) MSC, is the Compliance Officer of ED&F Mann Ltd, a major player in the London derivative markets. Having worked for four years overseeing the trading on the London Traded Options Market (LTOM), Mark moved into LTOM's Market Supervision Department for a number of years. From LTOM he spent one year with the SIB monitoring firms directly regulated by the SIB. Mark has spent the last four years with ED&F Mann Ltd.

Introduction

UK equity and futures exchanges have always had regulations governing their members' behaviour, particularly with regard to trading rules. Although many of the banks already employed Compliance Officers, it was only with the advent of the Financial Services Act (FSA) which came into force in 1988 that compliance became a well-known concept in the UK. Despite the short period of time since the FSA was introduced, the word "compliance" has led observers to believe that investment business is conducted within the confines of stringent, bureaucratic regulations. The reality is very different.

Before outlining practical compliance issues, the various legal and regulatory requirements which underpin much of the work of Compliance Officers need to be explained. After a series of public scandals involving investment firms, the government concluded that investors should be protected. The FSA created a framework for regulation of the financial industry within the UK. The FSA also provided the mechanism to create the Investor Compensation Scheme, designed to compensate private investors if they lost out as a result of a default by an investment firm up to a maximum value of £48,000. Finally, rules were established which required investment firms to keep the assets of private investors segregated from those of investment firms.

There have been a number of changes since the FSA came into force although the Securities and Investment Board (SIB) has remained the designated agency of the government in relation to the regulation of the financial services industry. This separation from direct governmental oversight has been criticized as political expediency whereby the government potentially avoids some responsibility and accountability for any regulatory problems which occur within the UK. The recent furore over the misleading advice given on the matter of personal pensions is a case in point. In addition to reducing its direct responsibility, the Government created the regulatory system at no cost to the taxpayer as it was designed to be self-financing, i.e. paid for by the investment firms. Whether investors and shareholders in investment firms appreciate the resulting increased costs is another issue!

The SIB originally played an important role in setting policy and rules to ensure consistency of practice throughout the industry. As the regulatory system has evolved, this has become less important. The SIB also acts as the parental overseer of the Exchanges and the bodies that undertake the actual supervision and monitoring of the investment firms, the Self-Regulatory Organizations (SROs). The main SRO for firms trading and broking securities and derivatives in the UK is the Securities and Futures Authority (SFA). The SIB's remaining responsibility is to ensure that only regulated companies can conduct investment business in the UK.

Both the SFA and the exchanges carry out regular monitoring of investment firms' trading activity which is supplemented by regular inspection visits. These visits are increasing in number and becoming more investigative and are not designed merely to check that firms adhere to the detailed rule books. They involve testing the firms' own internal procedures and help to promote best market practice within the industry. In addition, the SFA monitors the financial soundness of its non-bank members to ensure their long-term viability. (Banks which are members of the SFA are supervised by the Bank of England.) As the monitoring and inspections become more focused, the role and the cost of the SIB in overseeing this process is increasingly being called into question by market practitioners.

Compliance Officer

Although the word "compliance" is immediately linked with the FSA, in most investment firms it is much more wide ranging. For example the Compliance Officer is likely to be involved in implementing legislation directly affecting the business, such as money-laundering provisions of the Criminal Justice Act (1993). The Compliance Officer is a key member of the management of any investment firm as they are often involved in every aspect of the business. This can range from educating the workforce, reducing legal risk as well as actively creating internal controls, and setting up monitoring programs and ensuring that they are adhered to.

However, for any investment firm to be fully compliant with regulations, there needs to be a compliance ethos running through the whole company. The Compliance Officer acting alone is unable to monitor the trading activity of every trader and therefore has to rely on members of staff to inform him of any potential problems.

Importance of key staff

To ensure that an investment firm develops good compliance practice, it is vital that the internal structure and controls are well-documented and known to all staff. The reporting line should be clear and the Board should contain a number of people fully conversant with all the products being traded by the firm.

Key control staff such as the Compliance Officer, Risk Manager, Credit Manager and so forth should be independent from the trading staff, preferably having a separate reporting line to the Manager Director, Head of the Legal Department, etc.

Checks and balances must be maintained between the trading staff (often referred to as the "front office") and the reconciliation and administration staff (often referred to as the "back office"). It is vital that the staff valuing traders' positions cannot be unduly influenced by traders whose bonuses depend on the profitability of their positions. The obvious example where this separation of duties appeared to have failed was at Barings Bank's Singapore subsidiary, where Nick Leeson acted as the head of trading as well as being in charge of the back office, and allegedly concealed losses totalling £860 million which led to the collapse of the bank.

Chinese Walls

Where investment firms trade for themselves as well as advising and trading on behalf of external clients, internal controls become even more important. In 1986 the Stock Exchange abandoned the concept of single capacity and allowed members to broke on behalf of their clients in addition to taking positions themselves. Such members are known as "broker dealers". Investment firms implement so-called "Chinese Walls" to ensure information concerning client positions or intentions are not divulged to traders executing orders on the firm's behalf or vice versa.

Although investment firms have attempted to enforce Chinese Walls, in some cases by physically housing the completing departments on different floors or even different buildings, there will always remain a suspicion that privileged information will be passed on. Although the temptations to breach Chinese Walls are great, there have been actually very few proven cases. However, one recent case highlights the conflicts involved.

In 1995 the SFA issued a board notice concerning Roger Nagioff, the head of an investment firm's proprietary trading desk, who received confidential information about a proposed issue of securities and his firm's likely involvement in the issue. Mr Nagioff told his staff to take positions in the related shares and stock options without the knowledge of senior management or the Compliance Department. Despite approval being subsequently requested (without revealing positions had already been opened), the firm's discovery led to Mr Nagioff's registration as a manager of his firm being terminated by the SFA.

Similar conflicts exist with the derivatives industry, especially on the market floors. Many staff employed by floor brokers are permitted to take positions for their own personal gain, perhaps with a percentage of any profits going to the investment firm concerned. As a result, exchange and compliance staff of each floor broker actively monitor the trading of such staff when trading both their own and client orders to ensure that clients are not disadvantaged. These efforts are enhanced by most of the exchanges video-taping all trading, recording all telephone conversations and using sophisticated software to check on trading activity.

Error accounts

Even where investment firms do not allow their staff to trade for profit, temptation still exists. Every firm has error accounts that are used to account for errors made in execution. Whenever there is human intervention in the trading process, errors can occur, although these errors are surprisingly low in comparison to the volume of trades executed and the speed with which the floor staff are expected to operate. In relation to futures trading they can occur for a number of reasons, including misunderstanding between the booth staff and the pit traders, counting errors in actual execution in the pit resulting in an excess or a shortfall in trades done, trades in the wrong delivery month, etc.

The remuneration of some staff is adjusted often to reflect the size of profit or loss on the relevant error account. In such cases, placing improvements on execution prices in the errors account, rather than offering them to the client will reduce losses in the errors account and thereby increase the potential remuneration of the employee.

Again an investment firm's compliance staff should actively monitor such accounts to ensure that they are used for genuine errors (and not by traders trying to make up for losses by taking positions) and that any improvement in the trading price obtained is always offered to the relevant client.

Audited accounts

To ensure that these controls are working in practice, investment firms are constantly reviewed. In addition to checks by the Compliance Officer, investment firms are regularly checked by internal and external auditors. These reviews not only ensure that the Compliance Officer is carrying out his functions correctly and that the investment firm operates efficiently, they also review internal controls which are designed to seek to reduce or prevent fraud by employees and clients or counterparties.

Risk Manager

Communication of risk to senior management is a key control. The Risk Manager must ensure that he can calculate the investment firm's exposure to a particular client, country, exchange or contract. This task has become more complex with the development of ever more exotic derivative products and 24-hour trading. It is only with the aid of computer technology that this can be achieved. Exposures should be compared with pre-set limits which act as triggers to highlight unduly risky positions.

The Risk Manager must ensure the valuations of all positions are correctly calculated on at least a daily basis. Many investment firms are attempting to implement on-line valuations that will operate 24 hours a day.

From the vast amount of information gathered, the Risk Manager must ensure that senior management receive summaries of the investment firm's exposure. Barings can again be used as an example where this would appear not to have occurred.

Credit Manager

Linked to the job of the Risk Manager is that of Credit Manager. Some derivative brokers will grant certain clients credit. Indeed when trading base metal futures and options on the London Metal

Exchange, most clients expect some form of credit. Even broker dealers on the London Stock Exchange are now used to granting credit to clients. This has resulted from the abandonment of the old account system and the introduction of rolling settlement.

As the period of settlement is gradually reduced to a target of two days, it has meant that clients will often be unable to settle monies due within the prescribed limit. The SFA allows firms to grant credit to clients if the investment firm has followed the relevant SFA guidelines.

In essence, the Credit Manager assesses the risk of each client who has requested a credit line and sets an appropriate limit. Compliance staff have to ensure this process follows the SFA's guidelines.

Legal risks

Whenever an investment firm agrees to act on behalf of a client, it is vital that the firm ensures that the client understands the risks involved and can legally enter into the deal. These risks, colloquially grouped under the title "Legal Risks," are highlighted in a number of recent cases. In the UK a number of interest rate swap agreements that were entered into by local authorities, such as Hammersmith and Fulham in the late 1980s, were declared *ultra vires* and the investment firms involved lost millions of pounds as the authorities refused to honour their agreements.

In 1995, trading on the London Metal Exchange was affected by the potential default of a number of Asian clients who owed large sums of money.

In the United States, a number of clients recently claimed that they were misled into entering into complex derivative transactions which they did not understand and were unsuitable for their needs. These clients were large corporations such as Procter and Gamble. In short, the previous understanding of *caveat emptor* is gradually being eroded.

Legal and compliance staff have to ensure that clients are made aware of the risks involved and that legally binding contracts are executed to reduce the chance of default.

Conclusion

As a result of the increasing sophistication of the products offered by investment firms, the increase in large defaults and the gradual tightening of the regulatory screw, compliance has become ever more important in the UK. A reduction in its scope seems unlikely; in fact regulatory controls may become even more complex.

In 1996 the European Commission's Investment Services Directive and the Capital Adequacy Directive will come into force. These directives will mean every investment firm will be subject to stricter financial supervision and potentially new conduct of business requirements being introduced in every EU country. Although these changes will undoubtedly improve regulation in many continental countries, it is unlikely that the UK investor will benefit to any great extent.

To conclude, I believe the present system of regulation of UK derivative and securities exchange business is both necessary and fundamental to good working practices in the financial industry.

Although I believe the present system is cost-effective and directed to where the real risks arise, it remains to be seen whether the present regulatory structure will survive in light of the criticism of the SIB and potential political changes.

The Securities and Futures Authority

David Jones, SFA

Here, David Jones, Public Relations Manager for the Securities and Futures Authority (SFA) gives an overview of the SFA's role and structure, explaining the different departments and their functions.

Introduction

The Securities and Futures Authority (SFA) is responsible for the regulating firms involved in the securities and futures sectors of the financial services industry. Its aim is to promote and maintain high standards of integrity and fair dealing in the carrying on of investment business, thereby providing effective protection for the investor.

The history of the UK's financial industry is well-documented. Banking, insurance, shares trading and futures dealing have developed into highly organized services and markets to make London one of the financial capitals of the world. As financial markets developed, rules were introduced and continually refined so that business could be conducted in an orderly and fair manner.

Of course, rules are not a guarantee of successful investment. There is risk. Nevertheless, professionals in the industry apply knowledge, experience and skill in order to make the best judgement for their clients and themselves. But there are those who through fraudulent or incompetent practice, place their clients' money in jeopardy. To combat this, in 1986 Parliament introduced legislation which heralded a new system of financial services regulation.

With the primary aim of improving investor protection, the Financial Services Act 1986 brought about a major restructuring in the way investor services are regulated. It became a criminal offence to carry on investment business if not authorized to do so. A new organization, the Securities and Investment Board (SIB) was established to oversee the implementation of the Act but it developed its authorizing powers, and the task of day-to-day enforcement was given to specialist "front line" regulators such as SFA whose job it is to ensure that firms and individuals that come within their scope meet appropriate standards in order to be permitted to undertake investment business.

2 · Market Structure

The objective is to help protect investors, both private and professional, from financial loss caused by firms' insolvency, incompetence, or deliberate acts of deception. Furthermore, good market practice is one of London's attractions for international business. SFA's aim is to deliver effective regulation which will not stifle innovation or be so restrictive that business would be driven to competing in international markets.

> **SFA's aim is to deliver effective regulation which will not stifle innovation or be so restrictive that business would be driven to competing in international markets.**

The industry

SFA regulates over 1,300 firms involved in dealing or advising in securities or derivatives, most of whom are directly active on many UK and overseas exchanges.

Their earnings make a significant contribution to the British economy. Their business can encompass dealing in shares, bonds, traded options, financial futures, commodity futures or corporate finance. Many of them have a long and successful business pedigree; others are newer ventures created in response to demand for new or specialized products and/or services.

Most firms are located in London where the organized markets are, some are in other UK cities and towns serving the needs of their regional client base. The "nationality" of SFA firms is a reflection of London's international status; around half are incorporated overseas, notably North America, Japan and Western Europe, with branches in the UK.

The process

The regulatory process undertaken by the SFA has four main parts:

Authorization
This is the initial vetting of a firm to ensure that it is suitable to be permitted to conduct investment business. Firms that seek authorization must provide information which demonstrates that they are adequately funded, have viable business plans, that their management and staff are suitably experienced and competent and that there is no history of malpractice. SFA check the information and if applicant firms are considered to be "fit and proper" they are granted authorization.

Authorization includes the individual registration of directors, managers and investment staff in the firm. Some will have to take an examination to show that they understand the fundamentals of market practice and regulation. Those who are not registered are not permitted to deal or to give customers advice. More than 40,000 persons are registered with SFA.

Monitoring
Monitoring is an important task for the SFA. Once a firm has been authorized, that is not the end of the regulatory story. They are obliged to comply with the SFA's rules. All firms are required to provide a wide range of financial and other information to the SFA on a regular basis and sometimes upon special request. Teams of inspectors make routine visits to firms to check on their compliance with the rules. In some cases, the visits may be made without warning.

If the monitoring process uncovers non-compliance with the rules, steps are quickly taken by the SFA to ensure that the investors' interests are protected. In most instances the "infringement" is only of a minor administrative nature offering no immediate danger to the investor. Firms usually put things right as soon as it is brought to their attention.

Investigation
Where a more serious breach of rules is suspected either as a result of routine monitoring, or from reports received from other sources, a more focused investigation is undertaken to gather the relevant facts. Monitoring and investigation may sometimes involve liaison with other UK and overseas regulatory authority.

Prosecution
If the investigators feel that a firm, or an individual, has committed a serious breach of the rules, or if other good reasons exist, the case is considered at a more formal level. If the judgement is against the firm, the nature of the breach will determine the penalty. It could be a warning, a fine, a temporary order to stop trading or expulsion from membership, i.e. de-authorization.

The SFA cannot undertake criminal prosecutions through the courts. Should such a prosecution be necessary, the results of the SFA's investigations are passed to a relevant body such as the Department of Trade and Industry or the police.

Complaints and Arbitration

Member firms are expected to service their customers' needs with skill and consideration. Occasionally things go wrong and a customer may have a complaint. Where the firm and the customer are unable to reach agreement between themselves, the customer can refer the matter to the SFA's Complaints Bureau. The Bureau will consider the complaint and attempt to resolve the dispute between both parties. Arbitration procedures are also available if the firm's customer is not satisfied with the findings of the Bureau.

The work of the Complaints Bureau is overseen by a completely independent Complaints Commissioner. His role is not to re-examine the details of the case, but to determine if they have been dealt with properly and fairly by the Bureau. The Commissioner publishes an annual report on the work of the Bureau which is widely circulated.

■ ■ ■

'The open outcry method of trading has evolved over time into a highly organized auction style system where trades are conducted face to face, in a designated area of the market floor known as a "pit", by traders shouting their buying and selling orders.'

3

Trading and Clearing

Introduction

Open outcry versus screen-based trading –
Andrew Reierson, financial journalist

FT-SE 100 futures trading

OMLX

Product development – Julian Perrins, OMLX

Marketing and promotional support –
Tony Hawes, Equity Products, LIFFE

Clearing and settlement –
Jacqueline Totley, Monument Derivatives Ltd

Introduction

By far the most common method of trading, at least among the major US and London futures exchanges, is the open outcry method. This has evolved over time into a highly organized auction-style system where trades are conducted face to face, in a designated area of the market floor known as a "pit," by traders verbally indicating by shouting their buying and selling orders.

Open outcry requires traders to shout their orders to the other traders. A trader wishing to buy will shout first the number of contracts required followed by the price, e.g. 15 at 10. He is willing to buy 15 contracts for a price of 10. On the other hand, a trader wishing to sell will announce the price followed by the number of contracts, e.g. 20 for 2. He wishes to sell two contracts for 20. Obviously, in a busy, noisy market it is not always possible for everyone to hear the orders, therefore open outcry is supplemented by the use of hand signals which physically signal the traders' intentions. Any trade agreed by open outcry is confirmed by the two traders completing dealing slips to show who, what and how many have traded.

> **The main advantage with electronic trading is that all prices displayed on the dealing screens are firm, up-to-date dealing prices and are not indicative as with open outcry.**

The second, and by far the newer, of the two trading systems is electronic trading. In recent years a number of new exchanges have been established with trading based on personal computers in the traders' offices linked by telephone lines to a central computer at the exchange. With screen-based trading the traders remain in their own offices and enter their trades into the computer. If and when two orders match, a trade takes place electronically within the system. The main advantage with electronic trading is that all prices displayed on the dealing screens are firm, up-to-date dealing prices and are not indicative as with open outcry.

LIFFE and open outcry

Trading in LIFFE's products takes place on the exchange's trading floor at their Cannon Bridge market and is conducted by the time proven method of open outcry. Open outcry relies on competitive face-to-face trading on the market floor. This is in contrast with trading on the London Stock Exchange where trading takes place over the telephone using price-information dealing screens in large, office-based, trading rooms.

Open outcry on LIFFE's market entails parts of the trading floor being designated for the trading of specific instruments. These areas are known as "pits" and are generally raised up off of the market floor.

> **Key features**
>
> ### Trading jackets and badges
>
> *To help identify the different participants and their roles, traders wear colored trading jackets and trading badges. Each firm's trading jacket is different in both style and color from any other firm. This is obviously an instant and valuable aid to recognition when trading in a busy and crowded pit.*

While trading jackets are a notable feature of trading on LIFFE, they do not confirm the right to trade or necessarily the role of the trader. The trading right is given by the trading badge worn by the trader. The badges not only identify the trader, but also identify which categories of contract he or she can trade in. The badge shows:

- A three-letter mnemonic, specific to that trader.
- A trading permit showing the LIFFE permit that their member firm holds.
- The different products the trader is allowed to trade.
- A photograph of the trader.

> **Definition**
>
> *The **open outcry system** used for options trading is an auction-style trading method that enables all traders to hear, see and participate in any trading that is taking place. The traders trade openly and verbally with each other in the pit.*

However, while all information – bids, offers and acceptance – must be communicated verbally, this can be backed up by hand signals. Hand signals help to clarify traders' open outcry information and can show if the trader is buying or selling, the price at which he wishes to trade and the number of contracts he wishes to trade.

In order for open outcry to work, all the traders in a particular market sector (e.g. all chemical stocks) stand together in one area of the market floor. This area is known as a pit and the traders in the pit are known as a crowd.

LIFFE equity traded options

The traders in equity traded options fall into two groups, market makers and broker dealers. Market makers act as wholesalers buying and selling options on behalf of their firms. This "wholesaler" approach is crucial to the market as there is rarely, if ever, a balance or perfect match between investors wishing to buy and/or sell in the market.

> **Definition**
>
> *The **market maker's** job is to ensure that when an investor wishes to buy, there is someone willing to sell to him and when the investor wishes to sell, there is, again, someone willing to buy from him. If this facility was removed, the option prices would move violently from one extreme to the other as investors tried to match orders with those on the opposite side.*

So not only do market makers facilitate business by increasing liquidity, they also reduce volatility, ensuring that prices stay close to their fair value.

All members of LIFFE who hold an appropriate trading permit are known as market makers and may make two-way (bid and offer) prices in their appropriate stocks (equity or index). Market makers can be either assigned or nominated in particular stocks. In return for accepting the commitments associated with the role being assigned or nominated, they are granted certain privileges.

Both assigned and nominated market makers are obliged to make continuous two-way prices (bid and offer) in all series, for the stocks they are registered in, upon inquiry by any other member of the crowd in a minimum size as laid down by LIFFE. The minimum size for each option can be different and is set by LIFFE to help facilitate business. The minimum size is known as the exchange minimum quote size (EMQS) and can be changed by LIFFE from time to time. While there is a minimum quote size for the market makers, there is no restriction if the trader making the inquiry wishes to trade in a smaller size, or indeed if he wishes to trade in a larger quantity.

In addition to the obligation of the EMQS, assigned market makers maintain an agreed level of presence on the market floor for the options they are registered in and to ensure that prices are regularly updated for all the series of his/her assigned options.

In return for these undertakings, assigned and nominated market makers receive certain privileges. These privileges take the form of reduced clearing fee on their trades and for assigned market makers certain trading priorities over other non-assigned market makers.

Market makers attempt to make their profits either by buying options at a low price and selling them at a higher level, the difference being the profit the market maker makes, or by trading in the underlying securities at the same time as trading in the options. This enables the market maker to lock in a profit or position until the expiry of the option. With market makers constantly trading in different series in the same stock, they can establish a number of different risk-free strategies and positions, locking in a profit, over a period of time which can then be removed from their trading book.

> *Stockbrokers on the options market, who deal on behalf of private investors and fund managers, who have no direct access to the market, are known as* **broker dealers**. *There are no laid-down rules or obligations for brokers, but they must trade within the general rules and regulations and the spirit of the market.*

Definition

Broker dealers make their profit from commission charged and in some cases by dealing in options for their firm's own account. Any broker dealer trading for their own firm's account is required, under SIB and SFA rules and regulations, to deal for their client's best advantage at all times. This is to ensure that the broker dealer gives priority and precedence to client orders over and above their own firm's orders at all times.

If for whatever reason a broker dealer member of LIFFE was to become insolvent, a compensation scheme has been set up under the FSA to enable a "private customer" under SFA rules to claim compensation.

> **Definition**
>
> *All traders on the market are qualified* **Registered Options Traders**. *To achieve this qualification the trader must have passed a number of examinations in the theory of traded options and undertaken a practical exam where the workings and dealings of the market are simulated, as well as serving an "apprenticeship" on the market.*

Trading in options

Trading is only allowed during official trading hours, 08.35 – 16.10, and is continuous throughout the day with no official breaks for lunch, etc.

At the start of business (08.35) the exchange official will decide how to open the stocks for which he is responsible. This may be by either an informal opening or by an opening rotation.

An informal opening will usually take place during periods of little or no interest in the options. Prices and trades may take place in any order and at numerous prices.

An opening rotation will be called by the exchange official if there is considerable interest and activity in the underlying security and option. The stock is opened series by series, starting with the near month calls. Once the calls have been rotated the exchange official will rotate the puts, again starting with the near month. Trades may only take place in the series being updated and only at one price.

When an investor passes his order to his broker (see Figure 3.1), it is checked for completeness and accuracy before being passed on to the floor broker. The floor broker in turn will enter the appropriate crowd and ask for a quotation in the option series he is interested in. The market makers will quote their buying and selling prices (at this time they do not know if the broker is buying or selling or the quantity the order is for). The floor broker will work out who is making the highest bid and the lowest offer prices and possibly in what size before accepting the bids or offers and buying or selling as instructed by the investor.

3 · Trading and Clearing

Order route

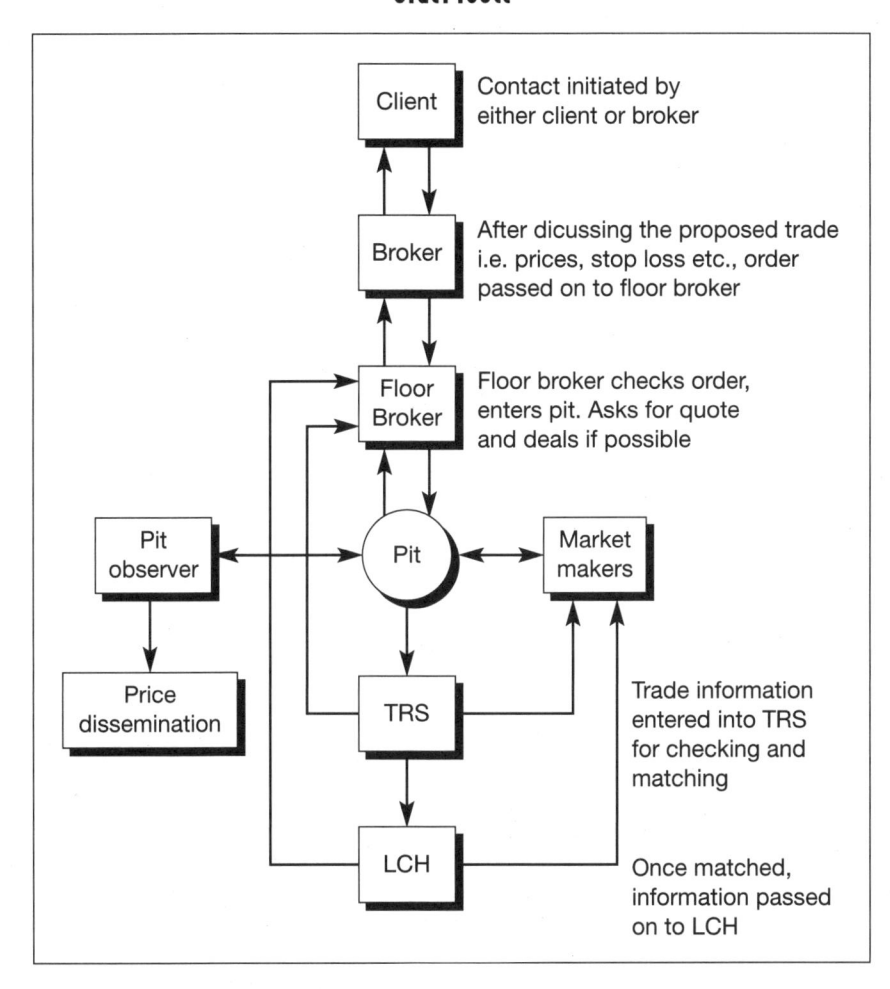

Fig 3.1

- Client — Contact initiated by either client or broker
- Broker — After dicussing the proposed trade i.e. prices, stop loss etc., order passed on to floor broker
- Floor Broker — Floor broker checks order, enters pit. Asks for quote and deals if possible
- Pit observer
- Pit
- Market makers
- Price dissemination
- TRS — Trade information entered into TRS for checking and matching
- LCH — Once matched, information passed on to LCH

When an option is deep out-of-the-money and has no value, most investors abandon their options as worthless. One reason for this is the fact that transaction costs and commission will be greater than the premium received from the sale of the option.

> **Definition**
>
> *However, some individuals and institutions need to quantify any losses for tax purposes. In order for this to happen, a facility exists to sell a deep out-of-the-money option for a nominal price of 1p per contract. This is known as "trading at* **Cabinet**" *or* "**cab**."

Public Limit Order Board

Key features

At best

Most orders from private investors are for execution at the market price (known as "at best"). While the investor is certain to deal, it may not be at the level he has decided is a fair price.

If an investor decides he wishes to trade at a particular price he can use the Public Limit Order Board (PLOB) if he cannot trade at his stipulated level straightaway. The PLOB allows the investor's price to be displayed to the market and then on to other users of the market via a quote vendor, encouraging other investors to enter the market and deal at the new PLO price displayed.

Definition

*A **Public Limit Order (PLO)** is a firm dealing order and will be represented in the market until either the end of the trading day, or when it is dealt or cancelled by the submitting broker. There is inevitably a time delay in the broker receiving instructions to cancel the PLO from the client and actually entering the market and doing so. If, during this time, the PLO is dealt the trade cannot be cancelled and will stand.*

Example

The price spread in the NFI May 330 call is:

60 – 65

60 is the price the market makers are prepared to buy at and is known as the "bid price," while 65 is the price the market makers are willing to sell at and is known as the "offer" or "ask price." An investor decides the fair value or price for the May 330 call is 63 and is prepared to buy five contracts at that price. The cheapest price he can purchase the options at in the market is 65. The investor decides that if he cannot deal at 63 he will enter his order on the PLOB. The new price spread will be:

> **63 – 65**
>
> The new 63 bid price being the investor's PLO for five contracts. This increase in the bid price may prompt holders of the May 330 calls to sell at 63 or, it may result in another investor deciding to make an opening sale at 63. If the investor can purchase five contracts at 63 he will have saved 2 per share or £20 per contract, enough to pay the commission charges.
>
> If the investor had purchased the options at 65 the bid price would have needed to increase to at least 66 for the investor to have made a profit (buy at 65, sell at 66). Having purchased the options at 63, the bid only has to increase to 64 in order for the investor to make a profit using the PLOB (buy at 63, sell at 64).

In most cases PLOB trades, at their stipulated prices, are given priority over market makers trading at the same price.

There are, unfortunately, a few drawbacks with the PLOB. First, if the investor wishes to purchase five contracts but the seller only wishes to sell one, the investor will have to buy the one contract. He must then wait and see if he can buy the remaining contracts at a later time during the trading day. Apart from the price and the maximum number of contracts, the investor can attach no conditions to the PLO.

The second drawback is that the investor may find himself chasing to price up or down. If, as in the example, the price spread is 60 – 65 the investor goes on the Board to buy at 63 and changes the spread to 63 – 65. The underlying security price rises, pushing the option's premium up to 64 – 68; the investor's PLO will not be fulfilled at 63 and he has lost the opportunity to buy the options at 65. He must now either submit a new PLO at, possibly, 67, buy his five contracts at 68 or walk away from the trade.

The Public Limit Order Board is extremely under-utilized on LIFFE. Less than 1 percent of business in the UK is conducted using the PLOB, compared with approximately 25 percent of business on the European Options Exchange in Amsterdam.

There is, unfortunately, a small additional charge for the use of the PLOB, but this is more than compensated for by the reduced premiums paid.

Trading halts

Under certain conditions trading of equity options on LIFFE may be halted by the exchange. The price of the underlying security is obtained from the London stock market from their trading system SEAQ (Stock Exchange Automated Quotation). While it is unlikely and extremely rare, there is the possibility of this link becoming unavailable or unreliable. In either of these two cases LIFFE may call a trading halt in the individual equity options affected or the equity options market in general.

Trading may also be halted in individual equity options if the London Stock Exchange has called a trading halt or suspended trading in the underlying security. If the calculation of the FT-SE 100 Index is, for whatever reason, prevented or unreliable, LIFFE may again call a trading halt in the index futures and option contracts. During a trading halt no trading whatsoever may take place in the option concerned. That means that no new positions may be opened or no open position closed. As soon as possible after the calling of a trading halt on the market floor, an announcement by LIFFE will be displayed on their trading systems. The announcement is then displayed, via all of LIFFE's quote vendors, to all information screens around the world.

Broker/client relationship

As the majority of users of LIFFE are not members of the exchange they are obliged to trade and have their trades cleared through the services of a floor broker and a clearing agent who are members of LIFFE.

Once the executing broker has transacted the business the trade is cleared through either the executing broker (if he is also a clearing member of the London Clearing House) or it is "given up" by the broker to a clearing agent.

Members of LIFFE act as principals and not as agents, as on the London stock market, to their clients (see Figure 3.2). Therefore when a broker executes a trade on behalf of a client a contract is established between the market and the broker and a second separate contract is established between the broker and the client. This ultimately results in the broker having a contract with the Clearing House, (LCH) and with the client.

Principal vs. agent

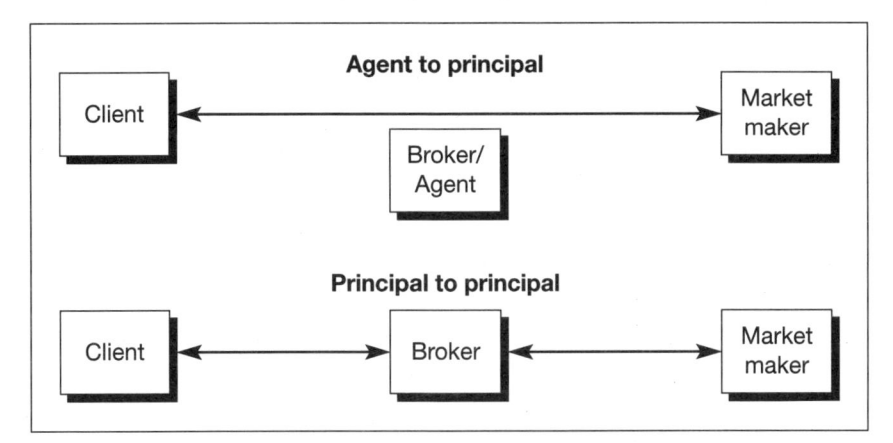

Fig 3.2

Agent to principal

Client ↔ Broker/Agent ↔ Market maker

Principal to principal

Client ↔ Broker ↔ Market maker

Definition

Autoquote *is a computerized option pricing system developed jointly by LIFFE and market participants. It is designed to give an indication of the level at which a particular option series is likely to trade, regardless of whether that series has been updated or not. The option variables, such as volatility, time to expiry and interst rates, are updated during the trading day by members of the market.*

Open outcry versus screen-based trading

Andrew Reierson, financial journalist

As more and more derivative exchanges are established, there has been an increase in the number of debates concerning the merits of the two main dealing systems – open outcry and screen-based trading. The older more-established exchanges in the US and the UK all operate on an open outcry system, well-established and extremely efficient, whereas the newer exchanges such as the DTB in Germany and SOFFEX in Switzerland have elected to operate an electronic dealing system from the beginning. Andrew Reierson, an independent financial journalist, describes the pros and cons of each system. Andrew started his financial career with the London Traded Options Market in early 1988. Since then he has gone on to work with a number of specialist derivative-related publications including Futures and Options World.

Introduction

The debate over open outcry versus electronic, screen-based futures and options trading has been going on since screen-based systems made their first appearance in the mid-1980s, and is likely to continue as long as both methods of trading exist. The debate has softened somewhat but some will argue that that is more a reflection of the growing maturity and pragmatism of the once-fledgling futures industry. There are still stark differences between floor and screen trading but the people involved are more focused on getting the business done rather than how it is done. For the end-user, the differences between the trading methods are largely academic and, in most cases, are hardly important as long as the order is being filled.

> There are still stark differences between floor and screen trading but the people involved are more focused on getting the business done rather than how it is done.

Screen trading is now enjoying a certain amount of co-existence with open outcry and this co-existence can be seen in differing degrees on all major exchanges around the world. Globex, the joint venture originally between Chicago Mercantile Exchange, Reuters and the Chicago Board of Trade to electronically trade the exchanges' products when their trading floors are shut, has enjoyed mixed success. The Chicago Board of Trade's Project A is experiencing growing success, and LIFFE's Automatic Pit Trading (APT), the after-hours trading supplement to its open outcry floors, is considered to be hugely successful.

It appears these systems are starting to work hand-in-hand, so what's the big difference?

What are the differences?

Until recently, such a debate existed because of the centuries-old tradition of futures being traded open outcry made any other way of trading unthinkable or even sacrilegious. The proponents of open outcry certainly do have a weight advantage. The mighty trading halls of the Chicago Board of Trade and Chicago Mercantile Exchange are testament to the success and durability of open outcry trading. Indeed, these exchanges have been used as the model for other floor-based exchanges set up around the world, and have seen open outcry success such as London's LIFFE, Paris' Matif, Singapore International Monetary Exchange and the Sydney Futures Exchange. Floor trading is successful for a number of reasons, but the main attraction is market transparency. The many different traders on the floor, whether they are locals trading for their own account, options market makers or brokers, ensure the best bid and ask prices are available at any given time and, most of all, one can see who – at least on the floor – is behind those bids and offers.

The bargains struck on the floor are immediately reflected in the trade information with all market participants, including those off the floor via information vendors, being fully aware of the trading activity. Customers using such exchanges have the confidence of knowing that they have their order filled at the best possible price at that time, determined by the supply and demand requirements of the pit, which in the case of the larger exchanges can be a few hundred traders.

However, much of the same can be said of screen-based systems where trade is conducted through an exchange terminal in the comfort of the members' offices. Prices and orders are input via the members' terminal and trades are executed under the same terms as open outcry, i.e. the best bid and ask prices are displayed usually with the collective bids and offer size at those price levels. The information is instantaneous, often quicker than open outcry, but customers, and even traders, may find it difficult to gauge who is behind the bid and offers.

Another advantage of open outcry is atmosphere. To the experienced floor trader, the mood of the market can be immediately sensed and trading decisions will be based on that "sense." For example, if large amounts of buy orders are coming into the pit, floor traders will be able to roughly determine their source by who is broking the orders and general floor gossip. If the buy orders are from several different sources, a bullish trend might be developing. However, if the buy orders are a hedge to protect cash market holdings, then a bearish tone might be setting in.

This type of market "feel" is less evident from screen systems where a trader's access to the outside world is through their dealing screen or the telephone to other traders and clients. A sudden influx of orders may not be immediately obvious through a screen, and a trader's reaction might be slow, whereas on an exchange floor the reaction would be instantaneous.

> **Dealing with people is good for getting a feel for the market but people are prone to errors, especially when it is busy.**

The face-to-face dealing on a floor does have its drawbacks. Dealing with people is good for getting a feel for the market but people are prone to errors, especially when it is busy.

The bond market fall-out of 1994 saw one of the busiest trading periods for futures and options exchanges in their history. However, for members of open outcry exchanges the peak of this period was also fraught with trading errors as clerks and traders had difficulty keeping up with order flow. Most of the common mistakes were down to incorrectly filled tickets, which is understandable given the thousands of orders an average-sized firm would have handled on the worst day. But this problem is doubled because floor trade is between two parties who must both fill in their tickets correctly before being matched at the clearing house. If tickets don't match, then in extreme cases it is difficult to prove that the trade ever took place, a disaster for the customer hedging a cash or swap market exposure to find out at the end of the day the order he or she thought was executed in the morning was never traded. It must be remembered that such instances are extremely rare. Fortunately, the fall-out from the bond market crash was minimal, but it did highlight some of the shortcomings of floor trading.

By contrast, screen traders had a relatively easy time of it. Inputting orders on to a screen is a precise action with client number, type of order, contract and size all entered before the trade is executed.

Some screen systems even query orders that have been keyed in incorrectly. While trading via keyboard probably involves new skills for most traders – "We look for typists instead of traders," jokes a member of screen-based Deutsche Terminborse in Frankfurt – it is accurate, quick and efficient. As far as bad trades are concerned, an audit trail is created from the time the trader inputs the order on the screen until it is settled and cleared at the clearing house. Discrepancies can and do occur, however, but less frequently than open outcry and with an audit trail that can easily identify the breakdown of the trade.

Screen-trading, efficient but charmless, is also relatively cheaper than open outcry. Most of the cost of running a screen-based exchange is in setting it up. There are maintenance fees and costs of upgrading and members must pay their line rental fees, and, of course, their membership fees.

On the whole, these costs are cheaper than those associated with setting up floor teams to trade on an open outcry exchange. The terminals are in the members' offices so there is no need to rent booth space. Also there is no need for extended floor teams as the screen trader conducts all aspects of trading at the terminal.

On the other hand, because of the sheer volume of contracts traded on the more established open outcry exchanges, often the cost-per-contract is cheaper than even the larger screen-based systems. However, the electronic exchanges are catching up volume-wise and costs are coming down. It won't be long before the customer has an even harder choice of where to put his or her business.

Another important plus for electronic trading is in listing new contracts. All exchanges are reluctant to launch products that might turn out to be a turkey, that nobody wants to trade. With floor-based exchanges, this is doubly important because valuable floor space can be wasted on dud contracts.

Nobody wants to launch unpopular products, but with screen systems this is not as great a problem. Getting a new contract on the system merely involves some software adjustment and if the contract proves unsuccessful, there is little, if any, cost to taking the contract off the system. However, there is also little cost in keeping the contract on the system. After all, some of the futures industry's most popular products spent long periods in the trading desert before coming into their own.

Space is also an important issue. Although the spectacular growth of the futures and options industry in 1993 and 1994 has tailed off somewhat, it is still growing. One of the big problems for open outcry exchanges is that the size of trading pits and the number of people they can accommodate is finite. Physical expansion of a trading floor is both expensive and disruptive, especially for an exchange established in a major financial center.

Screen-based exchanges boast that, theoretically, expansion is infinite. What this really means is that expansion is as large as computers will allow. Traders on the more popular screen exchanges are now used to slower trading times during busy periods, such as immediately after the release of economic data. However, the traders are also quick to point out that the delay is one of a few seconds at the most, much shorter than the delay that can be experienced in getting an order to a trading floor during the same busy period.

Summary

Both methods of trading are proving their capability in their own way. Combined, the systems have something for everybody. But as the trading industry gets more and more sophisticated, such old-fashioned prejudices against different trading styles will become just that – old-fashioned. Customers want to know that they are getting the best service available, whether this is on an open outcry or screen-based exchange is irrelevant.

However, the debate will continue. Competition amongst exchanges is just as fierce as it is among their member firms and differences in trading styles are easy targets, when drumming up market share. However, the market will vote with its feet, with some choosing the floor and some the screen – but most will be choosing both.

FT-SE 100 futures trading

Introduction

Unlike trading in options where there are separate functions and obligations for market makers and broker dealers, there is no official distinction between market makers and brokers in the FT-SE 100 and 250 futures contracts, and both are considered to be just traders. While there may be no market makers or brokers as such, in the futures pits the traders can be divided into those working for an exchange member firm and those working for themselves, known as locals.

The traders working for exchange member firms may be either transacting an order on behalf of a client or buying and selling contracts on behalf of his firm. While this may sound like a market maker and indeed he may be acting like a market maker there are, technically, no rules to stop him from executing client orders as there are in the equity options market.

> **Definition**
>
> **Local traders** *are individuals, who may sometimes be referred to as* **sole traders**, *who buy and sell futures on their own behalf and not for someone else.*

The main advantage for the exchange in having local traders is that they add liquidity to the market and so ensure that client orders are transacted with ease and speed. Most local traders will be unwilling to hold large positions overnight. This ensures that they are not exposed to adverse news or moves in overseas markets. Instead they will try and profit from very short-term movements and trends in the market.

Trading in futures

Unlike trading in the options market, which is a competing market-maker system allowing market makers to compete with one another as to who is making the best bid and offer, trading in the futures market is conducted under the order-driven system. This means that traders in the pit do not make a market or prices in the futures contract in order to entice investors to trade. If investors wish to trade they must decide at what price they are willing to trade and put their order to buy or sell into the market at their price.

Automated Pit Trading (APT)

While the open outcry trading finishes at 16.30, the FT-SE 100 futures contract continues to trade from 16.32 until 17.30 on the exchange's Automated Pit Trading system. This is an electronic computerized system designed to replicate open outcry trading after the market has closed.

Types of orders

When dealing in the futures market there are a number of different types of orders that investors can pass to their dealers. However, not all dealers will take all types of orders. The easiest and simplest type of order is the "at best" or "at market" order. This gives the dealer the authority to trade at the prevailing market price, whatever the level. While investors are guaranteed a trade, they may have been able to trade at a slightly better price by giving a different type of instruction to their broker such as a limit order.

By giving a "limit order" and specifying the price or level they are prepared to trade at, investors can ensure that if they do trade, it will be at a price they consider to be a fair price. However, by giving a "limit order" the investor may not be able to trade at all if no trader is prepared to buy or sell at the price they have stipulated. Obviously it is not always going to be possible to trade at the limit price given by the investor; in this situation dealers can be told to hold and work the order. He will then keep the order with him in the pit and trade it as and when it is possible. This may also result in the investor receiving a better price than originally given.

Definition

*A **"stop loss" order** is used to limit any losses that may occur if the market moves in the opposite direction than the investor anticipated. Suppose an investor buys the Footsie futures anticipating a rise in the short term, but is worried that a fall below a certain level will result in support being broken and the market falling further. In this case he can place a "stop loss" order just below the support level in case it is broken.*

Due to the nature of futures trading, one order that is not available to investors is the Public Limit Order Board. The speed at which futures are traded makes the guaranteed trading of PLOs impossible.

Quote vendors

The information from the dealing screens on the market floor is made available to private and professional investors alike through licensed quote vendors. While the information displayed by the quote vendors is almost always the same, the way in which it is displayed varies from one vendor to the next. The information available on each and every series on equity and index options traded on LIFFE includes:

- exercise price;
- expiry month;
- price of last trade;
- open interest at the close of the last business day;
- previous day's volume (number of contracts);
- closing mid-price for the previous day;
- current matched volume;
- price and size of Public Limit Orders.

In addition, the following information is made available from the London Stock Exchange:

- current bid and offer price for the underlying security;
- current volume for the underlying security;
- previous day's settlement price for collateral purposes;
- index value and change on day.

Settlement

TRS

Once a trade has been agreed by both parties, the broker and the market maker will enter the details on to a dealing slip or card (see Figures 3.3 and 3.4). The slip is in turn handed to members of the exchange who enter the details into a computerized matching system known as the Trade Registration System (TRS) to ensure both parties have exactly the same details. While there are exchange staff available to enter the details of trades into TRS, the majority

Mastering Exchange Traded Equity Derivatives

Fig 3.3 Dealing slip (1)

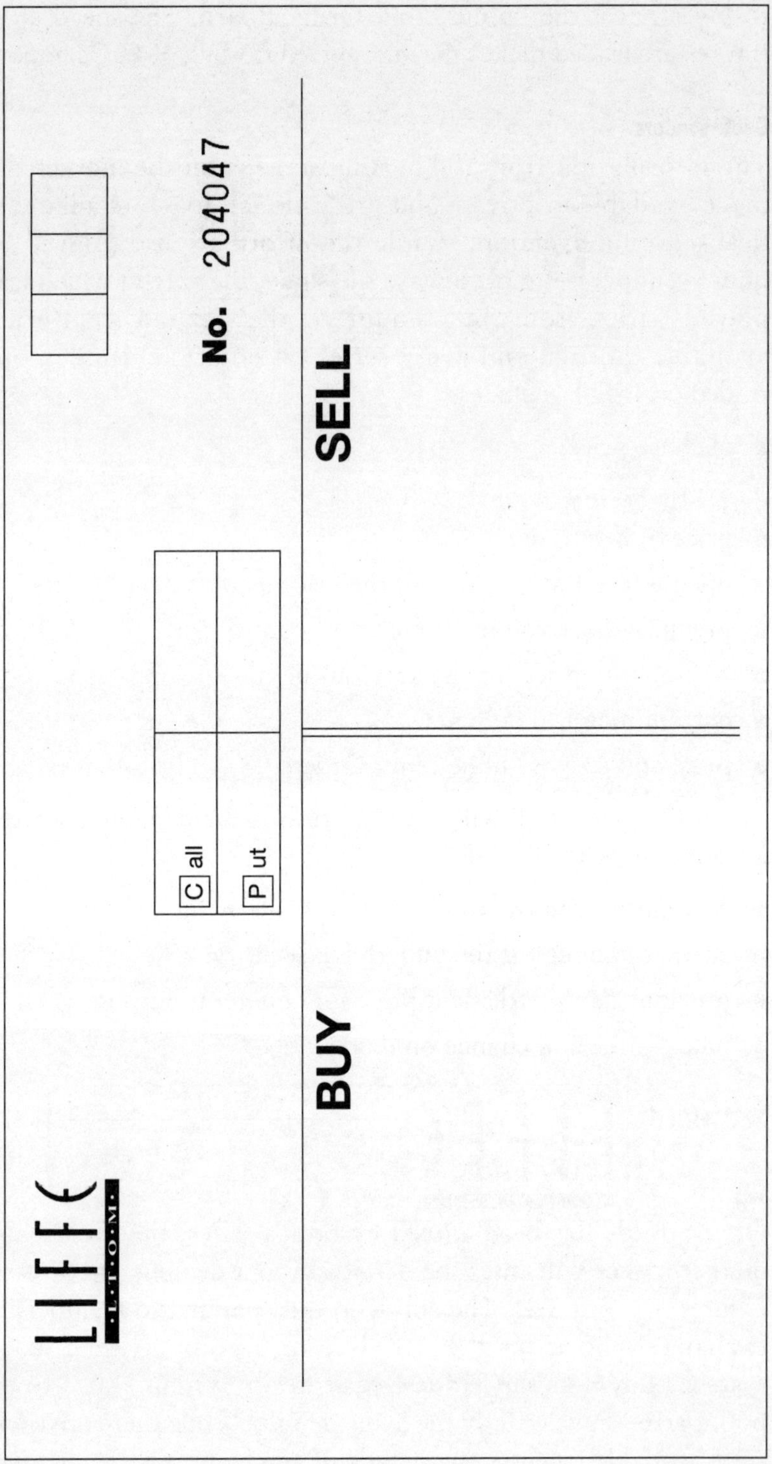

Dealing slip (2)

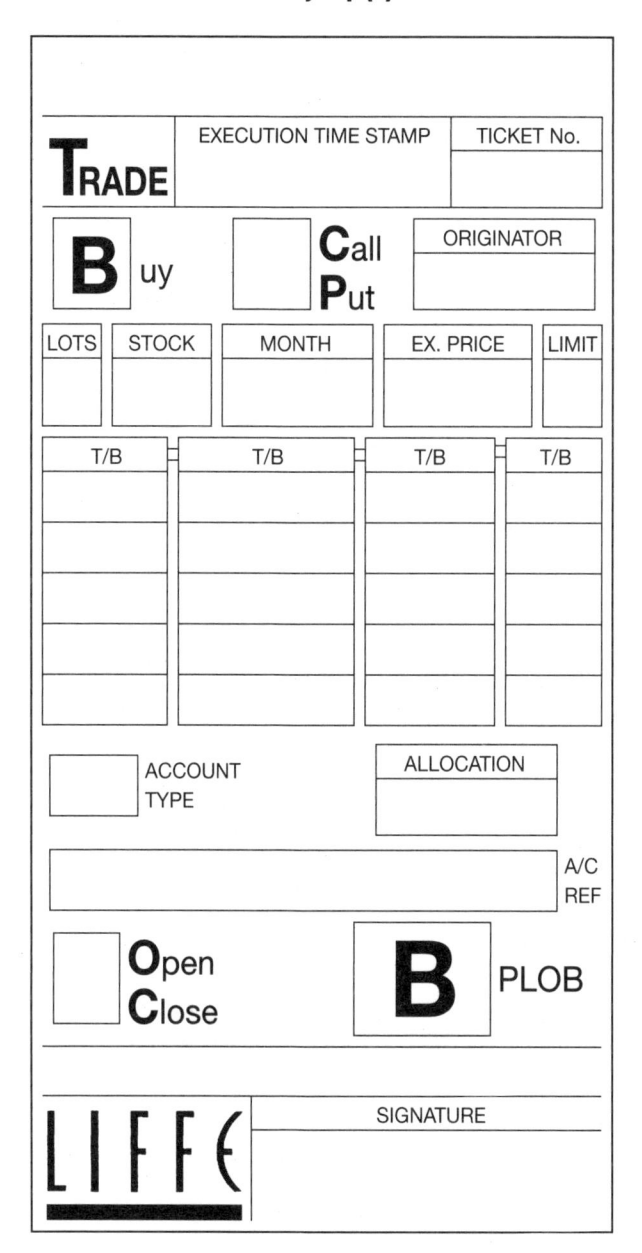

Fig 3.4

of member firms have their own access to the system and input the details of their trades themselves. This is known as Direct Member Input (DMI).

> **Definition** **TRS (Trade Registration System)** *is a real-time trade matching, allocation and registration system for all floor and Automated Pit Trading (APT) trades. TRS is split into several sections each concerned with one aspect of settlement and clearing.*

The first section trade information must flow through is Trade Matching where the details of the trades are checked and matched with the counter party's details.

From Trade Matching, the details pass on to Trade Allocation. It is possible that the trade is not for a direct client of the executing floor broker. In this case he will "give up" the trade and it will be allocated to and claimed by the other member.

Alongside Trade Allocation is Trade Claiming. Members must actively claim any trade allocated to them. Once the trade has been allocated and claimed, if necessary it is assigned to a specific account – House, Segregated Client, Non-Segregated Client, Local or Market Maker. Any trade that fails to pass any section within TRS for any reason is flagged as a mismatch for members' staff to resolve. As all of this is happening the trade may be reported back to the investor for his information.

CPS

From TRS the trade information is passed on to the Clearing Processing System (CPS). CPS provides member firms with real-time position-keeping and clearing functions, helping member firms to coordinate their trading settlement, margins and risk management systems. CPS is also used by the exchange (MSD) and LCH to monitor trading on a real-time basis throughout the day.

At the end of the trading day, once the trade has been matched, allocated and claimed, the details are passed from CPS on to the London Clearing House (LCH) for registration.

LCH

When the trade has taken place and matched there is a contractual obligation between the two parties (see Figure 3.5). Once the trade is registered with LCH, all links between the two trading parties are broken and any rights or obligations are between the investor and

Contractual obligations

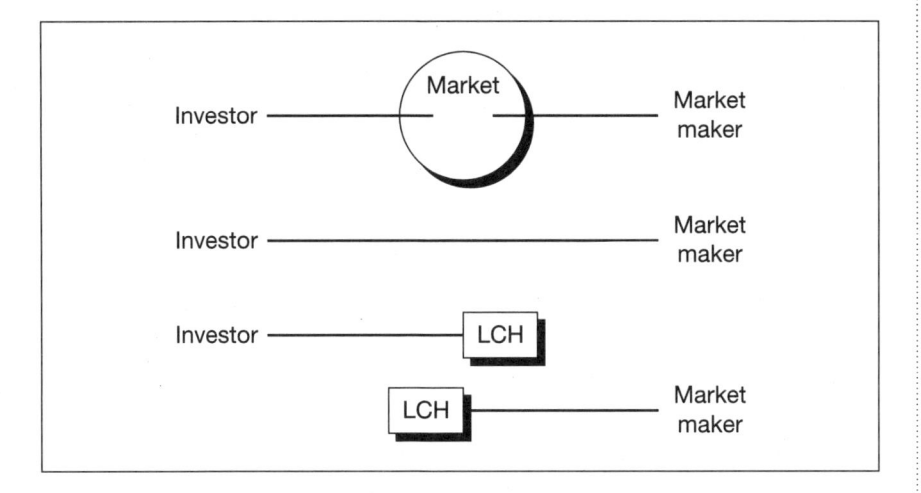

Fig 3.5

LCH. This system means that LCH is the guarantor for all trades on LIFFE and no one is at risk from counterparty credit ratings.

Payment for any options trade must be made to LCH by 10:00a.m. the following business day. However, most brokers will demand that most clients have sufficient funds on account with them to cover all purchases (including commissions) at the same time as accepting the order and trading.

At 16.10 the closing procedure starts. As with the opening procedure the exchange official can close the stocks in his charge by either an informal closing or a closing rotation depending on the amount of interest and price movements in the underlying security. Trading may continue in busier stocks as the prices are updated before being closed.

Exercise procedure

If a holder of an option wishes to exercise his rights and buy (call) or sell (put) the underlying security, he must instruct his broker to enter an exercise notice, to LCH, on his behalf. With the link between the buyer and seller having been broken, upon the submission of an exercise notice, LCH randomly assigns a broker to an investor who has written an option identical to the one being exercised, to either deliver (calls) or take delivery (puts) of the underlying security.

> **Key features**
>
> ## Computerized random selection
>
> *The computerized random selection process takes place overnight once all the day's trades have been processed. This allows for writers to close out their positions, during trading hours, without fear of being exercised against that evening.*

The selection by LCH will not identify an individual writer of an option, but a broker with at least one investor who has written an option identical to the one being exercised. The broker must then, again by random computerized selection, identify and notify the writer.

Once the option has been exercised, the details of the equity trade are entered into the London Stock Exchange's settlement system by the two brokers concerned. This is then matched as a standard share purchase and sale and settled on the appropriate Stock Exchange settlement day.

Equity options may be exercised on any business day and at any time until 17.20.

American-style index options may be exercised on any business day until 16.31. European-style index options may only be exercised on their expiry day until 18.00. On all expiry dates exercise times are extended to 18.00 to take into account the extra amount of exercise instructions received by LCH.

Clearing

All trades conducted on LIFFE, once checked and matched, need to be registered with a Clearing House. It is the Clearing House's responsibility to hold a register of all trades until the position is either closed, exercised or abandoned at expiry. Once registration has taken place the original counterparty agreement is broken and replaced with an agreement between the counterparties and the Clearing House. This process, known as "novation," has two important consequence. First, any counterparty credit risk is with the Clearing House not an individual or a firm who may not be considered a good risk.

> **It is the Clearing House's responsibility to hold a register of all trades until the position is either closed, exercised or abandoned at expiry.**

3 · Trading and Clearing

Second, with the Clearing House being at the centre of all trades, it allows a secondary market to be established, allowing options to be traded freely and openly.

The Clearing House for all trades on LIFFE is the London Clearing House (LCH) which is a Recognized Clearing House under the Financial Services Act (FSA) 1986. Under the FSA a Clearing House must have:

- adequate financial resources;
- monitoring and compliance procedures;
- high standards of integrity and fair dealing;
- and must cooperate with the Treasury and other regulators.

Membership of LCH (see Figure 3.6) is restricted to clearing members. These are firms who settle their own options business as well as being able to clear option business on behalf of other firms who are not members of LCH. Non-clearing members, usually smaller firms who do not transact sufficient business to justify the capital requirements of full membership of LCH, have an arrangement with clearing members for the clearing and settlement of their options business.

Margin

In addition to acting as the registrar and counterparty to all trades, LCH calculates and holds margin. Margin, in the form of securities or cash, ensures that a writer of options has the financial resources, if exercised against, to take delivery of and pay for, or deliver the underlying security. All clearing members of LIFFE and LCH are required to provide margin in order to cover the open positions of all of their clients, usually brokers. In turn, with LIFFE operating a

LCH Membership — **Fig 3.6**

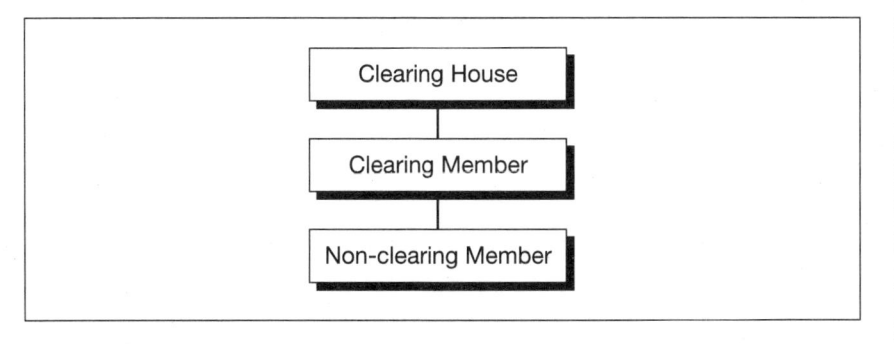

Clearing House → Clearing Member → Non-clearing Member

principal to principal system, all brokers acting for clients with open positions are required to provide margin to their clearing agents.

The margin provided by brokers to their clearing agents must be at least equal to the minimum margin requirements laid down by LCH. However, the margin charged by a broker to clients can be greater than that stipulated by LCH if the broker considers the client to be a poor credit risk.

SPAN

LCH uses a system called London SPAN to calculate its margin requirements. SPAN (Standard Portfolio Analysis of Risk) was developed by the Chicago Mercantile Exchange (CME) and adapted by LCH to meet LIFFE's requirements. The result is London SPAN.

London SPAN constructs a risk array of 16 different scenarios for changes in the price of the underlying security and for changes in its volatility (see Table 3.1).

The range is the largest move in the price of the underlying security that the Clearing House has identified as being likely in one day. For example, the scanning range set for XYZ Ltd might be 35 points. Therefore if XYZ Ltd is trading at 265, the 3/3 up range would go up to 300 and 3/3 down would be 230.

The volatility range is set to cover any change that might be expected in one day. If XYZ Ltd has a volatility of 12 percent, the "volatility up" scenario might value the option at 13 percent volatility.

The extreme move, up and down, is twice the normal scanning range.

LCH, after consultation with LIFFE, set all the parameters, such as scanning range, volatility and extreme moves. The para meters may be changed at any time to take into account changing market conditions.

Margin for short option positions consists of initial margin (calculated by London SPAN) and Net Liquidation Value (NLV).

Margin = Initial margin + NLV

NLV is calculated using the closing premium price of the series and is a negative figure for short positions and a positive figure for long positions.

Risk array — Table 3.1

1	underlying security unchanged	volatility up ↑
2	underlying security unchanged	volatility down ↓
3	underlying security up 1/3 range	volatility up ↑
4	underlying security up 1/3 range	volatility down ↓
5	underlying security down 1/3 range	volatility up ↑
6	underlying security down 1/3 range	volatility down ↓
7	underlying security up 2/3 range	volatility up ↑
8	underlying security up 2/3 range	volatility down ↓
9	underlying security down 2/3 range	volatility up ↑
10	underlying security down 2/3 range	volatility down ↓
11	underlying security up 3/3 range	volatility up ↑
12	underlying security up 3/3 range	volatility down ↓
13	underlying security down 3/3 range	volatility up ↑
14	underlying security down 3/3 range	volatility down ↓
15	underlying security up extreme move (cover 35% of loss)	
16	underlying security down extreme move (cover 35% of loss)	

If the closing premium for a short options position is 26p, the NLV will be £260 (premium × contract size × contract size).

> **Example**
>
> An investor is short 1 TBC Dec 360 call. The initial margin is calculated at −£97. The closing premium is 42p giving a NLV of −£420.
>
> Total margin = Initial margin + NLV
>
> = £97 + £420
>
> = £517 debit

Margin is also calculated on long option positions. However, the maximum loss a holder of an option can sustain is the premium paid for the option. Margin on a long position is a positive figure; it is not paid to the holder but may be used to offset margin requirements on short position in an option portfolio.

Position continues to be margined after the option has been exercised but before delivery takes place. This takes into account any price movement in the underlying security between exercise and payment for the stock. Delivery margin consists of contingent margin and initial margin. Contingent margin is calculated as the difference between the exercise price and the underlying security's closing price on the London Stock Exchange.

> **While LCH sets the minimum margin requirements brokers often require additional cover from their clients. This means the broker does not have to be continually approaching clients for additional cover.**

While LCH sets the minimum margin requirements brokers often require additional cover from their clients. This additional cover reflects the clients' credit risk and, since margin requirements can change daily, means the broker does not have to be continually approaching clients for additional cover. The broker can increase margin calls at any time, but may not reduce clients' margin requirements below that calculated by LCH.

LCH accepts a number of different forms of securities as collateral for margin. These include:

- cash
- certain UK shares
- UK Bank guarantees
- UK Treasury Bills
- UK Gilts
- £ Certificates of deposit
- US Treasury Bonds
- US Treasury Bills and Notes
- $ Certificates of Deposit
- German Government Bonds
- Italian Government Bonds
- Italian Treasury Bills

- Spanish Government Bonds
- Spanish Treasury Bills.

Securities put up as collateral must be registered into a nominee company controlled by the executing broker and their clearing agent. This gives the broker and the clearing agent legal rights over the securities should any default happen. All types of securities put up as collateral are liable to discounting by LCH to ensure their true market and saleable value is used when calculating margin. This discounting is known as a "hair cut" in the market.

OMLX

Introduction

OMLX is London's first and, to date, only fully computerized derivatives exchange. This is in addition to its electronic dealing link with OM Stockholm being the first example of two exchanges being linked electronically.

> **Definition**
>
> *The electronic dealing system, known as* **"OM CLICK,"** *consists of a central exchange to which all the traders are connected. The central exchange system consists of the actual "marketplace," an information dissemination subsystem that provides information about products and trades, and a further subsystem to capture information about deals made, before they are passed on to the clearing system.*

The system gets its name from the fact that the vast majority of functions are conducted by clicking on and off icons and menus using the mouse of the PC. This allows the trader to:

- place orders;
- conduct order maintenance, i.e. increase or decrease price and/or size of orders;
- activate or cancel orders.

Other features of OM CLICK include:

- an integrated order book;
- using different types of orders: fill or kill, rest of the day or until expiry;
- ranking orders in accordance with the rules, i.e. price and time order;
- the ability to trade combination orders;
- access to real-time market information;
- access full trade information and audit trails;
- colour coding of prices.

With trading on OMLX being electronic and with it operating an integrated Clearing House there is no need for a separate TRS system as on LIFFE. All orders placed into the trading system will only match and trade if all the information is present and correct and once any trade has taken place the system knows who has traded with whom.

Since 1991 OM CLICK has been in operation in Sweden, the United Kingdom, Austria and Italy.

Dealing process

The OMLX exchange is not at present open to private investors and is therefore a professional-only market. However, OM Stockholm is open to private investors, resulting in a rather lopsided order flow. While the market is not strictly a competing market-maker system, it is not an order-driven system either; in fact it falls some way between the two systems. Firm dealing orders are placed into the system and trade when matched, automatically, but, unlike a true order-driven system there are market makers to add liquidity to the market. The role and duties of the market makers on the OMLX depend to a certain extent on whether they are making a market in futures or options, but basically they are required to:

- maintain continuous firm dealing prices for the three at-the-money calls and puts;
- maintain a firm dealing price for all the contracts they are registered in if registered in futures contracts;
- quote additional firm prices if requested to do so by the exchange;
- make their firm prices in a minimum size of at least 10 contracts for both futures and options.

In return for complying with their obligations market makers receive a reduced clearing fee. The market makers are required to fulfill their obligation during the opening times of the exchange, 10.00 to 16.00 Swedish time. Unlike most exchanges it is possible for OMLX exchange members to trade with each other outside of these hours. If they do trade, and wish for the trade to be registered with the exchange, the terms of the contract must be identical to OMLX contracts and the trade reported to the exchange.

Once a trade has taken place within the system the details are automatically sent to the clearing department for registration and clearing. Unlike LIFFE, OMLX operates with a fully integrated clearing function within the exchange. Whereas on LIFFE, LCH becomes the counterparty to all trades, on OMLX the exchange itself is the counterparty and sets all margin requirements. This means that all trades are conducted with the exchange on the opposite side of the bargain as soon as the trade has taken place.

Margin

The exchange margining system is known as OMS II and is a portfolio-based risk analysis system first introduced in 1987. The most accurate and efficient way to calculate margin requirements is to look at the portfolio as a whole and see how an adverse move in the value of the underlying security would affect the entire portfolio. This is calculated by estimating the net cost to the exchange of closing the portfolio using the worst case move in the underlying security.

The actual formula for calculating the margin requirements for OMLX depends on the product, i.e. futures or options. However, there are a number of elements to the calculations which are the same for both futures and options.

Lead time

The lead time is the amount of time it would take the exchange to unwind or neutralize a position. This is usually set at three days as it may take this long to recognize that a firm has defaulted and then unwind the position. The lead time is used to calculate the size of the valuation interval.

Valuation interval

The valuation interval, also known as the scanning range, is the range of underlying values across which the portfolio is valued to determine the estimated worst case, to the Clearing House, or in OMLX's case the exchange itself, of liquidating the portfolio. The valuation interval represents the largest anticipated moves up and down over a given period, i.e. the lead time, from a given day's closing market price. The size of the valuation interval is dependent on past moves in the underlying security.

> **Example**
>
> If the valuation interval for the OMLX index is 10 percent + or – of the closing level and the index closed at 1387, the valuation interval would be calculated thus:
>
> upper limit   1387 + (10% × 1387) = 1525.7
>
> lower limit   1387 – (10% × 1387) = 1248.3

Therefore the OMS II system would calculate margins based on the assumption that the OMLX index would not go above 1525.7 or below 1248.3 during the lead time.

Valuation points

The extreme movements allowed for in the calculation are the upper and lower levels set by the valuation interval. This is then in turn subdivided into 31 valuation points, the mid-price of the closing market plus 15 valuation points on either side. At each valuation point the cost of closing out the position is calculated based on the value of the underlying security at that point.

The data used to calculate the margin requirements for both member firms and their clients is made available to exchange members in what are known as vector files to enable the member firms to calculate both their own and their clients' requirements, without having to wait for the figures from the exchange.

Futures

The stock futures contracts traded and cleared on OMLX are more like forward contracts and as such do not settle profits and/or losses on a daily basis. Instead they accumulate any profits or losses which are then settled, profits being paid out and losses received, usually at expiry. This means that the margin calculation must take into consideration the original price or the average price if contracts were purchased at different times and prices. This price is then compared with the estimated worst move, during the lead time, from that day's closing price.

Options

Since all options traded on OMLX are subject to stock type settlement of the option premium, i.e. settled the following business day, margin is only required for short or written positions. With a long position being able to be sold to realize a positive cash flow, the margin requirement for a held position is normally a positive figure. Alternatively, in certain circumstances where the value of the option is below a pre-set level it is deemed to be worthless and set to zero. Since the positive margin on a long position is used to offset any negative margin requirements for a short position, it is not distributed to the holder.

When calculating the option value, OMS II uses a number of models depending on what is being valued. The Black & Scholes model is used to value European-style calls and puts and American-style calls, The Black 76 model is used for index options and the binomial model for American-style put options. The volatilities used in the various models are the average of the closing implied volatilities of the three at-the-money exercise prices.

Obviously the higher the volatility the higher the value of the option. OMS II therefore sets a maximum limit on the volatility that can be used to value a long position and also sets a minimum volatility for a written option. An example of this is that long index options cannot have an implied volatility greater than 40 percent, whilst short index positions cannot have an implied volatility of less than 10 percent.

Cross margining

The majority of futures and options portfolios contain more than one position or contract type with the same underlying security. In this situation the risk involved is the risk of the combined position and not of the individual positions. OMS II takes these positions into account when calculating the margin requirements and produces a margin requirement for each underlying security.

Product development

Julian Perrins, OMLX

Whilst most people's impression of the workings of a derivative exchange is that of a passive market place merely offering a market floor for the trading of derivative products, the truth is that an exchange is extremely active and dynamic behind the scenes. The process of turning an idea into a successful product starts with market research and product development, and is continued with the marketing and promotional support for the product. Julian Perrins MA (Cantab), Business Development Manager at OMLX, looks at the process of product development. Julian started his career in derivatives with the London Traded Options Market (LTOM) overseeing the trading of the open outcry market before moving into product development, a position he also held after the merger between LTOM and the London Financial Futures Exchange. Julian is now the manager of business development with the Swedish OMLX Exchange in London.

Introduction

In 1994 over 50 new products were launched on various derivative exchanges worldwide. However, few of these products have actually succeeded in generating a constant stream of business. This highlights one of the problems product development departments have faced over recent years: so many new products have already been developed that it is difficult to find *the* one new product which has the potential to be a success. The ideal is to be as successful as the S&P 100 Index option contract traded on the Chicago Board Options Exchange (CBOE), the most actively traded equity derivative contract in 1994.

Despite the relatively high failure rate of new products the role of product development remains pivotol to exchanges. As financial markets and the needs of market participants change, so an exchange cannot afford to let its product range stagnate. Exchanges need to establish not only how they can develop new products, but also, how they can adapt their existing range of products to the markets' current and ever-changing requirements.

The purpose of this article is to give an overview of the work of product development within an equity derivative exchange, examine recent trends in the product development world and look at the reasons why new products may succeed or fail.

Product development trends

It is accepted that there are few blockbuster products out there waiting to be developed and listed on an exchange, therefore exchanges need to make their existing product range work harder. This can be achieved either by expanding the range of users of the existing products through simple marketing initiatives, or by expanding the range of expiry months available on a particular product. To this end, witness the recent introduction of serial months on certain of LIFFE's fixed-interest contracts and the existence of LEAPS (Long-Term Equity Anticipation Securities) on US exchanges.

In the last two years exchanges have taken this idea further with the introduction of Flex options. Flexible exchange options, to give them their full title, were pioneered by the CBOE. They are designed to provide investors with the best of the exchange-traded and the over-the-counter markets.

Flex options allow investors to set certain parameters of the contract themselves, such as expiry date, exercise price and exercise style, but the product is traded on an exchange and cleared and guaranteed by a recognized Clearing House. By their very nature Flex trades tend to be one-off transactions in large size. As such the Flex option way of trading can be, and will increasingly be, applied to those standardized contracts which are not liquid and may only be traded every other day or so.

A common way for an exchange to develop its product base is by setting up a linkage with another exchange. This broadens the products to which the members of each exchange may have access. Some linkages are across time zones, thus extending the trading hours of one contract, e.g. the CME and SIMEX link for the Eurodollar contract; others are in the same time zone, e.g. DTB and Matif. One of the problems which can face linkages in the same time zone is resistance from the exchanges' members, fearful that they will lose their share of business in their domestic products.

What makes a product successful?

The criteria for a product to be successful can be split into two parts; those relating to the nature of the product itself and those to its user base.

Product criteria

1. Clear rationale
To be successful, a new product must allow investors to do something which they cannot do using existing instruments or, if an equivalent instrument already exists, it must offer the same results but in a more cost-effective and resource-efficient manner, which compels them to change their practice. In short, there must be an economic need for the product.

2. Volatile underlying market
The underlying market for the new product, be it a share, equity index, a commodity etc., should be volatile. If there is no movement in the underlying instrument, then it is unlikely that the investor will wish to hedge their exposure to it or speculate on future price movements by using the derivative instrument.

3. Liquid underlying market
It is important for the likely success of the product that the underlying market is actively traded. If there is no interest in the underlying market, then there will be no interest in the derivative contracts. For market makers in a new product, the liquidity of the underlying instrument is vital, because they will hedge their derivatives' positions in the underlying instrument. If they are unable to hedge at a competitive price, they may be reluctant to quote tight price spreads in the derivative instrument.

4. Large underlying market
The larger the underlying market, the more demand there should be for a derivative product, due to there being a greater user base.

5. Simplicity
The product design should be kept as simple as possible, the market's interest in a new product can be easily lost if layer upon layer of complexity is introduced. Intricate specifications should be the reserve of practitioners in the over-the-counter market, developing bespoke products to solve the problems of their clients. The simpler the contract specification the easier it will be for arbitrageurs to become involved.

Product users

Self-evidently there should be genuine demand for the product from a wide range of users; too many products fail because the demand for them has been oversold. The potential user base must comprise a range of market participants:

1. Hedgers

Hedgers will use the derivative instruments to offset a position in the underlying instrument, thus reducing risk. They are indifferent about future price movements in the underlying instrument because such gains or losses are offset by their equal but opposite position in the derivatives contract.

2. Speculators

Speculators are the opposite of hedgers because they are looking to take risk rather than reduce it. A speculator will look to profit from a view he has of the likely future movement of the underlying instrument by actively trading the derivative.

3. Arbitrageurs

Arbitrageurs are crucial to the success of a new contract. On occasions when the price of the underlying instrument and the price of the derivatives contract on that instrument fall out of line, due to factors such as supply and demand, arbitrageurs will enter the market and force the two prices back into line, thus keeping the derivatives contract linked to the real world.

The involvement of real end-users, either as hedgers or speculators, in a new product is also crucial. If the professionals see that there is genuine business coming into the product, then they will respond by actively providing two-way markets.

New products

There are other factors which help to make a product successful. For example, there are occasions when exchanges may vie to be the first to launch a particular new product. In some product areas, particularly the fixed-interest market, experience has shown that it is vital to be the first to list the product and establish liquidity. For this reason there is competition between LIFFE and the DTB for the German Bond derivative market.

LIFFE was the first exchange to list derivatives contract at the short (Euromark) and long (Bund) end of the yield curve and despite the DTB listing comparable contracts, LIFFE has held about 70 percent of the total market business. The DTB, however, was the first to launch a medium-term bond contract (Bobl) and has total market share, despite LIFFE listing a rival contract.

The timing of the introduction of the new product is also a major factor. If one is considering listing a derivative contract on an index, that index must have been accepted as a benchmark by the market for the segment of the market it is indexing. Also at the time of the launch it is important that the market is looking at that particular segment of the market, i.e. second tier stocks, small cap stocks etc. Of course this requires a large slice of luck, the final ingredient in making a product successful.

What are the steps an exchange must take when launching a new product?

The first step is to have an idea for a new product. There are normally two main sources for these ideas: market participants and other exchanges. One of the tasks of a product development department is to monitor developments at the exchanges and to assess whether any product innovation can be applied to the relevant domestic market. Brokers and market makers are excellent sources for new products ideas because they have first-hand knowledge of developments in the market and can see where there is a requirement for a new product.

Once a new product area has been identified, an exchange needs to assess how viable it is to launch such a product. An initial analysis should focus on how the new product fits in with existing product range and the exchange's stated strategy vis à vis new developments. For example:

- Will the new product develop an existing product area?
- Will the new product involve a new product area? If so, is this an area which we want to move into? Does this fit in with the stated goals and objectives of the exchange? Does the exchange have any experience or expertise in this area?
- Is the target market for the product the same as that already trading with the exchange? If not, the exchange will need to

devote time and resources to marketing new contracts and developing a customer base for the product.

Feasibility study

Once the exchange has decided that this new product fits in with its strategic goals, then it will undertake a feasibility study. This involves undertaking a calling program around the exchange's members, both the sales side and the proprietary trading side. In discussions with market participants, the exchange will assess the demand for the product and try to find answers to questions such as: who will use it? why will they use it? and how often will they use it? This can be a tricky exercise because experience has shown that while market participants will always claim there is a demand for a product, once it is launched, this demand may be slow to materialize!

Also, one needs to be sensitive to the different needs and views amongst the exchange's membership. For one member, or group of members, a new product may compete with a successful over-the-counter product, but for another group of members a new product may offer a new area of business for them to expand into. An exchange needs to be sensitive to the politics of its membership.

For an exchange to decide to launch a new product, it will need some visible evidence of support from its members for the product. This normally takes the form of market-making support, i.e. members will undertake to make two-way prices in a minimum number of contracts for an initial period in order to give customers the comfort that there is a liquid market from day one.

As part of this program, the exchange will agree with practitioners a contract specification for the product in such areas as contract size and expiry months.

As well as undertaking external market research, the product development team will also need to assess the likely impact upon other departments within the exchange. For example:

- Are there any legal or regulatory implications arising from the introduction of the new product?
- Will any systems changes be required?

- How is the product going to be cleared and margined?
- How is the product going to be marketed?

Once this analysis has been completed a cost/benefits analysis can be performed. This involves creating a spreadsheet to model various "what if" scenarios, using projected levels of income based on the number of contracts traded and the costs of setting up the product and on-going maintenance costs. This analysis should show what level of business there needs to be in the new product for the exchange to recoup its costs and make an operating profit.

When the feasibility analysis has been completed, the exchange will decide whether to list the new product. Assuming the decision to list, a project team will be set up comprising of representatives from each of the main departments. The role of the project development team is now essentially one of project management, making sure that everything is done at the right time to ensure a timely launch. All that is now left is for the development team to sit back and, hopefully, watch the product trade. Then the process begins again.

Marketing and promotional support

Tony Hawes, Equity Products, LIFFE

Following on from the article by Julian Perrins on product development, Tony Hawes, Business Development Manager, Equity Products, LIFFE, looks at the marketing and promotional support for derivative products. Tony has been involved with equity and index options for over nine years. He started with the London Traded Options Market in 1987, regulating market trading for four years before moving into business development. After the merger between LTOM and the London Financial Futures Exchange, Tony continued in business development and for the last three years has been the manager responsible for private client business with equity and index products at LIFFE. He has recently taken on the responsibility for overseeing the transition of LIFFE's equity products from an open outcry market to a screen-based market.

Who is the end user?

The end users of equity based derivatives in the UK have historically fallen into three quite distinct camps. These are:

- "institutional" in the shape of fund managers, corporate treasurers and the like;
- "professional" in the form of equity market makers and proprietary traders (often Exchange members); and
- "retail" in the shape of private investors.

Whilst markets in the UK and overseas typically share these key user groups, the degrees to which each participate in the market vary significantly. Users of index futures, for instance, tend to be drawn almost entirely from the institutional and professional camps with the split of business in the UK being heavily in favor of the institutions.

Despite the picture painted by many commentators, the majority of derivative use is fairly unsophisticated and most of the institutions will only be using index futures as an asset allocation tool and index options for portfolio enhancement and insurance (hedging). Although most of the top 40 UK investment institutions are now thought to use derivatives in one form or another, and there has been a significant increase of late in their use of index options, there is much to suggest that considerable scope exists for them to increase that use.

Being geared toward institutional users, index futures tend to be of a size which prohibits use by retail (private) investors. The large size of these contracts means that most private investors will rarely have the wherewithal to own the underlying instrument (all stocks in the FT-SE 100 Index for instance) and would therefore be exposed to potentially unlimited risk.

However, some retail investors make extensive use of both equity and index options. As one might expect, their activity tends to be fairly uncomplicated and leans considerably toward straightforward limited risk speculation. Indeed, in a recent survey conducted by LIFFE, 62 percent of private client option users indicated that their main reason for trading options was speculative.

> In a recent survey conducted by LIFFE, 62 percent of private client option users indicated that their main reason for trading options was speculative.

Private investors also tend to prefer individual equity options and the same survey showed how less than one-third of their business was in index options. This is possibly as a result of the higher levels of comfort that exist when dealing with the same shares of companies with which they are familiar.

Who should the end user be?

Institutional

Despite a number of unquestionable benefits afforded by equity derivatives, many UK institutions are restricted from making further use, and some from making any use at all, of them. Regulation of funds in the UK has changed considerably over the last five years and now enables the use of derivatives for efficient portfolio management. Any restrictions now imposed are generally those resulting from the attitudes of fund managers and trustees.

All of LIFFE's products are marketed actively to institutional investors and the Exchange spends considerable time and effort pursuing changes in attitude, along with suitable changes in the various regulations. In terms of the fund managers and trustees – as with any other potential derivative user – the thrust of the marketing effort is of necessity built upon developing their understanding of the opportunities afforded by what many see as "new fangled" products.

In promoting products to the institutions the Exchange will often work closely with institutional brokers, perhaps on joint client visits or in-house seminars. Most exchanges, and LIFFE in particular, will also work closely with regulatory and professional bodies to encourage mutual understanding and make the appropriate use of derivatives as accessible as possible for all institutional users.

In all of these activities it is clearly important for exchange staff to have a good understanding of the regulatory environment and also to monitor closely any changes that may positively, or adversely, affect the ability of participants in the market to trade derivatives.

> In recent years there has been a significant increase in the use of both LIFFE's index futures and options contracts

Institutional users in the UK account for by far the majority of volume in equity derivatives. In recent years there has been a significant increase in the use of both LIFFE's index futures and options contracts and, in both cases, this is believed to be a result of wider institutional use. These institutions currently include insurance companies, unit trusts, investments trusts, hedge funds and pension funds.

Retail

Despite the fact that there already exists a hard core of private clients making extensive use of options in the UK, potential for growth in this area of the market, when compared to similar markets world-wide, is still very significant.

Although mostly anecdotal, evidence suggests that just prior to the Stock Market crash of 1987, private investors may have been accounting for over 30 percent of the total volume in equity and index options in the UK. However, following the crash and the resulting poor publicity suffered by the Stock Market in general, and the options market in particular, there was a rapid decline in the interest shown by the retail market.

Whilst it is difficult to accurately measure how much business emanates from private investors, it is generally accepted that in the UK today they account for less than 20 percent of the overall volume in equity and index options. This compares to figures of 50 percent and 70 percent in the US and Holland respectively. Indeed, in the fairly recent past, the figure for the US has been quoted as being closer to 80 percent and it is only the growth in institutional business there that has led to a fall.

To bring this further into perspective, it is worth noting that whilst the population of Holland is around a quarter of that in the UK, the European Options Exchange in Amsterdam trades considerably more equity and index option contracts than LIFFE.

The poor perception of the traded options market in the UK that has prevailed is possibly at its worst amongst the retail investment community. This perception was developed in the late 1980s early 1990s and seems to have been mainly brought about by "horror stories" of how private investors suffered at the hands of the options market. Whilst many of the stories undoubtedly had some basis of truth they were, almost without exception, the result of poor understanding and the employment of some extremely speculative trading strategies – many of which would, quite rightly, not be allowed by retail stockbrokers today.

> The poor perception of the traded options market in the UK that has prevailed is possibly at its worst amongst the retail investment community.

Equity and index options are unique amongst LIFFE's product range as all of LIFFE's other products are geared solely to the use of institutions. However, it is widely recognized that the private investor is important – if not essential – to the development of a successful market in equity and index options. LIFFE has therefore made concerted efforts to develop this sector of the market.

This approach has been to work in conjunction with stockbrokers to assist them in developing this area of their business – an approach which has been particularly successful in the US. Unfortunately, mainly due to the negative attitudes discussed above, many brokers have not been keen to pro-actively develop their option business. Indeed, at the time of the merger of LIFFE and the London Traded Options Market (LTOM) in 1992, a number of retail stockbrokers were withdrawing from the traded options market claiming that the products were either too risky and inappropriate for their clients or that the regulatory and administrative requirements were too onerous.

The Exchange developed a push–pull approach to retail marketing (similar to that adopted for institutional business) which has involved working both with proactive brokers to talk to their existing clients and also talking to private clients directly. Having only ever dealt directly with investors who, for the main part, would be considered "expert" or "professional" this was a significant departure for the Exchange.

This direct approach has manifested itself in the shape of a range of services, mostly of an educational nature, and has included the establishment of a dedicated private investor "information-line," an extensive range of literature and a series of seminars.

General business development

It is widely believed that the lack of understanding amongst both potential investors and market commentators is a major factor in hindering growth.

LIFFE offers a plethora of educational material in the form of a wide range of literature and seminars which are themselves promoted widely. These are widely recognized as being of a high quality and many are viewed as essential for those people coming to the market anew and may take the shape of open courses or may be specifically tailored for a given company.

Other restraining factors – although to a lesser extent than perhaps two or three years ago – are the problems that some participants face when trying to obtain information, including up-to-date prices and access to relevant services such as software for option pricing. It often falls, therefore, to the Exchange to source such information and publicise its existence and whereabouts to investors. As a vehicle for this LIFFE produces, and distributes widely, regular newsletters aimed at providing the various participants with regular updates on market activity and developments.

Whilst most institutions will have access to at least one, if not several, quote vendor services, it is only quite recently that costs for some such services have come down to a level where they are affordable for the serious private investor. However, it is still the case currently that many private investors are reliant upon historical (i.e. previous day) information from newspapers or a limited service provided though teletext systems which are updated only infrequently.

> **Wider dissemination of any information that makes it easier for investors to participate is clearly in the interest of the Exchange and important to the marketing effort.**

Wider dissemination of any information that makes it easier for investors to participate is clearly in the interest of the Exchange and important to the marketing effort. As such LIFFE works closely with quote vendors to ensure availability of accurate and timely price information and also maintains relationships with a wide range of service providers.

The development of relationships with the press are also naturally very important to derivative exchanges and the industry in general. The derivatives industry is widely regarded as very new (despite the fact that its origins can be traced back beyond the Middle Ages) and as a consequence is subject to particularly close scrutiny at the first sign of difficulty. A number of stories have broken in the last two years which have resulted in just such scrutiny and despite the fact that most do not even concern exchange traded contracts, the public relations machinery at LIFFE and other exchanges must go into overdrive to educate the commentators and eradicate misconceptions.

The process of encouraging support and developing understanding amongst financial journalists is therefore an ongoing and very important one. As well as frequent press launches of new products, regular courses and open days are held at the Exchange.

Similar efforts are made to establish relationships with a wide range of regulatory and professional bodies, including trade associations, involved in the development and monitoring of both institutional and retail investment activities. Once established, such relationships are often built upon with the production of joint ventures in the shape of briefings and seminars for members.

Both institutional and retail marketing activities also involve ongoing one-on-one visits to both end users and brokers as a means of researching requirements and ways in which they, and their clients, might like to see the market develop.

With the relentless progress of technology, information and the ability to trade all manner of investments, products become more widely available by the day. Coupled with the ever-growing demand for a wider variety of products, this leads to a continually growing and changing user base. As a consequence, the marketing of these products now requires, and is likely to require for some time to come, an extremely flexible approach.

Clearing and settlement

Jacqueline Totley, MSI (DIP) of Monument Derivatives Ltd

The settlement or "back office" function within many city firms is often thought of as unglamorous and boring. However, while settlement may not have such a high profile as trading, its role within the industry is just as important and has the ability to save the firm millions of pounds by the timely spotting of dealing errors. Below, Jacqueline Totley, MSI (DIP), of Monument Derivatives Ltd, looks at a number of issues and how they affect clearing and settlement. Jackie has spent over 15 years in the derivatives industry, including time with a Clearing House, an exchange, A European bank and a major international securities house. She is now a director of Monument Derivatives Ltd, a specialist derivatives broker.

Clearing services

There is an increasing trend towards using specialist clearing companies to provide clearing and settlement services. Many clearing companies offer global clearing facilities, which means that they are members of all the major markets or have established a network of links with clearers on the other exchanges worldwide. Other clearing companies set themselves up as providing an effective and tailored service in one market, while some users prefer to establish direct links with local specialists.

Clearing and settlement, including risk management, is certainly as important as execution. Clearers provide extensive daily documentation and information to their customers. This information should not be used solely by the "back offices"; it is extremely useful for the dealing desk in reviewing clients' positions and giving advice, and for senior management in monitoring positions and risk management. The information provided may include:

- the collection and collation of new trades
- the registration of trades
- position keeping
- settlement
- daily margin calculation
- collateral maintenance
- the process of exercise and assignment.

The relationship between the broker and a specialist clearing firm is normally established according to two basic structures. The first is where the broker has the sole relationship as principal with the clearing firm. This will typically take the form of a clearing services agreement between the two firms. Both of the firms will be conducting investment business and will therefore both be regulated under the Financial Services Act.

The clearing firm will look solely to the broker for payment of all monies and all instructions concerning positions in the account. The clearer will have no knowledge of the identities of any of the underlying clients, as the broker will maintain the relationship with the clients.

The clearing service may however include a provision of a sub-account facility to assist the broker in analyzing positions. In such instances, while the clearing firm will undoubtedly have internal monitoring procedures, it is unlikely to set formal limits and all business will be settled on the business day after the day of trade. This type of service is often known as a "model A" service.

The other main service is where the broker acts as an introducing broker to the clearing firm. In this instance, both firms will have a contract with the underlying clients, the broker providing the dealing and advisory services and the clearing firm the clearing and settlement service. This will result in the clearer acting as the counterparty for all such services for each client under the terms of business entered into with each customer.

The terms of the Introducing Broker Agreement between the broker and the clearer may provide recourse by the clearing firm to the broker in the event that a client introduced under the agreement subsequently defaults. The broking firm and the clearing firm will typically work together to establish an account opening procedure and set required minimum balances and monitoring procedures for each customer after considering their likely trading pattern and resources. This is known as a "model B" service.

The general trend to rationalize clearing services has also led to the increased separation of clearing and floor execution functions. While firms will typically use only one clearing firm, at least per centre if not worldwide, many use more than one executing broker, either due to their specialization in different products, long-established relationships or simply to spread business. A whole structure of arrangements therefore exists with floor brokers, who execute trades on the market floor and then give up the trades to the clearing firm acting for the broking firm.

Certain clearing firms also specialize in providing clearing services to independent traders, better known as "locals." These are entrepreneurs who commit their own capital and stand in the trading pit on a daily basis with the aim of making an overall profit, or more correctly, being right more times than they are wrong.

Locals provide the essential liquidity to the market, typically executing numerous transactions during each day with the majority always ensuring that they end the day "flat," that is to say with no open long or short positions held overnight, the main reasons for this being that many could not afford the margin requirements on open positions or simply wish to avoid overnight exposure.

Locals are typically self-employed and under the Locals Agreement they will be registered to the clearing firm who will be responsible for their activities on the market. The agreement will contain a series of trading restrictions both intraday and overnight which will be monitored by clearing personnel on the trading floor and in the office. Limits are typically linked to funds available on the account at any one time.

Systems

Few firms develop their own systems for clearing and settling trades. There are a number of systems houses that provide cost-efficient systems which can be operated either on a bureau basis or licensed in-house. The major advantage is that the development and continuous updating costs are spread over a number of users and the systems are capable of handling "all markets," with the supplier producing regular updates as new products and markets are launched. Any firm's major systems resources are either enhancements to the "basic" clearing service or devoted to the development of "front-end systems," that is proprietary models designed on technical or quantitative bases to provide valuations intended to highlight particular trading opportunities.

Compliance

It is important that everyone who works in the industry has an understanding of the regulatory environment and compliance requirements.

"Know your customer" is a cornerstone of the UK regulatory structure, meaning that at any time a firm intending to conduct investment business for a customer is aware of the full legal title of the customer and is in a position to categorize the client. The categories essentially separate private and non-private, or business, customers with a separate classification for market professionals, that is other market participants. This classification in turn defines the notifications and warnings that the customer must receive and regulations that the firm must follow in providing services to the customer.

The actual Customer Documentation must meet regulatory requirements, which for derivatives business are regulated by the Securities and Futures Authority.

Client money rules

The client money rules play a key role in the overall purpose of the Financial Services Act, namely the protection of investors. The purpose of the client money rules is to protect clients' money from the claims of creditors in the event of liquidation of a firm. The client money rules also cover "other assets," for example, collateral lodged by clients as cover for positions.

Where money requires client money protection, it must be held in client money bank accounts, separate from the firm's own money. All client money bank accounts must be properly established and subject to trust status arrangements, whereby the bank acknowledges that the money is being held by the firm on trust for its clients.

Likewise where a firm undertakes margined transactions for its clients, client transaction accounts must be established with Exchanges, Clearing Houses and Intermediate Brokers.

The initiation of a relationship with a provider of clearing services or a customer needs to be supported by written procedures and documentation to ensure that the respective rights and obligations of each of the parties is understood. It should also detail the regulatory requirements, establish the services to be provided and set the framework for the on-going monitoring and control of the arrangements.

The LIFFE market

Prior to March 1992 the London Traded Options Market was part of the London Stock Exchange and operated as part of the Stock Exchange framework with all business transacted on the traditional agency basis.

In March 1992 the LTOM was merged with the LIFFE market to form the London International Financial Futures and Options Exchange.

Like most derivatives exchanges LIFFE operates on the basis of a principal-to-principal market, that is, all business traded is as principal. Of course, LIFFE recognizes that much of the business transacted is actually for an underlying client. However, the concept is one of a series of back-to-back principal-to-principal contracts with each participant contracting with their customer or client as principal "down the line."

This ensures that LIFFE, as an exchange, can identify a principal to each transaction from within its membership.

All LIFFE members can be further subdivided as either clearing or non-clearing members. All non-clearing members must be linked to a general clearing member who is ultimately responsible for all their trades. Another feature of most derivatives exchanges is the existence of a central Clearing House which guarantees the performance of all business transacted.

Once a LIFFE contract has been executed, the two floor participants have established a contract between them. They then enter the trade for checking and matching.

All trades once matched are then registered with the London Clearing House, LCH. At this point two new contracts are created which replace the exchange contract, one between LCH and the Buying Clearing Member and another between LCH and the Selling Clearing Member.

On registration the Clearing House becomes a counterparty to each trade of a clearing member, that is, it becomes the buyer to every seller and the seller to every buyer.

The Clearing House also guarantees the performance of each trade to the clearing member, the major advantage being the elimination of direct credit exposure to trading counterparts. It is important to note that the Clearing House guarantee of performance only extends to Clearing House members and not beyond.

In order to support this guarantee of performance, the Clearing House provides a daily mark to market calculation and requires margin to be in place from clearing members to cover both initial and variation margin by 10.00a.m. on the day after the day of trade. All calls for margin cover are made through the protected payment system PPS. All clearing members are required to open a special PPS account from which the Clearing House can draw funds on a daily basis. LCH can also make intraday margin calls if required and all members must be able to respond.

The concept of margin flows down through the participants forms the basis of the SFA client money rules for margined transactions, requiring all member firms to hold sufficient margin from clients in the segregated account to cover aggregate margin requirements, and if there is a shortfall to top up the client money account from their own resources.

A daily calculation must be performed for derivatives to ensure that:

- All money held from segregated clients is segregated – that is all client monies are held in trust and protected in the event of the insolvency of the firm.
- The total amount segregated is sufficient, if positions are unwound, to meet gross liabilities to clients – and if not the firm is required to top up the client money account from its own resources.

The calculation is therefore, essentially a comparison of assets and liabilities.

Premium and Margin

All equity and index options on LIFFE are traded on a premium-paid basis, which means that premium amounts will be debited or credited to the account in full on the day after the day of trade.

The Clearing House, in association with the exchange, sets initial margin levels and is responsible for making calls for initial and variation margin on a daily basis. In addition LCH can make intraday margin calls if required.

The initial margin rates are parameters and may be changed from time to time in the light of changing market conditions.

In essence, the rate is set after considering historical price moves and volatility and reflects the amount that is considered sufficient to cover a one-day price movement. Only a one-day price move needs to be considered since LCH makes daily calls.

SPAN

The margining system used on LIFFE is known by the acronym SPAN, being Standard Portfolio Analysis of Risk. This, as the name implies, is based on an analysis of an overall portfolio rather than, for example, the other main alternative type of margining system generally referred to as strategy-based, which seeks to identify and "extract" specific strategies.

> **Definition**
>
> **SPAN** *is designed to emulate how a given portfolio would react to changing market conditions and the margin required is the largest loss that could occur for the portfolio under the set of conditions and parameters used in the calculation.*

A portfolio in this context is a group of positions relating to a single underlying asset. Thus all Zeneca Options would be grouped together, and the SPAN would be calculated. In this way SPAN offsets position risk wherever possible to produce a net margin. In order to match initial margin to risk, LCH needs to select the basis parameters of the model.

The scanning range is the full one-day price movement that LCH seeks to cover. For example, if the current scanning range for a stock is 30p, it means that cover is required for a change, upwards or downwards, of 30p in the current underlying stock price. In this example, if the underlying price is 300p, the scanning range would take an underlying price movement range from 270p to 330p.

The current requirement for FT-SE is 100-point move in the index. So if FT-SE closes at 3500, the scanning range would be from 3400 to 3600.

The volatility measures stock price variability, that is the amount the price moves up and down – the underlying price instability expressed as a percentage.

For each product the parameter is set for the change in volatility to be covered – an increase or decrease. For example, if the current implied volatility for ASDA is 60 percent and if the current parameter for a change in volatility of a series in ASDA is 10 percent, the cover required is for a change of volatility up to 66 percent and volatility down to 54 percent.

The exchange also selects the theoretical options pricing model that best suits the type of instrument; for instance, Black for futures, Black and Scholes for European-style Options and binomial-type models for American-style options.

Risk management

As a final topic I would like to put together some points and consider ways in which a firm can review their risks on a daily basis.

The key to successful risk management is in understanding the risks and how they may change, then assessing the amount of cover required against these risks at any time.

> **SPAN** — *Key features*
>
> *SPAN is a very sophisticated system; it takes a set of positions, develops a worst-case scenario based on historical movements and derives a figure of the amount required to cover this worst case.*

The calculations are produced by an authoritative source and are readily available on a daily basis and although they do not take account of positions in other markets, these also are likely to be readily available. All firms are required to call the SPAN calculations as a minimum from their clients.

The question you should ask is – IS SPAN SUFFICIENT?

Under the SPAN parameters the worst case scenario is based on a 24-hour move. This is considered sufficient since all clearing members are required to provide value for margin calls by 10.00a.m. the next day. Many clients are likely to be able to meet this timescale. As a simple calculation, take the scanning range and multiply it in full for the positions held, then multiply by 2 or 3 for the number of days you might expect it to take to receive funds.

In the case of a local, the normal assumption made by the clearing firm is that the existing account balance is all there is and real time on floor and systems-based monitoring is geared around this concept.

Customer business is normally handled somewhat differently, and starting with the basic "know your customer," coupled with strong settlement procedures and a clear segregation of duties and management reporting structure with relevant internal controls.

Above all, it is essential that the firm, or rather key personnel within the firm, have established various trading limits that are reviewed before a trade is executed and parameters against which total positions can be monitored. That senior personnel fully understand the products being traded and the risks involved in particular positions and how those risks may change is essential.

■ ■ ■

'It is important to break through the mystery and terminology surrounding derivatives as early as possible.'

Basic Characteristics of Options and Futures

Introduction

Traded options

What is a futures contract?

Option pricing

Basic trades

Futures trades

Flex options

Index traded options

Introduction

Derivatives, as with most specialist areas, whether investment, engineering or computing, can unfortunately be surrounded by mystery and their own unique terminology. It is important to break through the mystery and understand the terminology as early as possible in order to get a clear and concise picture of what is being discussed. Once we understand the basics, we can begin to see what futures and options are all about and how they can be used by both private and professional investors alike. Not only will this chapter explain the terminology surrounding index and equity futures and traded options, it will also lay the foundations for understanding how and why index and equity futures and options are used and how they work. Initially we will concentrate on equity traded options before moving on to futures contracts.

Traded options

It helps when trying to understand the basic concept of options to move away from stocks and shares to begin with and have a look at something we can all relate to from our everyday life, in this case buying a house.

An investor decides he wants to buy a new house. He goes along to a number of estate agents and after careful consideration, with regard to location, size and future potential, places a deposit on the house of his choice.

The terms of the deposit will normally specify that he is buying a house, the location, the cost of the house, together with the amount of the deposit and how long the deposit is valid for.

Once he has paid his deposit, the investor has secured the purchase price of the house, regardless of what happens elsewhere in the housing market or the general economy. There are now two choices open to him with regard to his deposit. He can:

1. Use his deposit and buy the house.
2. Do nothing and lose his deposit.

Having paid his deposit, the house purchaser has secured the right to purchase the house, but he is not obliged to do so. This means the prospective purchaser can, if the housing market or the general economy moves against him, walk away from the proposed house purchase, losing nothing more than the deposit already paid. The deposit giving the holder the right but not the obligation, to purchase the house is the same as an equity traded option based on a company's shares. A traded option is simply a method of securing either a purchase or sale price of shares.

After carefully considering the price and future prospects of a company's share, an investor decides he wishes to purchase an option. He approaches his broker and places his order. The price of the option will depend on the type of option it is, the purchase or sale price it secures and the time or life of the option. Each option specifies:

- what type of option it is (to buy or sell the shares);
- the number of shares involved (the contract specifications);
- name and type of shares (the underlying security);
- the purchase or sale price (the exercise/strike price);
- the amount of deposit (cost or premium of the option);
- how long it is valid for (its expiry date).

Once the option has been purchased, the holder has the same choices to make, about the option, as the investor with the deposit on the house. He can:

1. Take up his deposit and buy the shares (known as "to exercise" the option).
2. Do nothing and lose his deposit (known as "to abandon" the option).

However, a traded option is a security in its own right and may be bought or sold in the market at any time during its life. The option's price fluctuates as the price of the underlying security – the shares the option is based on – moves up or down. This means the holder of a traded option has a third choice; to sell the option back into the market for a profit or, if his decision was wrong, to limit his potential loss. The vast majority of investors trade their options back into the market, rather than exercise or abandon them.

> **The option's price fluctuates as the price of the underlying security – the shares the option is based on – moves up or down.**

> **Key features**
>
> ## Option trading
>
> *Option trading is a form of certificateless trading which means that no certificates are issued by company registrars. Instead, evidence of ownership is via a contract note issued by the investor's broker, but more importantly records of ownership are maintained on computer by the London Clearing House.*

Terminology

Before we go on, we need to look at the formal definition of an option and some of the terminology used.

> **Definition**
>
> *The definition of a **traded option** states: "An option is an agreement between a **buyer (holder)** and a **seller (writer)** giving the buyer the **right**, but **not the obligation**, to **buy** or **sell an asset** on or before a **given date**, at a **specific price** in return for a **consideration**."*

The buyer of the option, also known as the holder, has purchased the right to either buy or sell shares at a fixed price before a certain date. This means that the buyer or holder of the option has the right to decide what to do, and is not obliged to do anything. Just like the house buyer, the holder of the option can use the option and buy/sell the shares, trade the option back into the market or abandon it. On the opposite side of the trade is the seller or writer of the option who has no rights, only an obligation to either sell or purchase the shares if the holder chooses to exercise his rights. In other words the writer must sit tight and wait to see if the holder uses the option.

Whether the holder has acquired the rights to buy or sell will depend on the type of option purchased. There are two types or classes of options – calls and puts.

4 · Basic Characteristics of Options and Futures

> **Definition**
>
> **Call options** give holders the right, but not the obligation, to purchase the shares, if they wish to. If they want the shares they are "calling" them and thereby exercising the option.

> **Definition**
>
> The other type of options are **put options** which give holders the right, but again not the obligation, to sell the shares. In this instance holders do not want the shares and are therefore "putting" them on to someone else.

The shares that the option is based on are referred to as the underlying security or asset.

The fixed purchase or sale price secured by the option is known as the exercise or strike price and is set by the exchange with regard to the underlying security's price and a laid down table.

The prices in Table 4.1 are for UK equity options traded on LIFFE.

When an option is introduced to the market, whether it is due to the expiry of an old option or it is being introduced for the first

Table 4.1

Exercise prices for UK equity options

50	140	330	700	1150
60	160	360	750	1200
70	180	390	800	1250
80	200	420	850	1300
90	220	460	900	1350
100	240	500	950	1400
110	260	550	1000	1450
120	280	600	1050	1500
130	300	650	1100	1600

time, there will always be two exercise prices above and below the market price of the shares. In addition, if the underlying security price is the same as or near to an exercise price, that exercise price will be introduced with the next two exercise prices in the sequence above and below.

During the life of the option it may be necessary to introduce new exercise prices if the price of the underlying security rises or falls. If the market price of the underlying security falls below the second-lowest exercise price, or rises above the second-highest exercise price, the next exercise price in the price table will be introduced.

New exercise prices may also be introduced, at the discretion of the market officials, if the market traders request their introduction to aid trading in any way.

If the holder of an option decides to take up their rights and buy or sell the underlying security, it is known as "to exercise" the option. When a writer on the other hand is notified that they must buy or sell the underlying security to/from the holder, it is known as "being assigned."

Traded options have a finite life, the maximum time being nine months for equity options and 12 months for FT-SE 100 Index options. The date an option ceases to exist is known as its *expiry date*. This means that traded options are a wasting asset and after the expiry date the option ceases to exist and cannot be traded or exercised.

Expiry dates

There are always three expiry dates to choose from, with three months in between the dates, therefore, as already stated, the maximum life of an option is nine months. When an equity option is initially introduced to the market, it is allocated to one of three expiry cycles. The cycle it is allocated to will depend on when the company issues its interim and final results. The three cycles are:

1. Jan   April   July   Oct
2. Feb   May   Aug   Nov
3. Mar   June   Sept   Dec

> **Example**
>
> It is early January and an option on XYZ Ltd is trading on cycle 1 with expiry dates of Jan, April, and July. Once the Jan options expire, a new expiry date of Oct will be introduced, keeping three expiry months with three months in between. When the April option expires, a new expiry month of Jan the following year will be introduced. And so the cycle rolls on.

The expiry date for equity options is always the third Wednesday of the expiry month.

> **Definition**
>
> *The price paid for an option is known as its **premium** and is expressed in pence per share. However, it is not possible to trade options on just one share, they are in fact traded in contracts of, normally, 1,000 shares. ("Normally," because option contracts have to be adjusted to take into consideration rights issues and other corporate events.) This means that to calculate the cost of an option the premium must be multiplied by the contract size.*

> **Example**
>
> The premium of a XYZ Jan 360 call option is 18p. The contract is the normal contract size of 1,000 shares. The cost of the option, excluding transaction costs, is £180 (18p × 1000 = £180).
>
> The combination of an underlying security, expiry date, an exercise price and class is known as a series, e.g., ABC May 460 call.

An investor who, when buying an option, either opens a new position or increases an existing position, is transacting an opening purchase and becomes the holder of an option. When they sell some or all of the holdings they are closing their position and transacting a closing sale.

An investor who opens a new position or increases an existing position by selling an option is transacting an opening sale and becomes the writer of an option. When they buy back some or all of the options they have written, thereby extinguishing their obligations, they are transacting a closing purchase.

Underlying security

Traded options have been introduced on some of the most highly capitalized stocks on the London Stock Exchange and have all been, at the time of their introduction as traded options, members of the FT-SE 100 Index. By using only the most liquid stocks on which to list traded options, LIFFE ensures that there are firm, continuous two-way (bid and offer) prices on the underlying security.

In addition, the prices available on the underlying security are made in sizes that will allow the users of the traded options to hedge their position, with the underlying security, without the prices being moved substantially. Nearly all UK stocks have prices below £10 with the vast majority having prices of £5 or less. This helps to ensure that the stocks have sufficient liquidity in the stock market.

The liquidity of an underlying security is important when traded options are listed on it. If the liquidity of the security is restricted it is possible that speculators could use the options to gain control over sufficient stock to manipulate the share price. If this was the case, LIFFE would have to introduce position limits. These limits prevent investors, either individually or in groups, acquiring control of more than a certain number of options. The limits are normally, if imposed, dependent on the market capitalization of the underlying security. However, due to the liquidity of all of the underlying securities that have traded options based on them, LIFFE does not impose any position limits.

While there are no position limits imposed by LIFFE, if any individual investor or group of investors have control, including stock controlled by traded option, of more than 3 percent of the underlying security, the holding must be notified to the London Stock Exchange.

What is a futures contract?

Having already looked at a traded option, the concept of a futures contract is relatively simple. Just as a traded option can be looked on as a deposit securing either the purchase or sale price of the underlying security, so can a futures contract. However, with futures contracts there are no call or put contracts to determine whether the investor wishes to buy or sell the underlying security/asset. Instead, if the investor thinks the underlying security, in this case the FT-SE 100 Index, will rise, he buys a futures contract (he is going long of the future) and if he believes the index will fall, he sells the future (going short).

Once the investor has bought or sold the future, he has the same decisions to make as the holder of a traded option. He can either:

- exercise the contract;
- sell it back into the market (if he is long);
- buy it back from the market (if he is short).

If the investor exercises the futures contract and either buys (if long) or sells (if short), the underlying security settlement, as with the FT-SE 100 traded option contract, is for cash. However, as with traded options, the vast majority of contracts are never exercised. Instead, the positions are closed out by the investor taking an equal but opposite position in the market.

So if investor A had bought two Footsie futures contracts giving them a long position, they are then required to sell two Footsie futures which will result in the investor having a short position. This will mean that as far as the Clearing House is concerned the investor is both long and short of two contracts.

These two positions are then filed away together netting one off with the other. Not only will this result in investors having no outstanding position in the futures, but will also enable investors either to realize their profits or reduce their losses.

While up to now futures contracts sound exactly the same as traded options contracts, there are two very important differences. First, futures contracts cannot be abandoned. With a traded option that is worthless, the holder can decide to abandon it, allowing it to expire unexercised and worthless. However, an investor with a position in the futures, whether long or short, must close it out before expiry. This is because the holder of a traded option has the right, but not the obligation to exercise, unlike the holder of a futures contract who has an obligation to exercise, at or near to expiry, and can therefore not abandon a position he holds.

The investor must trade out of any position that is moving against him, limiting his losses, before expiry takes place. If, for whatever reason, the investor fails to trade out of the position, the exchange will automatically exercise the futures contract at expiry. This will result in the investor acquiring either a long or short position in the underlying security/asset.

Not being able to abandon a futures contract when it is out of the money at its delivery date means a futures contract has a different profit and loss profile from a traded option.

The second difference between futures and traded options is in the method of payment. With traded options the buyer pays the premium for the option in full by 10.00a.m. the following business day, with the writer receiving the options premium, again in full, by 10.30a.m. However, with futures contracts, transactions are paid for using a margining system with the full cost of establishing the position not paid for or received until the position is closed out.

Once a position in the FT-SE 100 Index future is established, the investor must lodge an initial deposit with his clearing agent, and through them on to LCH. This deposit is known as the initial margin and at present is £2,500 per contract. The position is then marked to market every evening after the market has closed. This ensures that the value of the position is adjusted each evening to take into account any movements in the price of the underlying security/asset.

Any profit or loss that has arisen due to the market movements is then received from or paid to LCH. This daily movement of money is known as variation margin and is designed to ensure that the value of the initial margin stays at the same level in relation to the underlying security/asset after taking into account market movements.

Underlying asset

The exchange, when introducing a new contract, cannot just say "This futures contract is based on this asset or that commodity," as all sorts of anomalies can and will develop. The underlying asset or security of the futures contract must be specified in detail so as not to leave any confusion or ambiguity as to what is being traded and what will be delivered if the futures contract is exercised. The details must include the quality or grade of any commodity.

4 · Basic Characteristics of Options and Futures

Examples

- The Italian Government Bond (BTP) Future traded on LIFFE is for ITL 200,000,000 nominal value of a notional Italian Government Bond with a 12 percent coupon. The contract standard specifies that delivery may be made of any Buoni del Tesoro Poliennali (BTP) with 8–10½ years remaining to maturity as at the tenth calendar day of the delivery month, provided that any such BTP has a minimum amount in issue of ITL 4,000,000,000,000. Delivery will take place through the Stanza di Compensazione Titoli in Italy and must be via a financial institution that has an account in its own name in the Stanza di Compensazione Titoli.

- The Long Gilt Future traded on LIFFE is for £50,000 nominal value of a notional Gilt with a 9 percent coupon. The contract specification are:

  Delivery may be made of any Gilts on the list of deliverable Gilts in respect of a delivery month, as published by the exchange on or before the tenth business day prior to the First Notice Day of such delivery month. All Gilt issues included in the list will have the following characteristics:

  1. having terms as to redemption such as provided for redemption of the entire Gilt issue in a single installment on the maturity date falling not earlier than 10 years from, and not later than 15 years from, the first day of the relevant delivery month;

  2. having no terms permitting or requiring early redemption;

  3. bearing interest at a single fixed rate throughout the term of the issue, payable in arrears semi-annually (except in the case of the first interest payment period which may be more or less than six months);

  4. being denominated and payable as to the principal and interest only in pounds and pence;

  5. being paid or in the event that the Gilt issue is in its first period and is partly paid, being anticipated by the Board to be fully paid on or before the Last Notice day of the relevant delivery month;

  6. not being convertible;

> 7. having been admitted to Official List of the London Stock Exchange; and
>
> 8. being anticipated by the Board to have on one or more days in the delivery month an aggregate principal amount outstanding of not less than £500 million which, by terms and conditions, if issued in more than one tranche or tap or issue is fungible.

Contract size

Not only must the exchange specify the quality or grade of a particular asset, commodity, or security; they must also specify the quantity to be delivered if exercised. When an exchange develops a new futures contract, it must take into consideration the wants and needs of potential users and the liquidity of the underlying instrument in the cash market.

If the contract size is too large, investors wishing to hedge small holdings or speculate with a relatively small position will be deterred from using the contract, and the exchange and its members will have lost business. If, however, the contract is too small, trading will become too expensive for the larger users, due to dealing and exchange costs and again the exchange and its members will lose money.

However, not all contract specifications are so complicated and involved. The FT-SE 100 contract specification is:

> Cash settlement based on the Exchange Settlement Delivery Price!

Option pricing

Option pricing variables

Understanding how options are priced will allow an investor to appreciate the fair value of an option and to understand how and why different events have different effects on options premiums. This in turn will help investors understand how and why different strategies work.

When pricing traded options, there are six main inputs or variables used in calculating the fair value of an option's premium:

- stock price
- exercise price
- time to expiry
- volatility
- interest rates
- dividends.

Intrinsic value

By using the first two variables, we can calculate the option's intrinsic value and time value. Therefore we can say that value of an option is equal to its intrinsic value and its time value.

$$\text{Premium} = \text{Intrinsic value} + \text{Time value}$$

Intrinsic value is the real or tangible value of an option.

> **Example**
>
> If the underlying security price is 269 and the SEP 240 call option must be worth at least 29. Having the right to buy something worth 269 for 240. This is the real or intrinsic value of an option.
>
> Underlying security price − Exercise price = Intrinsic value
>
> 269 − 240 = 29

> **Key features**
>
> ### Call option
>
> *A call option has intrinsic value when its exercise price is below the underlying security price. In other words, a call option with intrinsic value gives the holder the right to buy the underlying security at a price below the current market level.*

Call intrinsic value = Underlying security price − Exercise price

The higher the price of the underlying security in relation to the exercise price, the greater the option's intrinsic value and therefore the value of the option.

> **Key features**
>
> ## Put option
>
> *A put option will have intrinsic value when its exercise price is above the current market price of the underlying security. This gives the holder the right to sell the underlying security above the current market level.*

Put intrinsic value = Exercise price – Underlying security price

Intrinsic value is also the amount that an option is in-the-money. An option with no intrinsic value is out-of-the-money. The intrinsic value of an option is always a positive figure. If, for a call option, the underlying security price is above the exercise price, the intrinsic value of the option will be zero. For a put option the intrinsic value will be zero if the underlying security price is below the exercise price.

The intrinsic value can best be illustrated by Table 4.2.

> **Example**
>
> The 360 call option gives the holder the right to buy the underlying security at 360. With the share price at 422, the 360 call option has an intrinsic value of 62, the difference (or real value) between the exercise price and the current underlying security price. The 390 call option has an intrinsic value of 32, again the difference between the exercise price and the underlying security. The 420 has an intrinsic value of 2, while the 460 call option has no intrinsic value as its exercise price is 38 over the current share price.
>
> If we look at the puts, the 360, 390 and 420 puts have no intrinsic value as their exercise prices are below the current market price of the underlying security. With the share price at 422, the 460 puts have an intrinsic value of 38.

> **Definition**
>
> *Any option with intrinsic value is known as* **"in-the-money."** *An option without intrinsic value is known as* **"out-of-the-money."** *An option with an exercise price equal to the underlying security price is known as* **"at-the-money."**

Table 4.2

Intrinsic value

Exercise price	Call		Put	
	Int. Value	Prem.	Int. Value	Prem.
360	62	67	0	½
390	32	40	0	3
420	2	18	0	12
460	0	4	38	40

Share price: 422

Time value

As all investors know share prices can and do move up and down on a daily basis. This movement of the share price has the possibility of moving an option into the money from an out-of-the-money position. Market makers and other writers of options require an "insurance premium" to cover this possibility, which is known as time value. If the intrinsic value of an option is subtracted from its premium, the figure remaining is time value.

> **Definition**
>
> **Time value** *is the difference between the option's premium and its intrinsic value. Time value represents the remaining life of an option and the possibility of price movements in the underlying security, and subsequently the option's premium, before expiry.*

An option's time value will be greater the longer the option has until it expires. This increase is due to the increased opportunity for price movements, in the underlying security price and the option expiring in-the-money, i.e. with intrinsic value. As the option moves closer to expiry, so its time value will erode at an ever increasing rate. Initially, this erosion will be slow and almost undetectable but, as the option approaches expiry, time value will erode at an ever-increasing rate.

Using Table 4.3, we can work out the time value element of the option's premium. We know that the 360 call has 62 intrinsic value which, when subtracted from its premium of 67, gives a time value of 5. The 390 call with an intrinsic value of 32 leaves a time value of 8. The 420 call with its 2 intrinsic value and a premium of 18 has a time value of 16 and the 460 call has no intrinsic value, so the whole premium is made up of time value.

With the puts the 360, 390 and 420 puts have no intrinsic value and their premiums represent just time value. The 460 put has 38 intrinsic value leaving a time value element of 2.

From Table 4.3, we can see that time value is greatest when an option is at-the-money (exercise price closest to underlying security price) and decreases the further the option becomes either into- or out-of-the-money. This is due to the uncertainty of whether the option will move into- or out-of-the-money. The deeper an option is in-the-money the greater the probability of it expiring in-the-money. The deeper an option is out-of-the-money the greater the probability of it expiring out-of-the-money.

However, when an option is at-the-money it is possible for it to move either into or out-of-the-money. The extra time value is to compensate the writer of the option for this possibility.

Time value can be thought of as a form of insurance, against the possible price movement of the underlying security, that is payable by the buyer of the option to the seller (writer) of an option. As

Table 4.3

Time value

| Share price: 422 ||||||
Exercise price	Call			Put		
360	62	**67**	5	0	**½**	½
	Intrinsic value	Time value		Intrinsic value	Time value	
390	32	**40**	8	0	**3**	3
420	2	**18**	16	0	**12**	12
460	0	**4**	4	38	**40**	2

4 · Basic Characteristics of Options and Futures

Table 4.4

Time value increase

Underlying security price: 269			
Exercise price	Sep	Dec	Mar
260	12	21	24

with all insurance policies the longer the insurance is to run for, the higher the premium paid (a 12-month house insurance policy will be more expensive than a 6-month policy).

Table 4.4 shows how the premium of options with the same exercise price increases when the life of the option is increased.

The time value element of an option's premium can be plotted on a graph (see Figure 4.1). The graph shows that when an option is at-the-money, the time value element of its premium is at its greatest. As already stated, this is due to the uncertainty of whether the option will move into- or out-of-the-money.

> Time value can be thought of as a form of insurance, against the possible price movement of the underlying security, that is payable by the buyer of the option to the seller (writer) of an option.

Fig 4.1

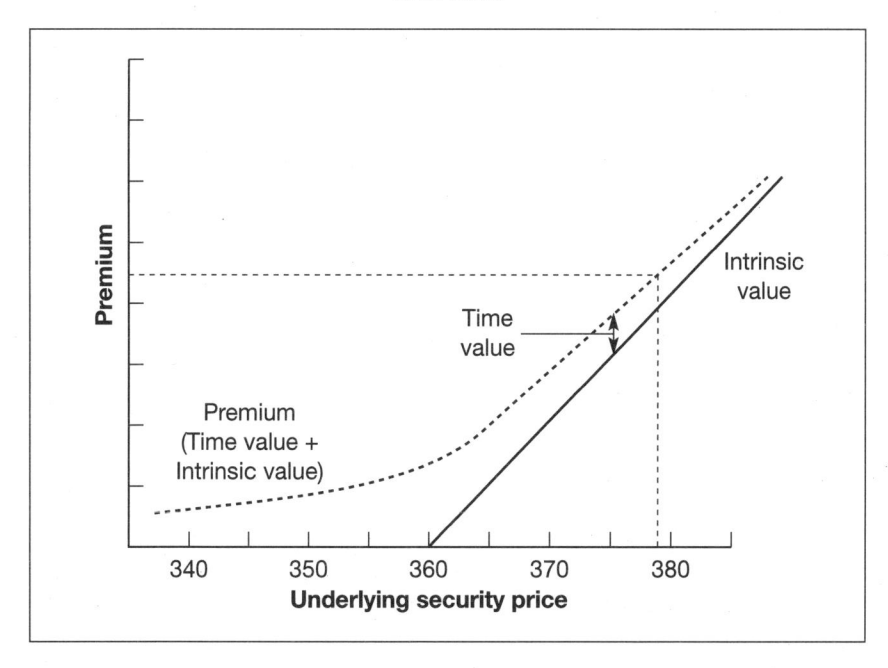

Time value

115

The graph shows the premium make up for a 360 call option. If the underlying security price is at 320, the premium is made up entirely of time value. The same is true when the underlying security price is at 360. However, the time value has now increased in recognition that the option is moving towards gaining intrinsic value.

When the underlying security is at 390, the 360 call premium is made up of 30 intrinsic value plus time value. As the option goes further into the money, so time value diminishes. This is due to the near certainty that the option will expire in-the-money.

Time decay

An option's time value erodes as it approaches expiry. To begin with this erosion is slow and almost unnoticeable due to the length of the life of the option. But, as the option draws nearer to expiry, so the erosion of time value increases. The decrease in time value continues at an ever-increasing rate until, on expiry, there is no time value left and the option's premium is made up entirely of its intrinsic value. Approximately 60 percent of time value erodes in the last 30 percent of an option's life span.

This erosion of time value works against holders of options and in favour of writers. Erosion of time value cannot be stressed too highly when buying near month options.

During the life of an option, an in-the-money option's premium comprises its intrinsic and time value, an out-of-the-money option has no intrinsic value, so its premium will be made up entirely of

Fig 4.2

Time value decay

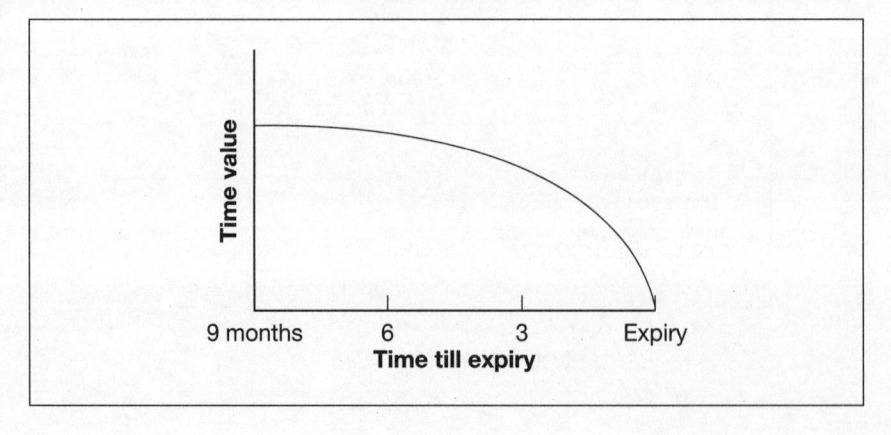

time value. At expiry, an in-the-money option's premium will comprise entirely of its intrinsic value and an out-of-the-money option's premium will be zero. This is due to the fact that at expiry there is no time left for an option to gain intrinsic or tangible value, an out-of-the-money option is worthless.

Volatility

> **Definition**
>
> **Volatility** *is a measure of fluctuations in the underlying security's share price over a given time. The greater the volatility of an underlying security, the greater the possibility of the option gaining intrinsic value and expiring in-the-money.*

If an underlying security has a high volatility, a buyer of the option can expect to pay more for it than for an option on a stock with low volatility.

Types of volatility

There are several different ways of looking at volatility:

- Historic volatility looks at the past performance of the underlying security. It is known and can be easily measured. However, past performance is no guarantee of future performance.
- Forecast volatility tries to anticipate what will happen in the future.
- Implied volatility is the volatility implicit in the prices being traded today.
- Future volatility is the one every one wants to know.

> **Key features**
>
> ### Increase in volatility
> *An increase in volatility will increase premiums, due to the additional uncertainty of the underlying security's price movements. The increased price movements will affect the option's chance of expiring in-the-money.*

Fig 4.3 — Volatility increase/decrease

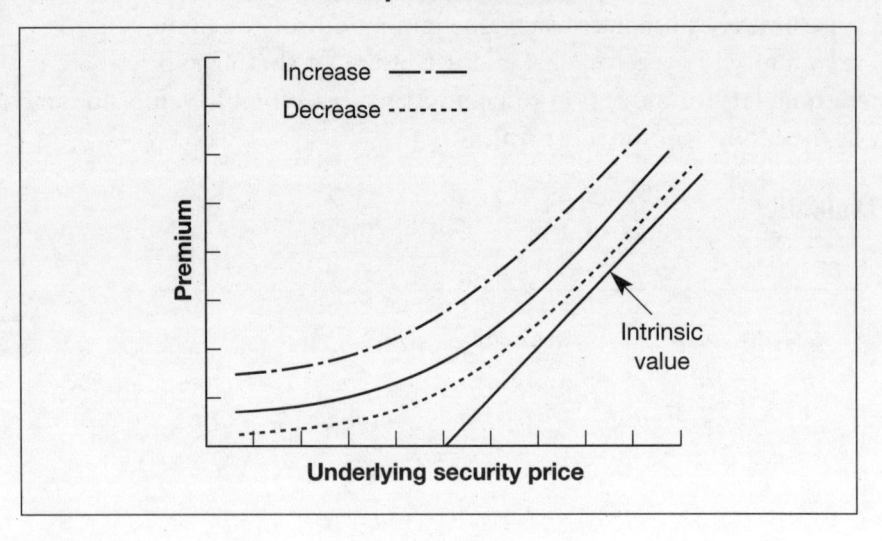

Graph showing Premium vs Underlying security price, with curves for Increase and Decrease in volatility, and a line indicating Intrinsic value.

As with time value, volatility can be plotted on a graph. Figure 4.3 shows the effect of an increase and a decrease in volatility.

> **Key features**
>
> ### Decrease in volatility
> *A decrease in volatility will result in a decrease in premiums as the chance of an option expiring in-the-money has diminished.*

Dividends

Holders of traded options are not entitled to any dividends paid on the underlying security and therefore dividends have no DIRECT effect on premiums. However, dividend payments are gradually built into the price of the underlying security. On ex-dividend date the underlying security price will normally be reduced by the amount of the dividend payment. This reduction will affect the option's premiums and result in call prices being reduced and put prices increased. The underlying security can be marked ex-dividend on the first business day of a week as long as the London Stock Exchange has been notified by the previous Thursday. Dividend dates and expected payments are usually forecast well in advance and should therefore be built into any prices and strategies used.

Interest rates

Interest rates have a bearing on options premiums when calculating what is known as the "cost of carry." This is a complicated formula for calculating the cost of borrowing money and purchasing options. Cost of carry is important to large traders such as pension funds, unit trusts and market traders and unimportant to private investors.

The theory of options pricing suggests option premiums are affected by interest rates in a second way. If interest rates are increased call premiums should also increase and put premiums decrease. Calls are looked upon as a delayed stock purchase, the money saved by buying calls can be placed on deposit to earn interest. Puts are looked upon as a delayed sale of stock that will result in the investor forgoing any interest that may have been earned from the sale of the stock.

However, in reality, an increase in interest rates will affect the underlying security market to a far greater degree, driving down the market with the result of call prices decreasing and put prices increasing.

Pricing models

The six input variables we have just looked at are used together with a pricing model. Two of the best known are the Black-Scholes and the Cox-Ross-Rubinstein models. The prices generated by these models are known as "fair values" and are not necessarily what the options are trading at in the market (Figure 4.4). The market price is derived from the "fair value" plus supply and demand, anticipation and the traders "book." However, armed with the fair value an investor can decide if an option is over- or under-priced and buy or sell accordingly.

Movements in the variables

Obviously movement in any one, or any combination, of the variables will have an effect on the premium of an option.

Key features

Share price movement

If there is an increase in the share price, the call premiums will increase and the put prices decrease, while a decrease in the underlying security price will result in call prices dropping and put prices rising.

Key features

Exercise price movement

An increase in exercise price will result in call prices decreasing and put prices increasing. A decrease in the exercise price will force call prices up and bring put prices down.

Key features

Volatility

If volatility increases, both call and put prices will increase, while a decrease in volatility will decrease both call and put prices.

Fig 4.4

Option pricing model

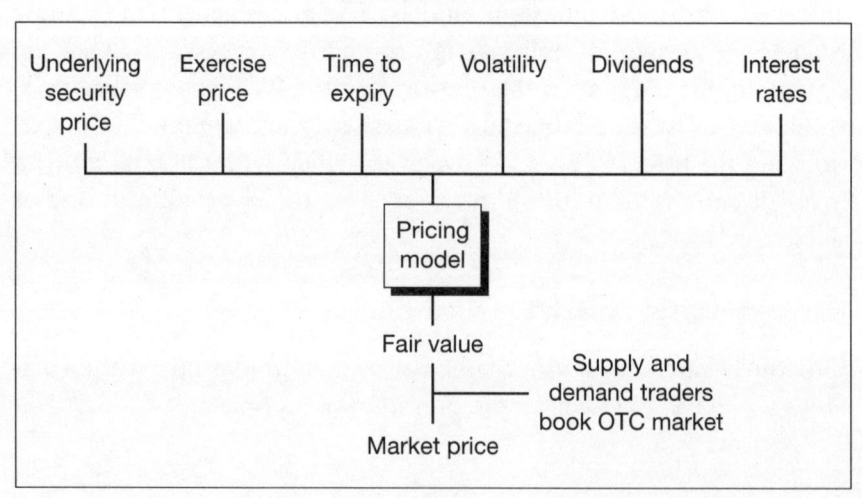

Underlying security price | Exercise price | Time to expiry | Volatility | Dividends | Interest rates

↓

Pricing model

↓

Fair value

Market price

Supply and demand traders book OTC market

> ### Expiry date
> *The longer until expiry will result in increased call and put prices. The closer to expiry an option is, the lower the call and put prices will tend to be.*

Key features

> ### Interest rates
> *If interest rates are increased, because of the effect on the underlying security market, call prices will decrease and put prices will increase.*

Key features

Above we have looked at the variables that are used in a pricing model to calculate the fair value of an option. In this section we look at some of the ways of using the prices generated for the possible outcome at expiry of the option. We will also look at options sensitivities.

Pricing Models

The two main pricing models available are the Black and Scholes analogous model and the Cox, Ross and Rubinstein binomial model.

The Black and Scholes model was the first pricing model to be produced and allowed the options markets to be properly priced for the first time. The model is based on a non-dividend-paying European option, it also assumes there are only two possible stock

Movements in the variables — Fig 4.5

	Stock price	Exercise price	Time to expiry	Volatility	Dividends	Interest rates
Call premium	↑	↓	↑	↑	↑	↓
Put premium	↓	↑	↑	↑		↑

Increase in variable

prices at the expiry of the option. This is obviously a very inaccurate picture of what does happen in reality. The Black and Scholes formula is represented by the equation:

$$(C = SN(d1) - Ee{-}rtN(d2)$$

where
$$d1 = \frac{\ln(S/E) + (r + 1/2\ \&2)t}{\&/t}$$

$$d2 = d1 - \&/t$$

C	= Call option premium	r	= Interest rate
S	= Stock price	t	= Time to expiry
E	= Exercise price	N(d)	= Cumulative normal density function
&	= Volatility		

A more realistic pricing model for American-style options is the binomial pricing model first designed by Cox, Ross and Rubinstein.

The binomial model is, in very simple terms, a model that consists of two options or choices at the end of each stage or time period and can be drawn as a pricing tree. The life of the option is divided into a large number of small time periods. It is then assumed that the price of the underlying security can move up or down during the time period. In Figure 4.6, the underlying security price starts from point A; from there it can go up or down in the given time.

From each of these outcomes, or price points, the prices can again rise or fall producing a further three price points. So the process continues over the life of the option until a pricing tree is produced.

The time between each price point and the amount of price movement will determine if the stock has high, low or medium volatility.

The prices of a stock with high volatility will move up or down much further in the same time scale as a stock with medium volatility. A stock with low volatility will move up or down much slower over a longer time scale.

Fig 4.6

Underlying security price

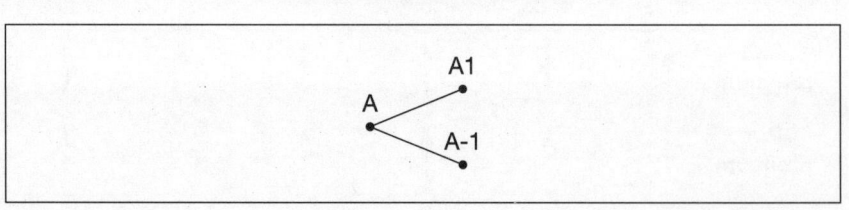

```
          A1
       A
          A-1
```

Pricing tree   Fig 4.7

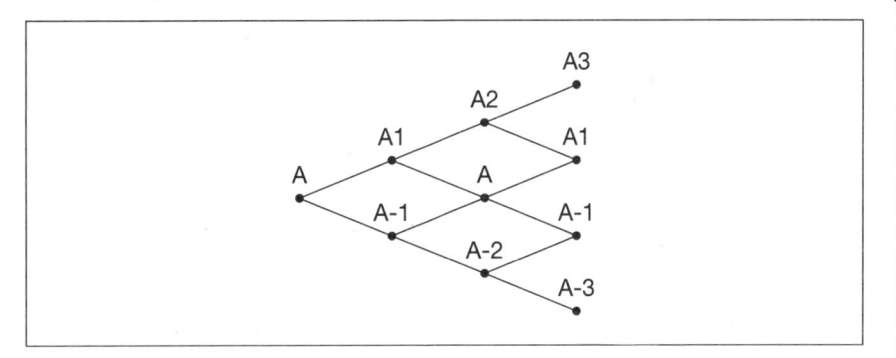

When a dividend is paid on the underlying security, the stock price will be reduced by the amount of the dividend. This can be shown in the pricing tree by a drop in all of the lines connecting the price points (Figure 4.8).

Using a binomial pricing tree, option prices are calculated by starting at the end of the tree and working backwards. At the end of the tree, the option is valued at its intrinsic value only. At any earlier price points the value of an option is the greater of:

1. the option's intrinsic value

   or

2. the value if held for a further period of time.

The option's intrinsic value is the amount the option is in-the-money. If the option is held for a further period of time, its value is its expected value at the end of that period.

Binomial pricing with dividend   Fig 4.8

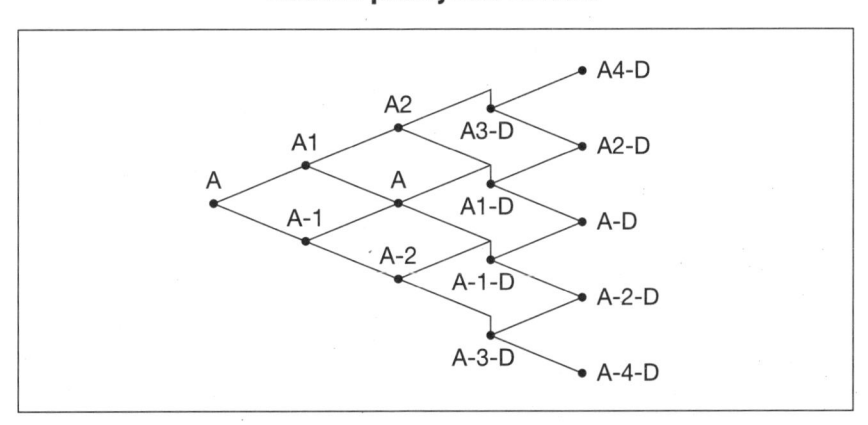

Option sensitivity

Option prices, as we have discussed, are arrived at by a pricing formula and six variables. Not only will a pricing formula give the price of an option for any given combination of variables, they will also show how the price generated will change for a particular change in one of the variables. These changes are known by Greek letters and are referred to as an option's sensitivities.

Delta

The first and the most common is Delta. Call options have a positive Delta between 0 and 1, with 0 for deep out-of-the-money series and 1 for deep in-the-money series. Put options have negative Deltas and are between –1 and 0. Deltas can be explained in four ways.

1. **The rate of change in an option's theoretical fair value for a one penny change in the underlying security price.** Table 4.5 shows how a call option premium changes for a 1p rise in the underlying security. Put premiums, with their Delta being negative, would fall for a rise in the underlying security.

   The first series with a Delta of 0.25 is a deep out-of-the-money series. A 1p change in the underlying security will not effect the premium. The second series is at-the-money and has a Delta of 0.5. For every 1p change in the underlying security the premium of an at-the-money option will change at half the rate, i.e. 0.5. The last series with a Delta of 1 is deep in-the-money option and for every 1p change in the underlying security there will be a 1p change in the premium.

2. **The ratio, of the underlying security to option contracts, required to establish a neutral hedge.** Rather than buying stock 1–1 with option contracts as a hedge, for example, the seller of

Table 4.5   **Call option premium changes**

Underlying	Security premium	Delta	New premium
255	30	0.25	30.0
255	30	0.5	30.5
255	30	1.0	31.0

an option buys stock in the ratio indicated by the Delta value. If an investor sells 10 contracts with a Delta of 0.3, he would buy 3,000 stock to hedge the position. If the investor purchased one call option with a Delta of 0.75 he would sell 750 shares in the underlying contract.

3. **The theoretical share position for an option's position.** The holder of a call position is theoretically long of the underlying security; for a put position the holder is theoretically short. For example, if an investor buys a call option with a Delta of 0.25, he is theoretically long 25 percent of the underlying contract, 250 shares. This definition can also be referred to as the theoretical or equivalent share position.

4. **Approximately the probability, given constant and stable volatility, that the option will expire in-the-money.** An option with a Delta of 0.5 has a 50 percent chance of expiring in-the-money. An option with a Delta of 0.9 has a 90 percent chance.

An option's Delta is not a constant figure but changes with every price movement of the underlying security. The amount by which it changes is known as the Gamma.

Gamma

The Gamma is the theoretical rate of change of an option's Delta for a one penny change in the underlying security. For example if a call option has a Delta of 0.25 and a Gamma of 0.05 for a 1p rise in the underlying security the Delta will change to 0.30. For a 1p fall the Delta will be 0.20. The Gamma of an option is also known as its curvature.

The Delta of an option can be described as the speed with which an option's premium moves, in respect to the changes in the underlying security price. The range of speed is from 0 percent (for a deep out-of-the-money series) to 100 percent (for a deep in-the-money series) or from 0 percent to −100 percent for puts. Gamma can then be thought of as the rate of acceleration or deceleration of the Delta.

Theta

With options being a limited life security, it is important to know how much theoretical value an option will lose for each day that passes with no movement in the underlying security. This theoretical loss in value for each day that passes is known as Theta. An option with a Theta of 0.005 will lose 0.005 in theoretical fair value for each day that passes with no movement in the underlying security. Theta is better known as time decay.

Vega

Volatility is a particularly important factor in the pricing of options. The sensitivity of an option fair value to changes in its theoretical volatility is measured by its Vega. An option with a Vega of 0.75 would gain (lose) 0.75p for each percentage point increase (decrease) in volatility. Vega is also known as Kappa, Epsilon and Omega.

Rho

The sensitivity of an option's fair value to interest rate movements is measured by its Rho. An option with a Rho of 0.03 would gain (lose) 0.03p for each percentage point increase (decrease). Rho is the least important of all the option sensitivities.

Basic trades

Buying calls

Call options give the holder the right to purchase the underlying security at the fixed exercise price in return for the payment of a premium. With the potential purchase price of the underlying security fixed by the call option, the value or premium of the option will rise as the underlying security price rises. The holder of the option then has the choice of either selling the option back into the market, at a profit, or exercising the option and purchasing the underlying security at the exercise price, below the current market level. Therefore with an expectation of a rise in the underlying security price, the call option should be purchased.

> **Example**
>
> It is late September, an investor expects the share price of XYZ Ltd to rise, from its present level of 268p, over the next two to three weeks. To take advantage of this expected rise, the investor buys a Dec 260 call option with a premium of 19p. The total cost of one contract would be £190 (19p × 1,000 = £190). The call option purchased has secured the right to purchase shares in XYZ Ltd at a fixed price of 260p, the exercise price, regardless of their price on the stock market.

> Over the next two weeks the price of XYZ Ltd shares have risen to 295p. Having the right to buy the shares at 260 must now be worth at least 35p. However, there is still time available for the share price to rise further, so the premium of the Dec 260 call option will now have risen to, say, 44p.
>
> The holder can now sell the call option back into the market for 44p, a profit of 25p, exercise the option and buy the underlying security at the exercise price of 260p, or wait and hope for a further rise in the share price and the option premium.

The potential profit or loss of any option position can be shown in two ways. The first is as a set of figures in table form. The second, and more common method, is as a simple graph. The profit/loss position for the trade in the above example is shown in Table 4.6. The same information is shown as a graph in Figure 4.9. The graph shows the possible profit or loss, of the Dec 260 call option, **at expiry**, for any given price of the underlying security. On the vertical axis is the profit or loss for the position and on the horizontal axis is the underlying security price.

Figure 4.9 shows that while the underlying security price is at or below 260 (exercise price) at expiry, the position is looking at a loss equal to the premium paid, 19p. If the underlying security price rises above the exercise price of 260, every 1p rise will eat into the loss by 1p, until the position breaks even at 279 (exercise price + premium). After the break-even point of 279, for every 1p rise in the underlying security there will be a 1p rise in the profit. The maximum loss for any long position is limited to the premium paid out, while the maximum profit is unlimited.

Advantages of buying calls:
- The maximum loss with a long call position is limited to the premium paid for the option.
- The profit potential for a long call is open-ended, i.e. unlimited.
- The premium paid for the option is a fraction of the cost of acquiring control over the same amount of stock, allowing the remainder to be invested elsewhere.

Table 4.6 — Profit and loss for long Dec 260 call

Share price	option +/−
220	−19
240	−19
260	−19
280	+1
300	+21
320	+41

- It is possible to make considerable gains in the option's premium for a relatively small movement in the underlying security price.

Disadvantage:
- The passage of time works against the time value part of the option's premium.

An investor may wish to use call options to take advantage of this rise in the value of the option for several reasons. The three most common being:

1. To gain exposure to the price rise for a limited outlay. This will also allow the investor to benefit from the options gearing effect.
2. To maintain exposure to future price rises after the sale of a stock holding.
3. To lock in a purchase price for the underlying security while awaiting funds to acquire stock.

To gain exposure (speculative trade)

The most common reason for buying call options is to gain exposure to an expected price rise in the underlying security. This strategy has the advantage over buying the shares of the underlying security of the limited outlay required. This means that with traded options it is possible to gain control over a large amount of stock without tying up large amounts of capital that can be used elsewhere. In addition, the gearing effect of options which allows for potentially, a large profit in percentage terms, for a

4 · Basic Characteristics of Options and Futures

Profit and loss for long Dec 260 call @ 19 Fig 4.9

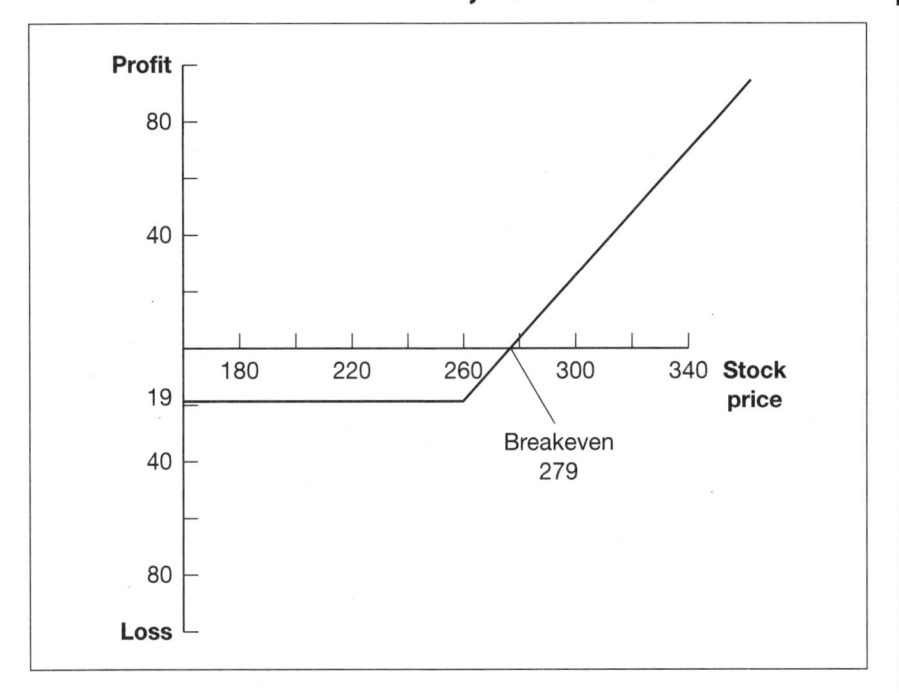

[Figure 4.9: Profit/loss chart with stock price on x-axis (180, 220, 260, 300, 340) and profit/loss on y-axis (80, 40, 19, 40, 80). Breakeven marked at 279.]

relatively small outlay and movement in the underlying security, is also very attractive.

The choice of series to purchase will depend on the investor's view of the extent and the timing of the expected rise. The timing of the rise, or more correctly the time the rise takes, is possibly the most important factor in the choosing the series. This is due to the possible erosion of the time value element of the option's premium.

> **The most common reason for buying call options is to gain exposure to an expected price rise in the underlying security.**

If the rise is expected over a long period, longer dated in-the-money options should be purchased. In-the-money options have both intrinsic value and time value and will respond to any rise in the underlying security penny for penny. While the time value element of the premium will erode at an ever-increasing rate, its percentage of the premium is considerably less than an out-of-the-money option where it will be 100 percent of the premium.

If the rise is expected to be relatively large and over a short period of time, out-of-the-money options should be considered. The premium of out-of-the-money options comprises entirely of time value and as the underlying security price rises, so the option moves towards acquiring intrinsic value, at an ever-increasing rate, resulting in a high percentage increase in the premium.

> **Example**
>
> On July 23, ABC Ltd shares are 476 and the Aug 500 call has a premium of 4. By Aug 11, ABC Ltd shares are trading at 531, a 55p increase or 11.5 percent. The Aug 500 call is now 33, a 29p increase or 725 percent.
>
> Once the option's value or premium has increased in value and is trading at a profit, an investor may decide to "walk up" the position. This is a strategy that allows an investor to realize a profit on the position and maintain an exposure to any future price rises in the underlying security. This is achieved by selling the option held and purchasing new out-of-the-money options, possibly with a longer expiry date, with some of the profits.

> **Example**
>
> An investor anticipates a sharp rise in the underlying security and so purchases an out-of-the-money call option. The anticipated rise takes place, forcing the option's premium to increase. The rise in the underlying security will lead to the introduction of new out-of-the-money series. The investor wishes to realize some of his profits, but is concerned that the underlying security will continue to rise and does not wish to miss out on further increases in profits.
>
> By selling his options, which are now in-the-money and using some of the profits to purchase new out-of-the-money options, the investor can realize his profits and maintain exposure to any continued price rises.
>
> | | |
> |---|---|
> | 1 August | Purchase 10 Sep 500 calls @ 4 |
> | ABC Ltd 481 | Cost of options £400 |
> | | |
> | 7 August | Sell 10 Sep 500 calls @ 22 |
> | ABC Ltd 515 | Profit £2200 – £400 = £1800 |
> | | Purchase 10 Sep 550 calls @ 2 |
> | | Cost £200 |
> | | Total profit £1600 + 10 Sep 550 calls |

Long Aug 500 call@4   Fig 4.10

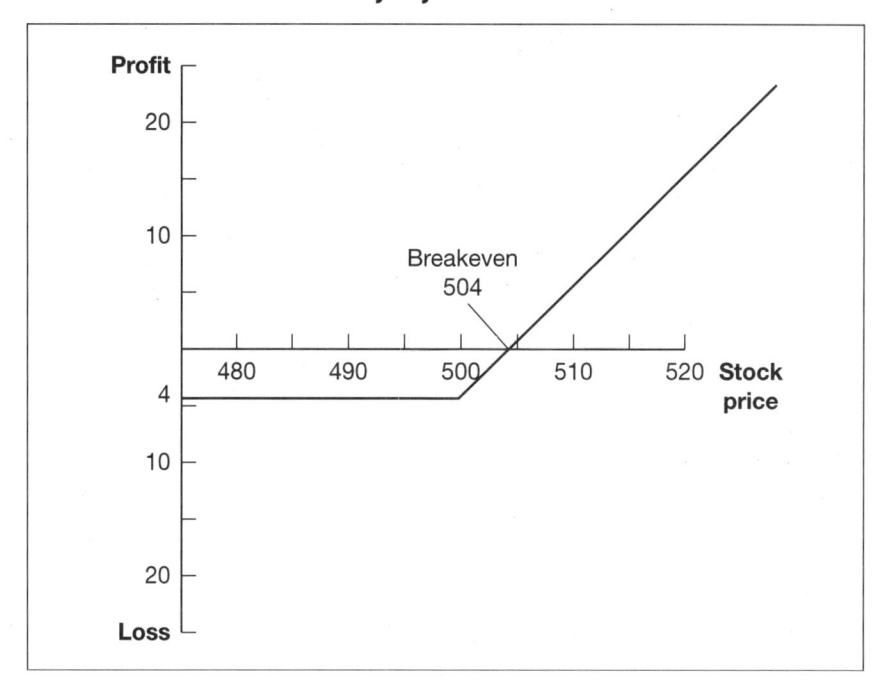

[Chart: Profit/Loss diagram for Long Aug 500 call @ 4, showing breakeven at 504, maximum loss of 4 below strike price of 500, and increasing profit above 504. X-axis: Stock price (480, 490, 500, 510, 520). Y-axis: Profit/Loss (20, 10, 4, 10, 20).]

Walking up

The strategy of "walking up" can be used to equal effect whether the investor is buying or selling calls or puts. As soon as an option has passed its usefulness, it should be sold (bought back) and another option purchased (sold).

To maintain exposure

It is not always possible for an investor to sell his holding in a company at the top of the market. The majority of the time the investor will sell too late, after the stock is past its peak. One method of ensuring that the investor receives the best possible price is to sell the holding while it is still rising and use some of the profits to purchase call options. (Investors should always sell into strength, i.e. a rising market).

By purchasing calls it is possible to maintain exposure to price movements in a stock after selling a holding.

> **Example**
>
> An investor purchased 5,000 shares in XYZ Plc at 126. The price has now risen to 158. The investor wishes to realize his profit, but is concerned that the price may continue to rise. By selling his holding at 158 the investor makes a profit of 32 per share (158 – 126). He can now use some of the profit to purchase 5 August 160 calls @ 8. In so doing the investor has locked in a profit of 24 per share (158 – 126 – 8 = 24). And will still be able to participate in any future rise in the share price through the call option.

Lock in a purchase price

Most investors have the majority of their funds invested, in one form or another, at any one time, while holding a small amount of cash for emergencies. A problem may occur when an investor identifies an investment opportunity but does not have sufficient funds available to take advantage of the situation for at least a month. In this situation the purchase of call options can expose the investor to any price rise in the underlying security and lock in a purchase price for the underlying security, to be used when additional funds become available.

An investor's expectation is for a rise in the share price of ABC Ltd, but he will not have sufficient funds available to purchase any stock for two months. Not wishing to miss the opportunity, the investor purchases a call option. The option, giving the investor the right to buy the underlying security at the exercise price at any time before the expiry of the option, has secured the buying price of ABC Ltd for the investor. If the price of ABC Ltd does rise the investor can either exercise the option and purchase the shares or sell the option back into the market, realizing his profit and purchase the underlying security in the stock market. By selling the option back into the market, the investor will receive the intrinsic value *and* any time value of the premium. If he had just exercised the option, he would realize only the intrinsic value.

> **Example**
>
> The share price of ABC Ltd is 218. An investor buys 1 Sept 220 call @ 7. The investor has locked in a purchase price of 227 (exercise price + premium) until Sept expiry. The share price of ABC Ltd rises to 242 and the premium of the Sept call rises to 24. The investor can now purchase stock in one of two ways.
>
> 1. Exercise option and purchase stock at 220 (exercise price). This gives it an effective purchase price of 227 (exercise price + premium).
> 2. Sell option at 24 and buy stock at 242 in the cash market. The investor has now effectively purchased stock at 225 (242 − (24 − 7) = 225 (premium received − original premium)).

When purchasing the stock through exercising the option, the investor received only the intrinsic value attached to the option. By selling the option back into the market, the investor receives both the intrinsic value and any time value in the premium. The only occasion that it would be ideal to exercise a call option early is immediately prior to a stock being declared ex-dividend and then only if the option is in-the-money.

On being marked ex-dividend the underlying security price will fall, normally by the amount of the dividend, causing the call to drop in value. If the dividend is large enough the fall in the option's premium may make it advantageous to exercise the option and acquire the dividend.

However, the investor must ensure the dividend is large enough to cover the original purchase price of the option and any commission charges. On all other occasions the option should be sold back into the market.

Writing (selling) calls

The writer of a call option accepts an obligation to deliver (sell) the underlying security, if assigned, at the exercise price in return for the option's premium. The premium received represents the maximum profit the writer of a call option can make. Call options should only be written if the investor's view of the stock is neutral (remaining stable) to slightly bearish (negative).

> **Example**
>
> An investor's view of ABC Ltd is that the share price will remain stable or fall slightly over the next two months. To take advantage of this expectation he decides to write call options. It is early September and the investor's view of ABC Ltd is that the price will fall slightly from today's level of 268p. In order to take advantage of this, he decides to write the Sept 260 call with a premium of 11p. The writer will receive £110 per contract (premium × contract size (11p × 1,000)).
>
> The writer is now obliged to deliver (sell) the underlying security at the exercise price of 260p if assigned. The premium received represents the maximum profit the writer can make on this transaction.
>
> By the September expiry, two weeks later, the underlying security price has fallen to 257p. With the underlying security price being below the exercise price, the holder will not exercise the option and buy the underlying security (the holder of the option could buy the underlying security on the stock market cheaper than by using the option).
>
> As the option is not exercised the writer can keep the option's premium and the underlying security as profit.

The profit and loss for the above example shows that as long as the underlying security price stays below the exercise price of 260, the writer will keep the premium for writing the call option as profit. As the underlying security price rises above the exercise price, the writer's profit will be eaten into until the position breaks even at 271 (exercise price + premium (260 + 11)).

If the underlying security price continues to rise above 271, the writer will lose 1p for every 1p rise: the writer is therefore looking at an unlimited loss.

Advantages of selling calls:
- The premium received for writing an option generates additional income and earnings.
- The passage of time works to the advantage of the writer.

Disadvantages:
- The option may be exercised early, obliging the writer to deliver the underlying security at a price below the market.

Fig 4.11

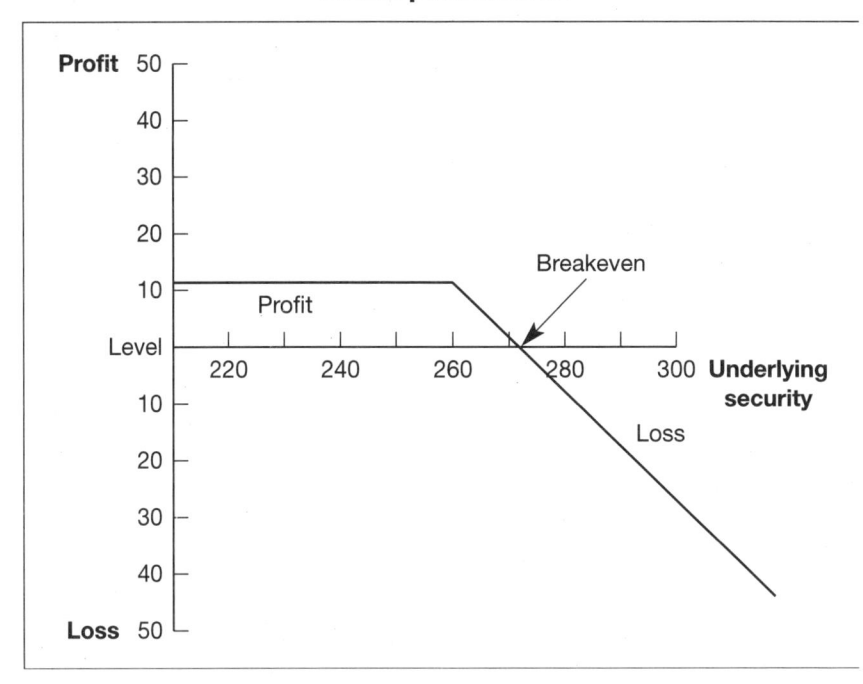

Short Sep 260 call @ 11

[Profit/Loss chart: flat profit line at 11 from 220 to 260, then declining through breakeven around 271, crossing into loss beyond 280, continuing down past 300 on the Underlying security axis.]

- The writer is facing the possibility of an unlimited loss if not holding the underlying security.

> **Definition**
>
> **Writing calls** *can reduce the risks associated with stock ownership and can make a portfolio less susceptible to volatile short-term market movements.* **Call writing** *can be aggressive or conservative depending on the series written and whether the position is covered or not.*

Call writing falls into two categories, covered and uncovered or naked writing. The covered call writer holds stock, or purchases stock at the time of writing the option, to cover their obligation. This counters any threat of being exercised against, as the writer already holds stock that can be delivered to the holder. The uncovered call writer does not hold the stock and must therefore buy the underlying security in the market at the time of assignment. The market price of the stock will be considerably higher than the exercise price of the option, otherwise it would not have been exercised, forcing the writer to trade at a loss. As the underlying security price continues to rise, the uncovered writer is faced with the threat of an unlimited loss.

There are several reasons and scenarios for writing call options, the four main ones being:

1. to enhance the performance of an existing portfolio or equity holding;
2. to offset the cost of stock purchase;
3. to secure a selling price and generate extra income;
4. to acquire downside protection, to the extent of the option's premium, in the event of a slight fall in the value of the stock.

Performance enhancement

The concept behind performance enhancement is to increase the earnings potential of a portfolio or an individual stock during periods of stable or falling prices. The premium received from writing options generates extra income, increasing the returns from a holding.

> **Example**
>
> An investor holds 5,000 TBC Ltd bought at 228. The share price has now risen to 246, but is expected to fall slightly in the short term. The extent of the expected fall does not warrant selling the holding or the purchase of puts. The investor decides to write call options. He writes 5 March 240 160 call for a premium of 13. The option will normally not be exercised unless the underlying security price rises above and remains above the 240 exercise price by the expiry date.
>
> The underlying security price falls slightly as expected, which will result in the option expiring unexercised, allowing the writer to retain the whole premium as profit, as well as keeping the underlying security.

The returns on such a strategy can be expressed in one of two ways:

1. The return if the option is unexercised at expiry.

$$\frac{\text{Premium} \times 100}{\text{Net investment}}$$

$$\frac{13}{215} \times 100 = 6.05\%$$

This return is from the period that the strategy was in place for and can be annualized to show a return of 24 percent.

2. The second way of expressing the returns offered by covered call writing is if the option is exercised.

$$\frac{\text{Premium} + \text{exercise price} - \text{original price} \times 100}{\text{Net investment}}$$

$$\frac{13 + (260 - 228)}{215} \times 100 = 20.93\%$$

Annualized this equals 83.72%.

A writer of call options should always know the returns from the position if the options are exercised or not. The selection of which series to write will be made easier with knowledge of the expected returns.

There will always be several different options series for the writer to sell. The choice of which one to use will depend on:

1. **The expectations of price movements in the underlying security over the life of the strategy.** If the investor is neutral as to price movement, then at-the-money options should be considered. At-the-money options will not usually be exercised, allowing the writer to keep the premium received. The premium of at-the-money options is made up entirely of time value which is at its greatest when the option is at-the-money. For a bullish expectation write out-of-the-money options. If the underlying security price does rise, the option should not become in-the-money and remain unexercised. If the expectation is for a bearish movement, in-the-money options should be written. The downward movement of the underlying security price will take the option from being in-the-money to at- or out-of-the-money and it will not be exercised.

2. **The amount of return required** will also determine which option is to be written. The higher the potential returns, the higher the risk of being exercised against. Writing in-the-money options offers the greatest return due to high premiums, but also carries the greatest risk of being exercised against and the stock being called away. The return from an out-of-the-money option will be less than an in-the-money option, but will carry far less risk of being exercised.

As the underlying security price moves, it is possible to walk down all or part of the position (this is also known as "rolling down"). An investor has written an at-the-money call against an existing stock holding. The price of the underlying security falls as anticipated, with the option moving to become out-of-the-money. The investor buys back the original at-the-money option at a profit and sells the new at-the-money options on the expectation of the underlying security either falling further or remaining stable.

Buy write

Definition

A buy write strategy is used to reduce the cost of a stock purchase. The investor, while purchasing stock, writes a call option using the purchased stock as collateral. The premium received from the sale of the option is used to offset the cost of the stock purchase.

Example

An investor wishes to purchase 5,000 shares in XYZ Ltd as a long-term investment at 189. Simultaneously to reduce cost, he sells 5 Mar 200 call @ 12. The premium received (12) has resulted in an effective purchase price of 177.

Buy 5,000 XYZ Ltd @ 189 = £9,450

Sell 5 Mar 200 calls @ 12 = £ 600

Net cost	£8,850
Cost per share	177p

> If the option is exercised, the investor must deliver stock at 200 (exercise price). However, the investor has an effective purchasing price of 177, giving him a profit of 23 per share or 13 percent.

Securing a selling price

It is possible to use a written call option to secure the sale price of the underlying security. Although puts are used to secure a sale price in a falling market, writing calls can secure the sale price in a rising market. The writer of the call also has the advantage of receiving the premium from the buyer, whereas the holder of a put must pay the premium.

> **Example**
>
> An investor holds stock at 415. If the stock reaches 460, it is considered overvalued and should be sold. The investor sells a Feb 460 call for 2. If the stock reaches 460 at or before expiry, the option will be exercised and the investor will have an effective selling price of 462 (exercise price + premium). If the underlying security does not reach 460, the option will not be exercised and the investor will keep the underlying security and the premium received as extra income.

Downside protection

Option writing may be used to provide downside protection in the event of a slight fall in the market. The amount of downside protection is limited to the premium received and the amount of premium will depend on the series written.

> **Example**
>
> Mega Bucks Ltd is trading at 245 and the following calls exist:
>
> | Exercise price | May |
> |---|---|
> | 220 | 32 |
> | 240 | 15 |
> | 260 | 6 |

Writing the May 220 calls (in-the-money) would give downside protection to 213 (underlying security price − premium (245 − 32) = 213). The 32 drop in the value of the underlying security would be offset by the premium received for writing the option. However, if the underlying security price does not drop below 220, the chance of being exercised against is very high.

Writing the May 240 calls (at-the-money) would provide downside protection to 230 (245 − 15). Again any drop in value of the underlying security will be offset by the premium received. The underlying security price now has to drop to 240 to avoid the possibility of being exercised against.

The May 260 calls (out-of-the-money) only provide protection down to 239 (245 − 6), but the likelihood of being exercised against is remote unless the stock rises to 260 (Figure 4.12).

Key features

Margin

Writers of traded options are required to lodge margin with their broker. Margin acts as a form of insurance to ensure the writer has sufficient funds or the stock to deliver the underlying security if exercised against.

The funds, in the form of cash, UK Gilts, US Treasury bills, German Government bonds and certain UK equities are lodged with the broker for the duration of the position.

The minimum margin requirement is governed by the London Clearing House (LCH). Typically, individual brokers set their own minimum requirements that are higher than those set by LCH. Margin requirements can and do change daily. By holding a higher minimum requirement than LCH stipulates, brokers are saved from the need of constantly demanding additional margin from writers as the market moves up and down.

Downside protection with written calls Fig 4.12

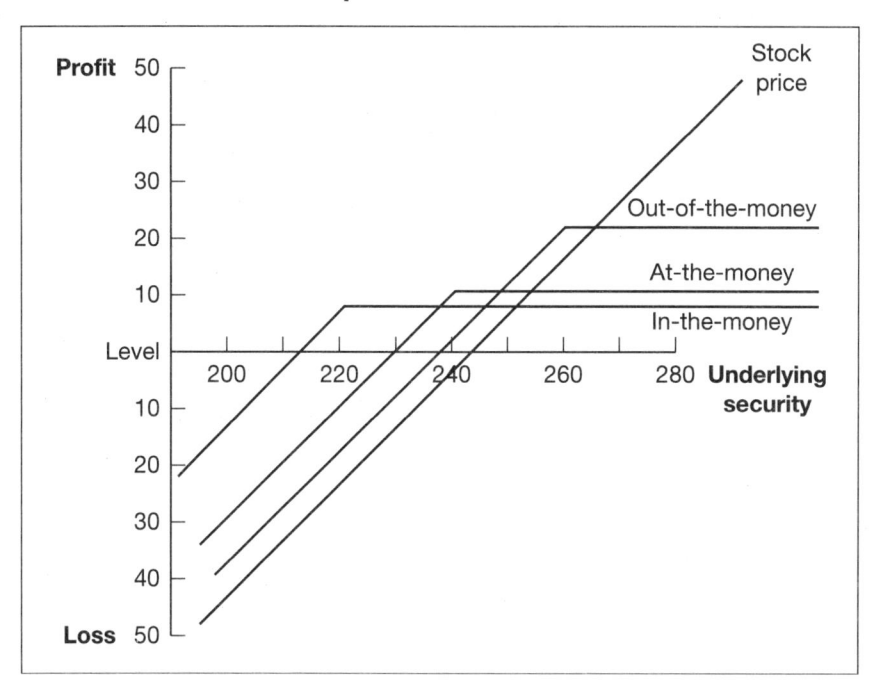

[Graph showing profit/loss curves for Out-of-the-money, At-the-money, and In-the-money written calls against underlying security price from 200 to 280, with Stock price line for reference.]

Buying puts

> ### Put options
> Put options, giving the holder the right to sell stock, at the exercise price, are generally purchased in the expectation of a fall in the underlying security.

Key features

This fall will result in an increase in the value of the put, having secured the sale price of the underlying security, allowing it either to be exercised and the stock sold above the market price or traded back into the market, for its premium, at a profit.

Example

It is March and an investor expects the price of NFI Ltd (467p) to fall. In order to take advantage of the expected fall, the investor buys an April 460 put option for 14p, giving the right to sell the underlying security at the exercise price of 460 on or before the expiry of the option. The price of NFI Ltd falls to 432, the value of the 460 put rises to, say, 32p. Having the right to sell something worth 432 for 460 must be worth at least 28p, but with time remaining until the expiry of the option, there will also be time value on the option.

The profit and loss profile shows that if the underlying security is above the exercise price of 460 at expiry, the option will expire worthless and the holder of the option will make a loss equal to the premium paid for the option. This loss is the maximum loss the holder can make. As the underlying security price falls, the loss will be eaten into until the position breaks even at 446 (exercise price – premium (460 – 14)).

If the underlying security continues to fall the investor will make a profit equal to the amount the underlying security price is below the break even price. The profit is limited by the fact that the underlying security can only fall to zero.

Advantages of buying puts:
- A put option allows an investor to profit from a falling market.
- The maximum loss with holding a put position is limited to the premium paid out.
- The profit potential is limited by the fact that the underlying security can only fall to zero.
- The gearing of options mean that the investor can make considerable gains for a relatively small outlay.

Disadvantage:
- The passage of time works against the holder and the time value element of the option's premium.

Like calls, buying puts can be used for several reasons, the most frequent ones being:

- to gain exposure to and thereby profit from a fall in the price of the underlying security;

Long Apr 460 put @ 14   Fig 4.13

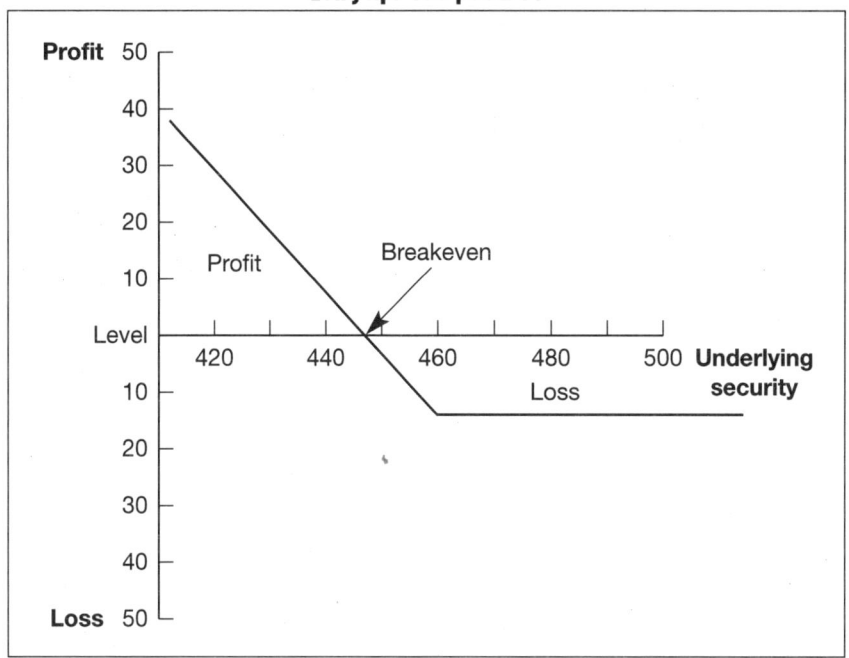

[Profit/loss chart: downward-sloping line from approximately (420, +38) through breakeven near 446, flattening at –14 for underlying security prices at/above 460; x-axis marks 420, 440, 460, 480, 500; y-axis Profit/Loss from 50 to –50 with "Level" at 0.]

- to hedge or insure an existing position against an adverse price movement in the underlying security;
- to lock in a sale price for the underlying security.

To gain exposure (speculative trade)

The advantages of buying puts options are the same as those for buying a call. The premium paid out is the maximum loss a buyer can sustain and the gearing effect can result in high percentage profits for a relatively small price movement in the underlying security.

The choice about which series to purchase is yet another similarity with call options. Not only must the extent of the fall be anticipated, but also the timing of the fall.

If the fall is expected to be substantial and over a short period, out-of-the-money series should be purchased. If the fall is less substantial and over a longer period in-the-money and longer dated puts are best.

It is possible, unlike calls, to purchase a long-dated put for little more than a short-dated put. This is due in part to puts being less popular than calls (supply and demand) and their profits being limited by the underlying security only being able to fall to zero. This situation can be an advantage if the underlying security does not fall at the speed the investor anticipates.

> **Example**
>
> It is 1 June and TBC Ltd is trading at 236. The expectation is that the share price will fall quite substantially over the next few weeks. To take advantage of this fall, an investor purchases a July 220 put option @ 2. Two weeks later the underlying security price has fallen to 224. The premium of the July 220 put has now risen to, say, 8. The investor can now sell the put option back into the market for a profit.
>
> While the option has not acquired any intrinsic value, the time value element of its premium has risen. This rise takes into account the fact that the option is now approaching being at-the-money where time value is greatest.

Once an investor is making a profit with a particular trade he may wish to walk up the position, realizing a profit but maintaining his exposure to future price movements. To do this, the investor must sell his options position back into the market, at a profit, using some of the profit to purchase more options with a lower premium and possibly a longer-dated expiry month. By walking up his position, the investor has recovered his initial investment at a profit and established a new position in a further out-of-the-money option at no cost. This new position can be looked upon as being risk free as its cost to the investor is zero.

To hedge an existing stock position

> **Key features**
>
> ## Buying puts
>
> *Buying puts can be used to act as an insurance against a fall in the price of an individual security or, when using FT-SE 100 Index options, the market in general. This strategy is known as insurance and places a floor under the holding through which its value will not fall.*

Any loss in the underlying security being offset by a rise in the value of the put option position. While call writing will provide a limited amount of downside protection, only the purchase of puts can provide cover in the event of a substantial fall in the underlying security.

> **Example**
>
> An investor holds stock at 467 and anticipates a fall in its value. For tax reasons he does not wish to sell the stock and realize any profit. He decides to purchase an April 460 put @ 14 to hedge his position. If the stock falls to 415, a fall of 45; the 460 put would have risen in value to offset this loss.
>
> | Stock | Stock +/− | Option | Hedge +/− |
> |-------|-----------|--------|-----------|
> | 410 | −57 | +36 | −21 |
> | 430 | −37 | +16 | −21 |
> | 450 | −17 | −4 | −21 |
> | 470 | +3 | −14 | −11 |
> | 490 | +23 | −14 | +9 |
>
> The effect of the hedge has been, at the expiry of the option, to limit the loss of the investor to a maximum of 21. He is still able to participate in any rise in the underlying security, although at a reduced rate equal to the premium paid out for the put option.

When establishing a hedge, it is necessary to determine the number of option contracts required. For a holding of 5,000 shares, five contracts would be required.

$$\frac{\text{Holding}}{\text{Contract size}} = \text{Number of contracts}$$

$$\frac{5{,}000}{1{,}000} = 5$$

This is the simplest type of insurance available and, depending on whether in-, at- or out-the-money options are purchased, will depend on the actual performance of the hedge. In-the-money options will respond penny for penny with a fall in the underlying security. At-the-money options will generally move at half the rate of the underlying security and out-of-the-money options will respond the slowest to any price changes in the underlying security. The amount of protection will depend on how much an investor is willing to pay.

If the fall in the underlying security is expected to continue after the expiry of the hedge, it should be rolled over into the next expiry month.

Lock in a sale price

Buying puts can also be employed to lock in the sale price of the underlying security. It is possible that due to an investor's tax situation, he/she is not able to take advantage of high share prices and sell his/her holdings.

> **Key features**
>
> ## Buying puts
> *By purchasing put options it is possible to lock in a sale price, to be used at a future date when an investor's tax situation may have changed.*

Writing put options

Puts are usually written with a neutral to slightly bullish view to price rises in the underlying security. The put will then not be exercised by the holder, thus allowing the writer to keep the premium received as profit.

> **Example**
>
> It is February and an investor expects the price of ABC Ltd to rise very slightly over the next few months. The expected rise is not large enough to warrant the purchase of call options so the investor writes put options as an alternative. The price of ABC Ltd is 544 and so the March 550 puts are written with a premium of 40p. If, as expected at expiry of the option, the underlying security price is above the 550 exercise price, the writer will not be assigned and will therefore be able to keep the premium of 40p or £400 per contract as profit.

The profit/loss profile shows that the writer will make a profit of 40p (his/her maximum) if the underlying security price is above the exercise price of 550 at expiry. The position will break even at 510 after which, if the underlying security continues to fall, the writer will make a loss equal to the amount that the share price is below the break-even price.

Advantages to put writing:
- Able to generate additional income and earnings.
- The passage of time works in favor of the writer.

Disadvantages
- The possible loss is limited only by the fact that the underlying security can only fall to zero.
- The writer may be assigned early and have to take delivery of the stock above the current market price.

Short March 550 put @ 40

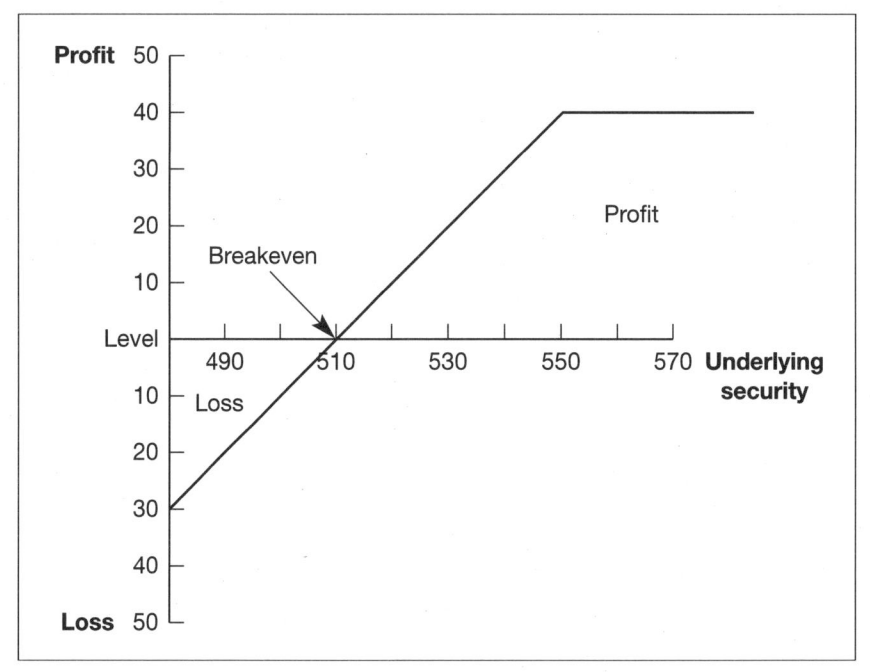

Fig 4.14

Writing puts, like writing calls, falls into one of two categories, covered and uncovered (naked) writers. However, in the case of puts, being a covered writer means having sufficient cash to purchase the underlying security if assigned.

The writing of put options can be used for two purposes:

- generating additional income;
- locking in a purchase price.

Generating additional income

Just as with call writing, selling puts can be used to generate additional income. The writer of a put receives the premium from the buyer. This premium represents the maximum profit the writer can make as long as the option remains unexercised at expiry.

The amount of additional income generated will depend on which series is written. An in-the-money series, with its high premium, will generate the highest returns, but runs a far greater risk of being exercised. Out-of-the-money options, with their low premiums, will produce the least returns but are considered a much safer proposition against the threat of exercise.

As with all option writing strategies, margin is an important consideration. Investors must check with their broker about what they will accept as collateral and the amount required.

Locking in a purchase price

An investor takes a long-term optimistic view of a stock. However in the short term there is the possibility of a fall in its share price. The investor wishes to acquire stock at the lowest level possible and so writes a put option at the level he thinks the stock may fall to.

If the stock does fall to, or below, the exercise price on or before expiry, the put will be exercised and the investor will be obliged to purchase the stock. The cost of the stock to the investor will be the exercise price minus the premium received, ensuring that the investor purchases stock at the lowest level possible.

If the underlying security does not fall to the anticipated level, the option will not be exercised. With the option unexercised, the writer of the put will keep the premium received from the sale of the option as additional income.

Which options to use

One of the most important aspects of dealing in traded options is knowing which series and class to buy. This naturally will depend on the investors' expectation for the stock and how much risk they are prepared to accept.

If the investors' expectations for the underlying security are bullish, they should purchase call options. With a willingness to accept a high degree of risk, an out-of-the-money series should be considered, or for a smaller degree of risk in-the-money options.

With a neutral to slightly bearish view, investors should consider writing call options. Again, depending on the amount of risk acceptable, either in-the-money options, high risk, or out-of-the-money options, low risk, can be used.

If the expectation for the underlying security is bearish, put options should be purchased. Again, the amount of risk investors are exposed to can be adjusted by the series purchased: out-of-the-money for high risk and in-the-money for low risk.

If the expectation is neutral to slightly bullish, writing put options can be considered, adjusting the series for the amount of risk acceptable.

Futures trades

While there are four different trades (buy call, sell call, buy put, sell put) that investors can transact with traded options, there are only two possible trades with a futures contract – buy or sell. If investors' expectations for the underlying asset are bullish, they should buy the future. If the expectation proves to be correct, the futures contract will rise in value allowing them to close out the position at a profit. If, on the other hand, investors' view the underlying asset as bearish, then they should sell the futures contract. If the view is correct, they will be able to buy back the futures at a lower price than they were sold for, the difference being the profit they have made.

Index futures contracts can be used to take a view on the direction of the overall market with the added advantage of gearing. With index options being exposed to just market or non-specific risk, investors do not need to have an option on the value of a stock but can use the futures to "play" the market.

Example

An investor takes the view that the FT-SE 100 index is about to rise after a period of consolidation. The index futures contract is trading at a spread of 3496 to 3498. The investor buys the futures at 3498. Over the next seven working days the index rises to 3589 and the investor then sells the futures contract. The profit on the trade is the difference between the two index levels multiplied by £25. However, with the purchase of futures being on a margined basis, the flow of the profits takes place on a daily basis as described in the following table:

Day	Variation margin	Index	Action
1		3533	buy
2	Initial margin £2,500	3577	
3	44 × £25 = £1,100 received	3563	
4	14 × £25 = £350 paid out	3565	
5	2 × £25 = £50 received	3564	
6	1 × £25 = £25 paid out	3570	
7	6 × £25 = £150 received	3589	sell
8	19 × £25 = £475 received + initial margin		

A total profit of £1,400

The other possible futures trade is to sell or short the future. This involves the investor selling a futures contract that they do not own, in the hope that the index will fall and they can buy it back at a lower price than it was initially sold for.

Example

A fund manager is concerned that the economic data to be released over the next week could have an adverse effect on the index, so decides to sell the future in order to take advantage of this. The fund manager sells the future at 3510, the index falls to 3446 over the next week, the future is then bought back, and the contract makes a profit of £1,600.

4 · Basic Characteristics of Options and Futures

Day	Variation margin	Index	Action
1		3510	sell
2	Initial margin £2,500	3484	
3	+ £650	3489	
4	– £125	3494	
5	– £125	3475	
6	+ £475	3489	
7	– £350	3476	
8	+ £325	3446	buy back
9	+ £750 + initial margin		
Total profit £1,600			

Long future 3533

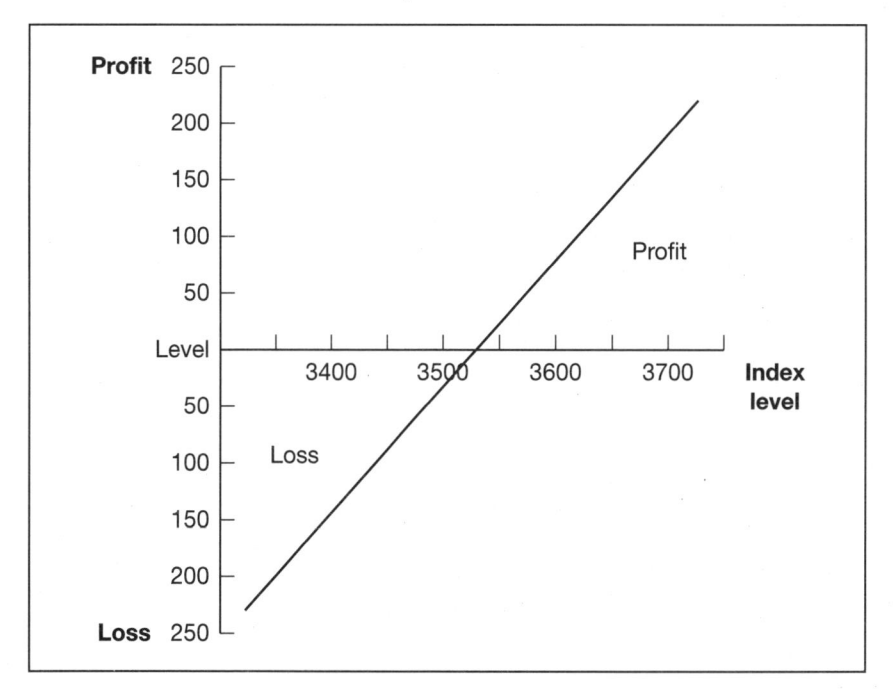

Fig 4.15

Fig 4.16   **Short future 3510**

[Chart: Short future 3510 payoff diagram, downward-sloping line from approximately (3300, +200) through (3510, 0) to (3750, -220); x-axis "Index level" from 3400 to 3700; y-axis "Profit/Loss" from -250 to +250]

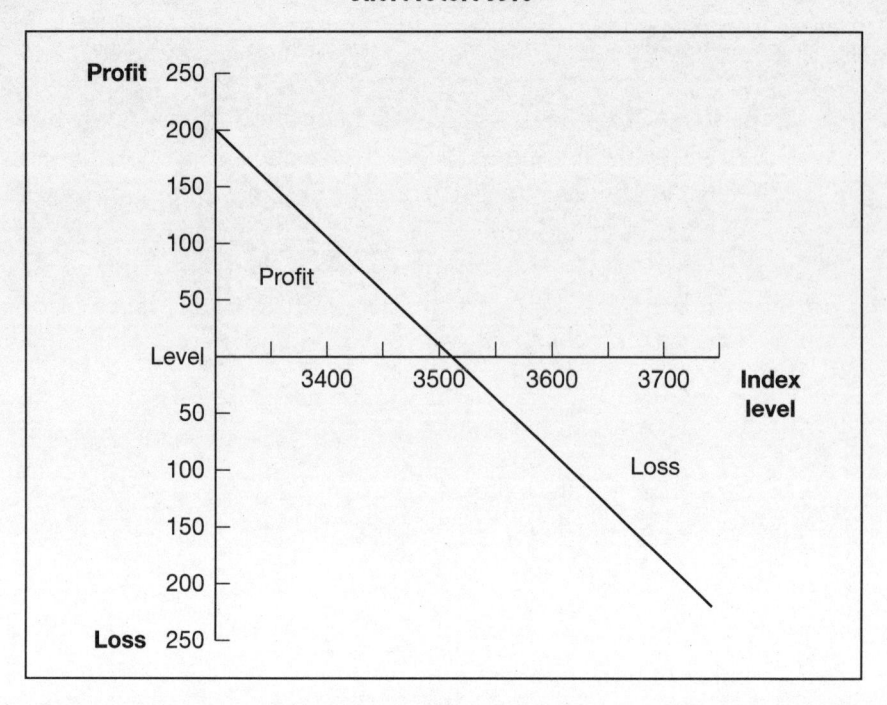

Flex options

While exchange-traded derivative products have increased their volume drastically over the years, an even bigger increase has taken place in the Over the Counter (OTC) market. OTC products are traded "off exchange," i.e. directly between security houses and banks over the telephone. One of the main advantages of OTC products is their ability to cater for contracts for quantities of an underlying asset, with an expiry date not available with a standardized exchange-traded contract. This means they are extremely flexible in their make-up.

However, there are a number of disadvantages to OTC products. First, the contract is directly between, and always with, the original counterparty, exposing the two sides to counterparty credit risk. Should the counterparty, for whatever reason, be unable to meet his contractual obligations, the other party has no course of redress but to sue in a court of law. In addition to counterparty credit risk, there is no secondary market enabling the buyer or seller to trade out of their position, therefore if the original counterparty does not wish to close the bargain at an acceptable price, the investor must enter into a second position, equal to, but opposite to, the first with another party.

As a counter to the flexibility of OTC contracts which takes business away from exchange-traded derivatives, both LIFFE and OMLX have introduced a new product known as "flex futures and options." First designed and developed in America in 1993 by the Chicago Board Options Exchange, with the introduction of flex options on the S&P 100 and the S&P 500 Indices, flex options allow investors to specify exercise price and expiry date. This enables the investor to tailor the product to suit his needs.

However, because they are traded on an exchange, the Clearing House becomes the ultimate counterparty, eliminating the credit risk associated with the OTC contracts. In addition there will always be a secondary market available allowing the investor to trade out of his position, if and when he wants to.

While both LIFFE and OMLX have introduced flex contracts there are a number of basic differences between them as shown in Table 4.7.

Index options

Indices are used to describe the value of a group of individual components. The index may show the rate of inflation as in the retail price index, the economic activity of purchasing managers as in the purchase managers index or the relative value of an equity market such as the Financial Times 30 Index.

While equity indices have been around for some time – the FT 30 was started in 1935 – it was not until quite recently that futures and option contract were available on them. The major factor contributing to their introduction was the advent of electronic screen-based trading. In order for screen-based trading to work, the prices for the individual components of the index must be entered into a central computer accessed by the market participants. The computer can then, using the individual prices, establish the relative value of the index.

Most indices are weighted averages of the individual prices, which are then used to adjust, either up or down, the relative value of the index. The index must have a starting value and this is usually set at an arbitrary value such as 1000.

Table 4.7   Differences between OMLX and LIFFE flex contracts

	OMLX Futures	OMLX Options	LIFFE Options
Underlying index	FT-SE 100, FT-SE 250, FT-SE Actuaries 350, FT-SE 350 Actuaries Industry Baskets*	FT-SE 100, FT-SE 250, FT-SE Actuaries 350, FT-SE 350 Actuaries Industry Baskets*	FT-SE 100
Exercise style		American or European	European
Unit of trading	£10 or £25 per index point	£10 or £25 per index point	£10 per index point
Expiry date & time	10.30 am on any business day	10.30 am on any business day	10.30 am on any business day
Exercise times		Between 08.30 & 16.30 on any business day for American style	By 18.00 on expiry day
Trading hours	08.30 – 16.30	08.30 – 16.30	09.00 – 15.45

Mineral Extraction: Extractive Industries; Oil, Integrated; Oil, Exploration & Production

General Manufacturers: Building and Construction; Building Material & Merchants; Chemicals; Diversified Industries; Electronic & Electrical Eqp.; Engineering; Engineering, Vehicles; Printing, Paper & Packaging; Textiles & Apparel

Consumer Goods: Breweries; Spirits, Wines & Ciders; Food; Manufacturers; Household Goods; Health Care; Pharmaceuticals; Tobacco

Services: Distribution; Leisure & Hotels; Media; Retailers, Food; Retailers, General; Support Services; Transport; Other Services & Businesses

Utilities: Electricity; Gas Distribution; Telecommunications; Water;

Financials: Banks, Retail; Insurance; Life Assurance; Merchant Banks; Other Financial; Property

The index is a weighted average in order to give more value to some companies than to others. This allows for the difference in market size and value between different companies. The most usual form of weighting is that of market capitalization. This is calculated by multiplying the company's share price by the number of its shares in existence.

Therefore a price movement in a company with a high market capitalization will have more of an effect on the value of the index than the same price movement of a company with a smaller market capitalization.

While a market capitalization weighted index takes into account movements in the prices of its constituents, it will not take into account any dividends or interest payments made by those companies. Therefore, it is only a price index and not a total return index.

In the UK the main index used to show movements on the London Stock Exchange is the Financial Times-Stock Exchange 100 Index (FT-SE 100 or the Footsie). The index consists of the top 100 listed UK companies by market capitalization. Obviously the market capitalization of a company is constantly changing with any change in its share price.

FT-SE 100

Key features

In order to ensure that the FT-SE 100 consists of the top 100 market-capitalized companies, the constituents of the index, and all other shares on the London stock market, are reviewed quarterly and changes made to the membership of the index if necessary.

If and when any changes are made to the constituents of the index, the base value of the index also needs to be changed, otherwise the index will show changes in price movements and in the capital structure of the constituents.

The value of the index is calculated every minute by the London Stock Exchange, using the share prices quoted by the market makers on SEAQ, (the share dealing system) and the arithmetical formula and therefore acts as a real-time indicator to the level of the UK stock market. The base level for the index was set at 1000.0 on 31 December 1983.

Unlike individual equity options which are settled by the physical delivery of the underlying security, if exercised, FT-SE 100 futures and options contracts are what is known as "contracts for difference." If exercised, there is no delivery or receipt of actual stock. Instead, the option is settled for cash. This process avoids the difficulty of delivering shares in each of the index constituencies. Not only would this be time-consuming, but it would also prove to be very expensive. In addition, if the individual shares had to be delivered, there is every possibility that their prices would be manipulated to some degree or other.

> **Definition** *For traded options the amount of cash received or paid is calculated by the difference between the exercise price and the index value when exercised (known as the **Exchange Delivery Settlement Price**) × £10.*

For the futures contract the process is slightly different. The amount is calculated by taking the difference between the price at which the futures contract was either bought or sold and the EDSP × £25.

Index traded options

There are two styles of index options available on LIFFE: European and American. European options can only be exercised at expiry, whereas American options can be exercised at any time, on any business day, during the life of the option. All equity options are American-style options.

Unlike equity options, where there are three expiry dates with three months between each date, index options have their own different expiry cycles. American-style index options expiry dates are the closest four months to today's date, plus June and December, as shown in the first example below. This cycle gives the index a maximum life of 12 months. European-style index options have

March, June, September and December, plus the two nearest months, and this style is used in the second example.

> **Example**
>
> It is 1 Jan and the expiry dates for the American-style index options are:
>
> > Jan, Feb, Mar, Apr, (being the closest four months) + June and Dec.
>
> When Jan expires May will be introduced. When Feb expires there will be no new month introduced as June is already in existence.
>
> When June is the closest month and about to expire, the sequence will be June, July, Aug, Sept + Dec. When June does expire, Oct will be introduced along with a 12-month June date.

> **Example**
>
> It is 1 Jan and the expiry date available for the European-style index are:
>
> Jan, Feb, (being the two closest months to today's date), plus March, Jun, Sept, and Dec.
>
> When Jan expires, April will be introduced, still giving the four standard expiry months, plus the two additional near months. When Feb expires, May will be introduced as the second additional near dated expiry month. When March expires, March the following year will be the new month introduced to maintain the four standard expiry months. No new near-dated expiry month will be introduced.

In order to prevent the possibility of manipulating the value of the index at expiry, all exchanges have procedures in place to ensure that the final EDSP is a fair and true representation of the index. On LIFFE, the FT-SE 100 Index expires at 10.30 a.m. on the third Friday of the expiry month. The value of the index is recorded every minute from 10.10 to 10.30. The three highest and lowest readings are discarded and the average taken from the remaining 15 readings in Table 4.7.

The settlement price of the Footsie is calculated in this manner to prevent any large investment houses from manipulating the index to their advantage and profit.

The FT-SE 100 can be used for both speculative and hedging purposes. Hedging, a type of insurance, compensates a fall in the value of the portfolio with a rise in the value of the option.

Example (speculative)

If we imagine it is 1 May and the index stands at 2860. This represents £28,600 (the index value × £10).

An investor buys a June 2850 call for 75. This gives the holder the right to purchase the index value at the close of business on the day of exercise for £28,500.

In June, just before expiry, the index is valued at 2935 (or £29,350). The holder of the June 2850 call has the choice to either exercise the option and purchase the index or sell the option back into the market for its premium. By exercising the option and buying the index at 2935, the investor will make £850 profit (purchase £29,350 for £28,500). Selling the option back into the market, the investor will receive the premium, which may be 87 or £870 profit.

Futures pricing

As discussed earlier with traded options, the difference between the option's intrinsic value and its premium or price is known as the time value. Time value represents the remaining life of the option and the possibility of movements in the price of the underlying security. With futures contracts, the difference between the futures price and the spot price of the underlying asset is known as its basis.

As with the time value of traded options, basis is greatest when the futures contract has the most time until expiry, when the time value of traded options and the basis of a futures contract will be zero.

4 · Basic Characteristics of Options and Futures

In other words, the derivatives price will converge with the spot or cash price of the underlying security at expiry. It is this convergence that will help keep prices in line.

While there are six factors that will determine the price of any traded option series (underlying security price, exercise price, time to expiry, volatility, dividends and interest rates), the factors affecting the price of an equity index futures contract, and therefore the basis, are money market rates, dividends (declared and forecast) and market sentiment.

> **Example**
>
> If we take an example with the index standing at 3400, money market rates at 7 percent and a gross dividend yield of 4 percent, what is the basis, and therefore the fair value, of the index with an expiry date in one year's time?
>
> The equation: **FP = SP + (OC – OL)**
>
> where: FP = Futures Price
> SP = Spot Price
> OC = Opportunity Cost
> OL = Opportunity Losses
>
> If we add into the calculation the figures
>
> $3400 + (3400 \times (7\% - 4\%))$
> $= 3400 + 102$
> $= 3502$
>
> Opportunity cost = the risk-free interest received.
> Opportunity losses = the dividend yield forgone.

The basis can be drawn as a straight line on a graph as in Figure 4.17. From this, it should be possible to calculate the basis, and therefore the fair value, of an index futures contract with any expiry date within one year.

Unfortunately, the straight line of the theoretical basis is not the case in practice. The problem is that the theory assumes that the dividends paid on the constituents of the index are evenly spread throughout the year, which in practice is not the case. In addition, money market rates can and do alter, depending on the length or time of the loan or deposit. These variables will affect the fair value of futures contracts with different expiry dates.

While it is possible to work out the theoretical basis, and therefore the fair value, for a futures contract as above, it is often the case that the futures contract will be trading at either a discount or a premium to the futures fair value.

> **Key features**
>
> ## Arbitrage
> *The most important principal in the pricing of futures contracts is that of arbitrage. If there are two identical financial instruments trading at the same time, but on different markets, they must trade at the same price. If there was any anomaly between the prices, i.e. one was trading at a higher price than the other, arbitrageurs would sell the higher-priced contract, buy the lower-priced contract and lock in a risk-free profit.*

The problem with the example is that it does not include any transaction costs, i.e. the bid-offer spread or commissions. Because of the transaction costs it is always possible to have relatively small differences between the two contracts. While it is quite acceptable to have a small difference in the prices of the two contracts there should be no opportunity for arbitrage.

If we take an example of an underlying security with a spot or cash price of 100 which, for this example, pays no dividend or interest, the only cost of buying the asset is the interest (5 percent) on the money used to purchase the asset. Hence the cost of buying the asset and holding for one year would be 105. If there were no transaction costs, i.e. bid offer spreads and/or commissions, the possibility of arbitrage would ensure the futures price was in line with its fair value.

If the future was trading at too high a price (known as trading rich), arbitrageurs would sell or short the future at, say, 108, while at the same time buying or going long of the underlying security at 100, using funds borrowed at 5 percent.

4 · Basic Characteristics of Options and Futures

EDSP calculation

Table 4.8

Index level	Time	Index level	Time
3196.7	10.10	3198.4	10.20
3195.6#	10.11	3199.1*	10.21
3197.8	10.12	3198.2	10.22
3197.5	10.13	3197.6	10.23
3198.1	10.14	3198.3	10.24
3197.2	10.15	3197.2	10.25
3198.8	10.16	3196.8	10.26
3198.7	10.17	3195.0#	10.27
3198.9*	10.18	3194.9#	10.28
3198.4	10.19	3195.8	10.29
		3199.3*	10.30

Exchange Delivery Settlement Price = 3197.7
* three highest readings
\# three lowest readings

In one year's time the futures contract would be exercised and the arbitrageur would deliver the underlying security (bought at 100) at 108. Having paid 5 percent interest, the arbitrageur would be looking at a risk-free, guaranteed profit of 3. This type of arbitrage is known as cash and carry arbitrage.

Looking at the reverse situation, where the future is trading at too low a price (cheap) to its fair price, at say 102, the arbitrageur would buy the futures contract at 102, while at the same time selling the underlying security at 100, with the proceeds of the sale of the underlying security placed on deposit at 5 percent.

At expiry of the futures contract, in one year's time, the arbitrageur would take delivery of the underlying security at 102. Having received interest at 5 percent on the sale of the underlying security the net cost of buying the underlying security with the futures contract is 97, giving the arbitrageur a guaranteed risk-free profit of 3.

Fig 4.17

Basis

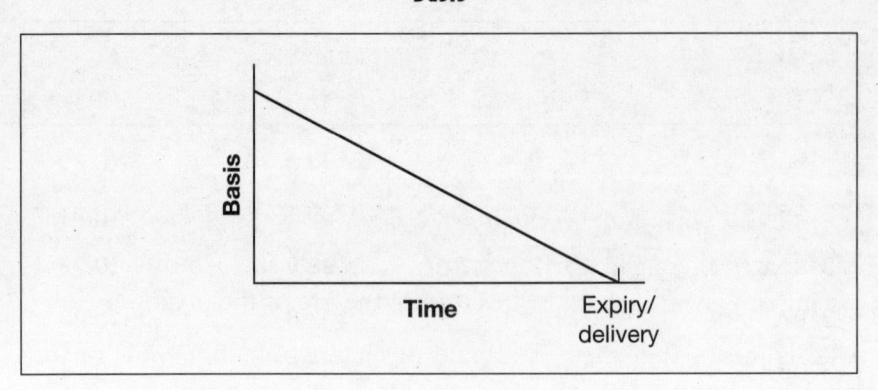

[Graph showing Basis decreasing linearly over Time to zero at Expiry/delivery]

This type of arbitrage, buying the future and selling the underlying security, is known as reverse cash and carry.

If either of these situations actually arose in the market, arbitrageurs would be quite happy to transact this type of business all day long, locking in risk-free, guaranteed profits. However, the volume of business in both the futures contract and the underlying security would soon force the prices back into line.

> **Definition**
>
> *If **cash and carry arbitrage** was taking place, the selling of the futures contracts would force the price down, while the underlying security price would rise due to the level of buying activity.*

> **Definition**
>
> *With **reverse cash and carry**, the buying of the futures contract would force its price to rise, while the underlying security price would fall, in line with the selling, forcing the prices back into line.*

The possibility of arbitrage will ensure that the fair price relationship between the futures contract and the underlying security is maintained.

As we have said, transaction costs, i.e. the bid-offer spread and commission, are barriers to arbitrage opportunities. In addition to the transaction cost, the theory of arbitrage assumes that there are no differences for borrowing or depositing money. In practice there is the money market's equivalent of the bid-offer spread, with borrowing rates higher than deposit rates.

Finally it is not always possible to borrow money for the whole duration of the arbitrage. This will necessitate the arbitrageur borrowing money at different rates during the life of the position.

All this means that there is a band or channel on either side of the futures contract's fair value within which risk-free arbitrage is not possible. The band is known as the arbitrage-free channel. This arbitrage-free channel will differ from one investor or trader to another depending on their ability to short the future or underlying security and the rate at which they can borrow or deposit funds.

A major consideration for any investor is their cash flow. When purchasing shares in the constituents of the FT-SE 100, the investor will have a large negative or outgoing cash flow due to the purchase of the shares. However, once the investor has been registered as the beneficial owner of the shares, there will be a positive or incoming cash flow from the dividends paid on the shares.

If, on the other hand, the investor purchased FT-SE 100 Index futures contracts, the initial outflow of funds would significantly reduce, as the only payment required is the initial margin payment. Unfortunately though, there are no dividends paid to holders of futures contracts. However, the savings made when using the futures contracts from the outflow of funds can be placed on "risk free" deposit ensuring a positive cash flow from the interest.

■ ■ ■

'The ultimate goal of any investor, whether a private investor or a fund manager responsible for a multi-million pound pension fund, is to maximize returns while minimizing risks.'

5

Uses and Benefits of Index and Equity Derivatives

Introduction

Risk

Portfolio protection

Asset allocation

Performance enhancement

Anticipatory hedging

Cash flow management – buy write

Introduction

When combined with a portfolio or an individual holding in the underlying security, index and equity futures and options offer an investor the opportunity to to improve the performance of their holding, combined with the ability to control a holding's exposure to risk. The use of index and equity futures and options by both private and professional investors include:

- portfolio protection – hedging and insurance
- portfolio enhancement
- asset allocation
- anticipatory hedging
- cash flow management
- synthetic strategies.

In other words, index and equity futures and options manage the risks associated with the holding of equity-based investments. Any strategy available on individual equities can also be used on stock indices and vice versa.

Risk

The ultimate goal of any investor, whether a private investor or fund manager responsible for a multi-million pound pension fund, must surely be to maximize their returns, while at the same time minimizing the risks, regardless of whether the aim of the portfolio is income, growth or a balanced return.

The risk associated with buying shares can be broken down into two components, specific and non-specific or market risk as shown in Figure 5.1. As the name suggests, specific risk is associated with the stocks and shares of a specific company. It may be attributed to the company's product, market place or style of management. Market risk affects the whole stock market and is more concerned with the economic outlook of the country and market sentiment.

5 · Uses and Benefits of Index and Equity Derivatives

It is possible to reduce specific risk to a minimum by holding a diversified portfolio. The more shares held, spread over a number of different sectors, will all but eliminate specific risk.

Market risk, on the other hand, cannot be diversified away. However, by using traded options, market risk can be managed in an effective and efficient way.

> **The more shares held, spread over a number of different sectors, will all but eliminate specific risk.**

The risk reward profile of an individual share or portfolio is illustrated in Figure 5.2. It shows the expected return for the holding (15 percent), as well as the possibility of a very low return (0 percent) or a very high return (25 percent). The bell shape of a company's risk reward profile is known as a normal distribution curve and shows the probability of various returns at a number of different share prices.

By using index and equity futures and options, it is possible to manage and alter the risk reward profile to achieve a more desirable result. However, when using index futures and options to manage the market risk of a portfolio, the index must have a high level of congruence, not only to ensure that like is being compared to like, but also to ensure that the fund manager does not fall foul of the regulatory bodies.

With the FT-SE 100 Index accounting for 70 percent of the market capitalization of the FT-All Share Index, the FT-SE 100 must be considered not have a high degree of congruence with a portfolio of broadly based equities.

Specific and market risk

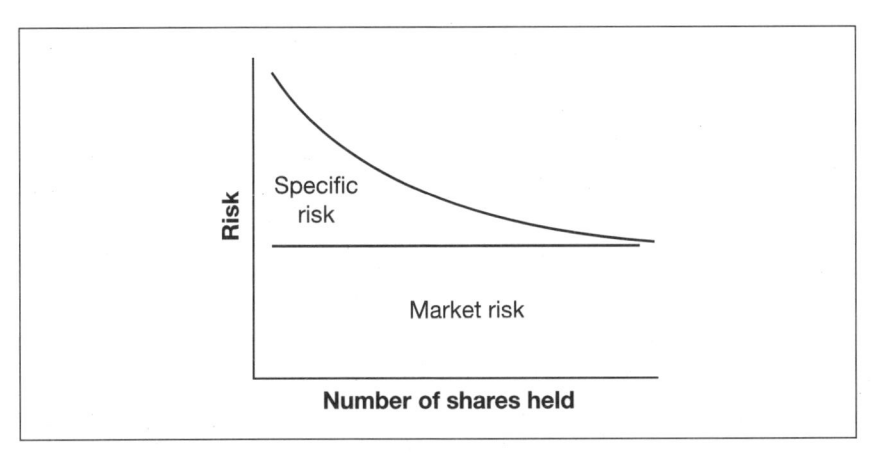

Fig 5.1

Fig 5.2

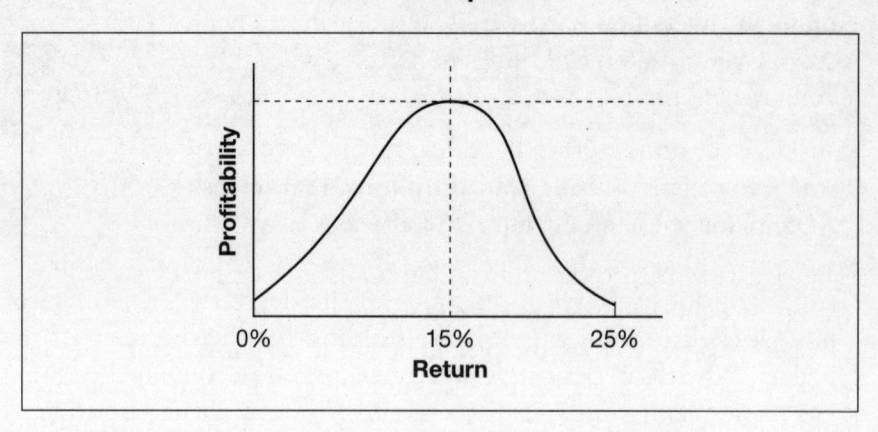

Risk reward profile

[Graph showing Profitability vs Return, with curve peaking at 15%, spanning 0% to 25%]

Definition *The relationship between the return on a portfolio of equities and the return on the market is described as its **Beta**.*

The Beta of a stock can be found by regressing the returns of an individual security into the returns of the market. The Beta of a portfolio is the value-weighted average of the Betas of the components of the portfolio. The Beta of the market is always one.

A portfolio with a Beta of one will mirror the returns and movements of the market. If the portfolio had a Beta of two, it would move twice as fast as the market, whereas the returns and movements of a portfolio with a Beta of 0.5 will be half that of the market.

By using the Beta of a portfolio a fund manager can tailor a hedge, or any other strategy, to suit the individual portfolio.

Portfolio protection

By using index and equity futures and options, it is possible to protect the value of either an individual holding or a portfolio. This is possible by using short futures positions or put options in order to manage the exposure of a holding/portfolio to price movements in the underlying asset. As the price of the underlying asset moves, so the futures or options price will move. The movement in the price of the derivative can then be used to offset the price of the underlying asset.

Hedging

The theory behind hedging a position is that any loss in the underlying asset is compensated for by an increase in the value of the derivative. However, if there is a rise in the underlying asset it is cancelled out by a fall in the value of the derivative. The investor has "locked in" the value of the holding for the duration of the hedge. As with all derivative strategies, once the combined position has passed its usefulness, it can be closed out at any time during its life. Most positions are hedged using short FT-SE 100 or Mid 250 futures contracts. Having sold the futures contract, if the underlying asset, the FT-SE 100 or 250, falls, then the short futures position will receive an in-flow of cash from the variation margin which will compensate for the fall in the value of the index. However, if the index rises, the investor with the short futures position will have to make the variation margin calls, cancelling out the rise in the index.

Example

A fund manager has a portfolio valued at £10 million, of broadly based UK equities from the FT-SE 100, which is used as the fund's bench-mark. After reaching a new all-time high, the fund manager is concerned that the index, and consequently his portfolio, will fall in the short term. Not wishing to liquidate the portfolio, the fund manager decides to hedge the fund's exposure to short-term adverse price movements by selling – going short – FT-SE 100 futures contracts. By selling the futures contracts against the fund, the fund manager has now "locked in" the gains the portfolio has made.

If the index, and hence the value of the portfolio, does fall, the fund manager will receive the variation margin, in the form of cash payments from LCH to compensate for the fall. Finally, the fund manager will be able to buy back the futures contracts at a price lower than they were originally sold for, finalizing and quantifying the profit.

> The quantity of futures contracts sold will depend on the value of the fund and the level of the index at the time of establishing the hedge. The formula is:
>
> $$\frac{\text{Value of holding/portfolio}}{\text{Index level} \times £25} = \text{Number of contracts}$$
>
> For this example:
>
> $$\frac{£10,000,000}{3552 \times £25} = 112.61 \text{ contracts}$$

Not being able to trade in fractions of a contract the fund manager must decide whether to slightly under-hedge and sell 112 contracts or slightly over-hedge and sell 113 contracts. If the fund manager under-hedges the portfolio as the index falls, the short futures position will not completely cover the fall, resulting in an underperformance of the hedge. On the other hand, if the fund manager over-hedges the portfolio as the index falls, the short futures position will increase in value faster than the index loses value. While this does not sound such a bad thing if the fund manager's view proves to be incorrect and the index rises, the short futures position will lose value faster than the portfolio gains in value, resulting in the value of the overall position losing money.

The fund manager's view proves to be correct and the index falls 150 points to 3402, a fall of 4.25 percent. The value of the portfolio has fallen in line with the index to £9,575,000. However, as the index has fallen so the short futures position has increased in value, and the fund manager has been compensated for the fall in the index by the positive cash flow of variation margin. The short futures position can now be closed out by buying back the futures sold, at a lower price than they were originally sold for, finalizing and quantifying the profit on the short futures hedge.

If, however, the fund manager's expectation for a fall in the index had proved to be wrong and the index actually rose, the value of the short futures position would have fallen, resulting in the fund manager having to make the cash variation margin calls to LCH. This negative cash flow to LCH would have cancelled out any gains in the value of the underlying portfolio. A hedged position, using short futures, "locks in" a value for the underlying portfolio, which

Short futures hedge

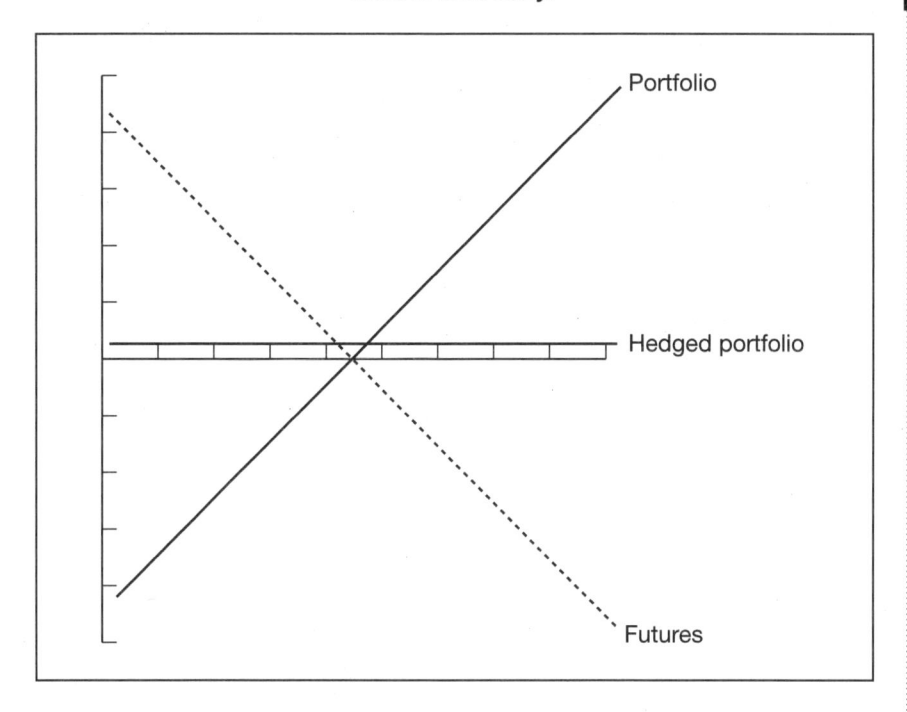

Fig 5.3

[Chart showing Portfolio (solid upward line), Futures (dashed downward line), and Hedged portfolio (horizontal line)]

should then not change regardless of the movements in the FT-SE 100 Index. While the downside is protected and indeed cancelled out, there is no upside potential should the fund manager's view prove to be wrong.

A fully and properly hedged portfolio will have a Beta reduced to zero.

Portfolio protection – insurance

If the fund manager had wished to insure the value of the portfolio, while at the same time being able to participate and benefit from any unexpected rise in the index, he should have considered purchasing put options on the FT-SE 100. By purchasing the put options, the fund manager places a "floor" under the portfolio under which the value of the fund will not fall. While the portfolio will not fall below the "floor" placed under it by the put option, there will be a slight fall in the fund until the floor is reached.

This fall will be equal to the premium paid for the option. With the maximum loss of a long option position being equal to the premium paid for the option, it is possible for the fund to participate and benefit from any rise in the index above this amount, i.e. the premium. Once the index has risen enough to cover the premium, any further rise will work through to the bottom line of the portfolio.

Example

If we use the same information as in the previous example, it will give a better comparison of the two techniques. A fund manager has a portfolio valued at £10 million of broadly based equities from the FT-SE 100 Index. The portfolio has a Beta of 1 and uses the FT-SE 100 Index as a benchmark to measure its performance. The fund manager is concerned about the possible fall in the index and so the portfolio. To counter this threat, the fund manager purchases index put options in order to place a "floor" under the value of the portfolio. The formula for designing the insurance is simular to the formula used in the short futures hedge. However, this time the index level is multiplied by £10 (the contract unit of trading) and not the £25 for the futures contract.

$$\frac{\text{Value of holding/portfolio}}{\text{Index level} \times £10} = \text{Number of contracts}$$

So in this example:

$$\frac{£10,000,000}{3552 \times £10} = 281.5 \text{ contracts}$$

As with the previous example, the fund manager must decide whether to under- or over-insure the portfolio. However, when using put options to insure the portfolio, if the fund manager decides to over-insure and his view proves to be incorrect and the index rises, the fund will still be able to participate and benefit from the rise, unlike in the previous example.

The fund manager decides to purchase the Nov 3550 put option with a premium 69p. The total cost of the options, excluding transaction costs, will be £194,580 (number of contracts × premium × £10). The fund manager has now placed a floor under the portfolio of 3481 index points (exercise price – premium). If the fund manager's expectation is correct and the market does fall, so the value of the put options will increase. The puts can then be sold to realize their profit, compensating the fund manager for the fall in the value of the portfolio. Table 5.1 shows the position of the insured portfolio if the put options are held until expiry.

Due to the fund manager over-hedging the portfolio by purchasing 282 contracts, the value of the insurance increases slightly as the index falls.

If the fund manager's expectation had proved to be incorrect and the market had risen during the life of the insurance, the portfolio would still have benefited from the rise, even if the put options had been held to expiry. In practice, the put position can be closed out at any time, so reducing any loss to a minimum and allowing the portfolio to participate fully in the market rise.

If the fall in the index is certain to happen, then a short futures hedge is the better value. However, if there is any chance of the expectation being wrong and the market rising, then put options offer the best alternative as they will allow the fund to participate in the rise.

Asset allocation

Asset allocation is the process of structuring a portfolio to achieve the desired results with regards to sectors and the weighting given to those sectors, and can be divided into two categories – strategic and tactical.

> **Definition**
>
> **Strategic asset allocation** *is concerned with achieving the desired results in the long term, whereas* **tactical asset allocation** *is concerned with short-term deviation from the strategic allocation to take advantage of short-term movements in different sectors and markets.*

> **Example**
>
> A fund manager has a portfolio of £100 million with a current asset allocation as follows:
>
> *Current allocation*
>
> | | |
> |---|---|
> | Equities | 70% |
> | Gilts | 25% |
> | Cash | 5% |

Mastering Exchange Traded Equity Derivatives

> However, due to expected short-term interest rate movements, the fund manager wishes to change the allocation to:
>
> *Desired allocation*
>
> | | |
> |---|---|
> | Equities | 60% |
> | Gilts | 35% |
> | Cash | 5% |
>
> In order to restructure the portfolio, the fund manager must decrease the fund's exposure to equities by 10 percent or £10 million and increase its exposure to Gilts by 10 percent or £10 million. To achieve this new allocation using futures, the fund manager must sell FT-SE 100 Index futures to reduce the fund's exposure, i.e. hedge the position, and at the same time purchase Gilt futures to increase the fund's exposure to price movements in the Gilts market.

To restructure the portfolio and make the necessary tactical asset switch in the normal manner in the equity and gilt markets would

Fig 5.4

Long put insurance

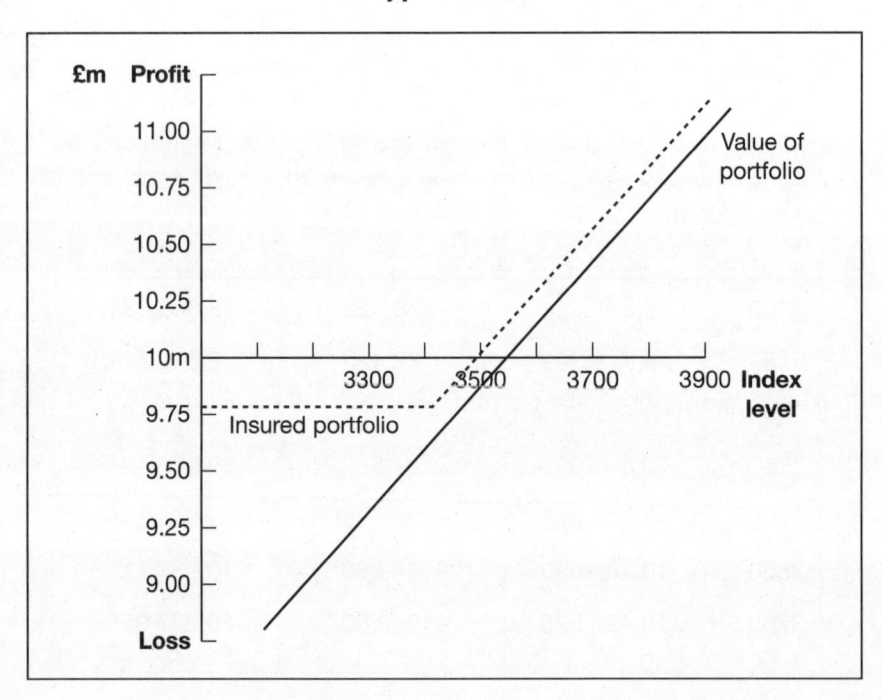

[Graph showing £m Profit on y-axis (ranging from Loss at bottom through 9.00, 9.25, 9.50, 9.75, 10m, 10.25, 10.50, 10.75, 11.00) versus Index level on x-axis (3300, 3500, 3700, 3900). Solid line labeled "Value of portfolio" and dashed line labeled "Insured portfolio".]

5 · Uses and Benefits of Index and Equity Derivatives

Insured portfolio distribution curve — Fig 5.5

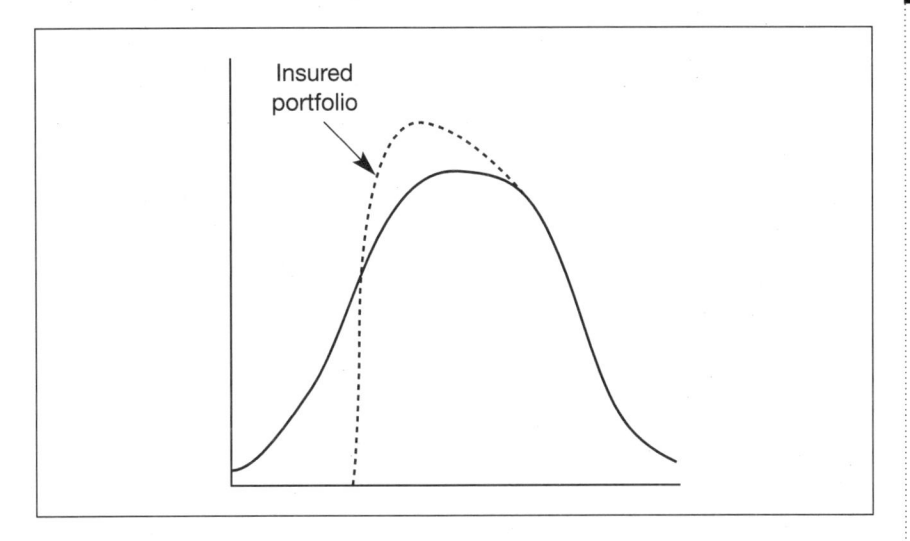

take time and leave the fund manager open to movements in the underlying assets, and any short-term liquidity problems. By using the derivatives markets, the fund manager can execute the switch in the shortest space of time, while leaving the underlying portfolio unchanged. In addition, and possibly more importantly, the costs involved with a tactical asset switch are much smaller in the derivative market than the cash markets.

Table 5.1

Index	Portfolio value £	Put option value £	Insured portfolio £
3400	9,577,464	+228,420	9,805,884
3450	9,718,309	+87,420	9,805,729
3500	9,859,154	−53,580	9,853,574
3550	10,000,000	−194,580	9,805,420
3600	10,140,845	−194,580	9,946,265
3650	10,281,690	−194,580	10,087,110
3700	10,422,535	−194,580	10,227,955

Table 5.2   **Transaction costs – Equities vs FT-SE 100 Futures**

	UK Equities	FT-SE 100 Futures
Bid/offer spread	0.90%	0.05%
Commission	0.40%	0.05%
Stamp duty	0.50%	–
Total	1.80%	0.10%

Once any asset allocation switch has been executed, the fund manager can choose whether to change the make-up of the underlying portfolio on a more permanent basis, in which case the fund manager can unwind the derivatives positions as the switches are made or leave the underlying portfolio unchanged, using the exposure gained through the derivatives to take advantage of any short-term strengths and weaknesses.

The advantages of using futures and options for tactical asset allocation switches are:

1. The switch can be implemented immediately.
2. The underlying portfolio does not have to be disturbed.
3. Liquidity in the futures and options market can be greater than in the cash market.
4. The reduced costs of dealing.

Performance Enhancement

Covered Call Writing

Fund managers and private investors can enhance the returns and thus the performance of the funds under their control by writing covered call options against either individual holdings or their complete portfolios. The object of covered call writing is to enhance the returns of a holding or portfolio and not to have the stock called away.

5 · Uses and Benefits of Index and Equity Derivatives

Definition

*The **writer of a call option** receives the premium of the option from the buyer and, in return for this premium, takes on an obligation to deliver a set number of shares or, in the case of the FT-SE 100 Index, make a cash payment, on or before the expiry date of the option, at the exercise price of the series.*

The writer of the option must be both able and willing to make the delivery if assigned. The option is only likely to be exercised and the writer assigned when the current share price is above the exercise price of the option and only then when the option is near to expiry.

Key features

Writing call options

Writing call options against an existing holding of the underlying security is regarded as a low-risk, conservative strategy. If the option is not exercised before its expiry, the writer will keep the premium received from the buyer as profit.

This premium will also protect the writer against a slight fall in the underlying security.

Covered call writing is very popular with large institutions and private investors with large holdings of stocks in the FT-SE 100 Index.

An additional advantage with covered call writing is that any dividends or other benefits attached to the underlying security accrue to the shareholder.

Example

It is early September and the shares of NFI Ltd are currently trading at 442p. An investor holds 5,000 shares purchased at 389p. After their short run-up, the investor expects the shares to consolidate at their present levels. The investor therefore writes five at-the-money calls against the holding. The investor writes the

> Jan 460 calls with a premium of 13p and receives £130 per contract or £650 for the five contracts.
>
> If the investor view proves to be correct and the share price for NFI Ltd is below 460p by the January expiry he/she will keep the premium received as profit. The £650 received represents the maximum profit the writer can make on this position.
>
> If, however, the underlying security price rises above the exercise price of 460p, then the chance of the option being exercised and the writer assigned increase. If the writer is assigned, he will have to deliver stock to the buyer of the option at the exercise price of 460p. However, having already received the premium of 13p, the writer will effectively be selling the stock at 473p. If the stock continues to rise, the writer will not participate or benefit from it above 473p. The 13p premium will offer some protection in the event of a fall in the underlying security down to 447p.

Covered call writing can be an extremely useful strategy to use during periods of static market condition. The eventual outcome for the strategy can be worked out for any price in the underlying security and is therefore known in advance. Whilst there is a possible opportunity loss if the share price rises, the premium received offers some downside protection.

It should also be remembered that should the underlying security price move against the writer, just as with all futures and options positions, he can close out the position at any time.

Covered put writing

Investors can also enhance their portfolio's return by writing covered put options.

> **Definition**
>
> *Unlike covered calls which are covered by a holding in the underlying security,* **covered puts** *are covered by a holding of cash. If the put option written by the seller is exercised, the writer is obliged to buy the underlying security at the exercise price.*

5 · Uses and Benefits of Index and Equity Derivatives

Covered call write   **Fig 5.6**

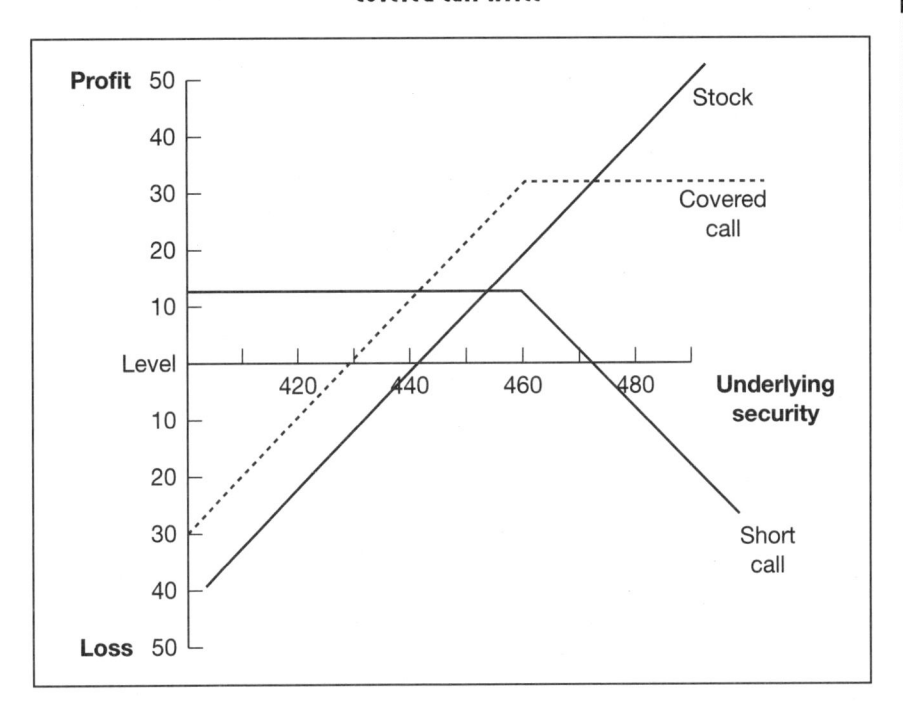

This obligation is covered by the cash already held. The objective of covered put writing is to enhance the performance of the portfolio and not to have to buy the underlying security.

However, writing covered puts can be considered a method of acquiring stock at a price below the current market price.

As with covered call writing, the writer of the puts (covered by cash) receives the premium from the buyer in return for accepting the obligation to buy the underlying security, at the exercise price on or before the expiry of the option. If the underlying security price is above the exercise price of the option at expiry, the option will not be exercised, allowing the writer to keep the premium received for writing the option as profit.

If the underlying security price is below the exercise price of the put at expiry, the option will be exercised and the writer assigned to buy the stock at the exercise price. However, having already received the premium for writing the put option, the writer will effectively be buying the stock at a price below the prevailing market level.

> **The objective of covered put writing is to enhance the performance of the portfolio and not to have to buy the underlying security.**

This strategy works best when the expectation for the underlying security is neutral to slightly bullish.

Anticipatory hedging

Index and equity futures and options can be used to secure the purchases price of an individual security or a basket of securities that will be purchased in the near future. This allows fund managers and private investors to participate in any price rises in between the the date of buying the futures or options and the receipt of the funds to actually purchase the securities. The general guideline concerning the time scales is that the receipt and/or expenditure of money is certain to take place and should be within one month.

Example

A fund manager knows that in one month's time he will receive £1.5 million. However, in between now and the receipt of the money he is concerned that the FT-SE 100 Index, and therefore the underlying securities, will rise in value. Not wishing to miss out on the expected rise which would mean paying more for the shares in the future, the fund manager can purchase either FT-SE 100 futures or call options.

By purchasing the futures or options, the fund manager is immediately exposing the fund to any future price movements, for a minimum outlay, without having to purchase the underlying securities. While it is possible to use futures to establish an anticipatory hedge, it is normal to use call options.

Call options are particularly attractive for anticipatory hedging and cash flow management, as the risk associated with long option positions is limited to the premium paid for the option, which is a fraction of the underlying security price. This compares with long futures positions where the downside risk is unlimited.

Once the index has risen, the call option premium will also have risen, allowing the fund manager to sell the option back into the market at a profit offsetting the increased purchase price of the underlying securities. Selling the option back into the market is preferred to exercising the option due to time value. If the option

5 · Uses and Benefits of Index and Equity Derivatives

is exercised and the underlying securities purchased by the fund manager, he will only receive the intrinsic value of the option. But by selling the option back into the market, the fund manager can receive the intrinsic value and any time value left on the option. That said, particular attention must be paid to the time element of the option's premium, as any increase in the index may be eroded, as far as the option's premium is concerned, by the passage of time.

Cash flow management – buy write

A writer of a call option receives the premium from the buyer and in return for this payment takes on the obligation to sell a fixed number of the underlying security, at the exercise price, on or before the expiry date if called upon to do so.

> **Definition**
>
> *When an opening sale of a call option is combined with the simultaneous purchase of the underlying security, the premium received can be used to offset the cost of the stock purchase. This strategy is known as* **"buy write."**

> **Example**
>
> A fund manager wishes to purchase 10,000 shares of WTB Ltd, even though his expectation for the stock is neutral to slightly bearish in the short term. To take advantage of his expectations, the fund manager writes 10 call option contracts at the same time as the purchase.
>
> | | |
> |---|---|
> | Buy 10,000 stock @ | 497 |
> | Write 10 July 500 calls @ | 10 |
> | Effective purchase price | 487 |
>
> If the expectation for the stock proves to have been correct and the underlying security price is below the exercise price of 500p at the expiry of the option in July, the option will not be exercised

Mastering Exchange Traded Equity Derivatives

> **Example**
>
> and the writer will keep the 10p premium as profit, reducing the purchase of the stock from 497p to 487p.
>
> However, if the expectation proves to have been wrong and the underlying security price is above 500p at the July expiry, the option will be exercised and the writer assigned. This will mean the writer will have to deliver the stock at the exercise price of 500p. However, having already received 10p premium for writing the option, the effective selling price will be 510p.

If the expectation for a security is that the share price will remain below the exercise price of the option written, until after the expiry of the option, a buy write strategy can be an effective way of reducing the cost of a stock purchase.

The option series chosen must be in line with expected share price movements and not due to high premiums, i.e. options should not be written at an exercise price that could result in assignment if the investor wishes to hold the stock on a long-term basis.

It should be remembered that, as with all traded option positions, if, during the life of the position, the share price moves against the investor, he can extinguish his liabilities by buying back (closing out) the option he has written at any time.

■ ■ ■

'Useful guidelines for fund managers and trustees dealing in futures and options.'

Important Guidelines

Check list for fund managers

Corporate events

Trading rules/guidelines

Taxation of options for private investors

The regulation and taxation of futures and options in UK funds

Barings

Check list for fund managers

The following guidelines should be used as a check list for fund managers and trustees and followed, along with their own specific dealing rules, before dealing in futures and options.

Authorization

- Ensure that senior management permit the use of futures and options.
- Ensure that the firm is authorized to deal in futures and options products and that the client mandates, trust deeds, scheme particulars, etc permit their use.
- Identify any specific steps necessary to obtain authorization, e.g. changing the trust deeds of a fund.
- Agree with the fund trustees the circumstances in which futures and options will be used.
- Ensure that the objectives for using futures and options are clear: hedging, asset allocation, cash flow management, income enhancement, etc.

Back office

- Ensure that the back office is in a situation to be able to deal with futures and options transactions.
- Decide if it is necessary to employ new staff and systems to deal with futures and options settlement and administration, and if the current staff need special training.
- If new systems are required, identify whether the company should buy a system that has already been developed (off-the-shelf package), or have one tailor-made to the specific requirements of the firm.
- Identify how a new system must be integrated with current settlement and administration systems.

Broker services

- Identify which broker(s) to use for trade execution and clearing.
- Identify the product knowledge and experience required of the brokers.

6 · Important Guidelines

- Identify the services required in:
  - execution and clearing
  - portfolio risk management advice
  - market research: quantitative and fundamental
  - statistical work and charts.
- Agree commission and fees with each brokerage firm.

Clearing

- Decide if it is necessary to open separate accounts for different funds with the clearing broker.
- Agree how to settle accounts with the clearing broker, i.e. agree balances each day and pay and receive cash daily, or deposit a suitable amount and top up if necessary.

> **Agree how to settle accounts with the clearing broker, i.e. agree balances each day and pay and receive cash daily, or deposit a suitable amount and top up if necessary.**

Initial margin procedures

- Agree which forms of initial margin can be deposited with each broker.
- Ensure that these arrangements fit with the portfolio requirements.
- Agree the level of interest the clearing broker will pay on the balance of the margin deposit.
- Agree multi-currency arrangements for margin.
- Agree how to deal with the varying margin procedures on different exchanges.
- Ensure that the firm is equipped to deal efficiently with sudden changes in initial margin levels triggered by changing market conditions.

Reporting structure

- Identify the types of trade reports and confirmations that are required.
- Identify all reports which are particularly needed for the company's internal administration.
- Investigate whether it would be helpful to have telex/fax business confirmations.
- Ensure that the internal reporting structure, front desk to back office, and vice versa, are in place.

Accounting and valuation

- Clearly identify the accounting procedures to be adopted for futures and options.
- Identify the regulatory/taxation requirements that must be addressed in the accounting procedures.
  - SRO requirements
  - fund regulation (e.g. unit trusts)
  - valuation procedures
- Identify how to deal with allocation of transactions and valuations across several funds.

Risk

- Ensure that the credit risk of the clearing broker used is clear to the firm.
- Ensure that your funds are held in a segregated account with the clearing broker.
- Identify what would happen if another of the clearing broker's customers defaulted.

Internal risk control

- Ensure that management procedures are in place for regular review and analysis of all forms of risk control.
- Ensure that the appropriate "red alert" systems are in place to assess the futures and options exposures to markets at any time, and in particular during volatile periods.
- Identify which employees are authorized to deal in futures and options, and how to control this.

Performance measurement

- Ensure that the appropriate method is used to show the effect of futures and options on the portfolio.

Quote vendor service

- Ensure that quote vendor and price information systems are in place (e.g. TOPIC, Reuters, Telerate, etc).
- Ensure that adequate in-house/external research facilities are available.

Corporate events

During the life of an option any corporate event on the underlying security will result in an alteration to the contract specification of the option. The most common corporate events which will be covered here are a capitalization issue, a rights issue, a takeover and a stock suspension.

Capitalization issue (bonus or scrip issue)

A capitalization issue, also known as a bonus or scrip issue, is an issue of shares, to existing shareholders, fully paid for out of company cash reserves. Historically shares in British companies have been priced under £5, making them attractive to private investors. If a company's share price rises above £5 and the company has sufficient cash reserves, it may consider a capitalization issue to help promote its shares to private investors. The issue is expressed as a ratio to the shareholder's existing holding. The options contract specification will be adjusted on the issues ex-entitlement date. The adjustment is calculated as follows:

$$\text{New contract size} = \text{Old contract size} \times (1 + x/y)$$

$$\text{New exercise price} = \text{Old exercise price} \times (1/1 + x/y)$$

where x = bonus entitlement.
       y = proportion of existing holding.

Example

ABC Plc announces a one-for-four capitalization issue. This means the company is issuing one new share for every four shares an investor holds. The new options contract size will be adjusted as follows:

$$1000 \times (1 + 1/4) = 1250$$

The option has exercise prices of 280, 300, 330, 360: these will be adjusted as follows:

$$280 \times 1/1+1/4 = 224$$
$$300 \times 1/1+1/4 = 240$$
$$330 \times 1/1+1/4 = 264$$
$$360 \times 1/1+1/4 = 288$$

> Any new series introduced after the ex-entitlement date will represent an option on 1,000 shares as per normal contract specifications.

If, during the calculations, the result is a fraction of a share the fraction is rounded to a whole number.

Margin

The value of shares pledged as margin will be adjusted proportionately on the ex-entitlement date.

For example, if the issue was a one-for-one by ABC Plc, then writers of traded option contracts with ABC Plc shares pledged as collateral would find the value of their shares halved and would be required to put up further margin to cover the deficiency. This could be done by pledging further shares in ABC Plc in respect of their new entitlement or by providing another form of collateral.

Rights issue

A rights issue is a method of a company raising capital, by offering its existing shareholders the right to subscribe to a new issue of shares, in proportion to their existing share holding. The issue is described as a ratio to the investors' existing holding, e.g. 3 for 7. This gives the investor the right to purchase 3 new shares, at the subscription price, for every 7 he already holds. The subscription price is normally at a discount to the current market price of the underlying security. The first calculation to be made is for the theoretical ex-rights price. This is the price the underlying security should be trading at after the rights issue and is as follows:

$$\text{Theoretical ex-rights price} = \frac{m \times P(cum) + n \times PR}{n + m}$$

$$\text{New contract size} = 1000 \times \frac{P(cum)}{P(tex)}$$

$$\text{New exercise price} = \text{Existing exercise price} \times \frac{P(tex)}{P(cum)}$$

Where

m = proportion of existing shares.
P(cum) = underlying security cum-rights price.
n = new shares to subscribed for.
PR = rights price.
P(tex) = Theoretical ex-rights price.

> **Example**
>
> XYZ Plc announces a 3 for 7 rights issue with a subscription price of 227. The day prior to the shares being declared ex-rights the cum-rights price is 234.
>
> The theoretical rights price is:
>
> $$\frac{7 \times 234 + 3 \times 227}{7 + 3} = 232$$
>
> The new contract size is:
>
> $$1000 \times \frac{234}{232} = 1009$$
>
> The new exercise prices are:
>
> $$200 \times \frac{232}{234} = 198$$
>
> $$220 = 218$$
> $$240 = 238$$
> $$260 = 258$$
>
> The result is that the holder of an old 220 series call option will now be able to buy the underlying security at a price of 218 × contract size (£2,199), virtually the same price as the original contract. The writer's position is that although he must now deliver more shares they are at a lower price per share. If he is a shareholder he will be able to participate in the rights issue, while if he is not a shareholder in the underlying security he will be delivering the shares in the ex-rights form by purchasing them cheaply in the market.
>
> The holder of a put option will now be able to sell 1,009 shares at the reduced exercise price and the writer of a put option will be obliged to take delivery of 1,009 shares at 218 instead of 1,000 at 220.

Takeover

If a takeover is announced on a security on which traded options are traded, and an option is exercised, the procedure will depend on whether the takeover offer has been declared "wholly unconditional" or not. If the takeover offer is not wholly unconditional and an option is exercised, the underlying security is delivered in "non-assented form."

In the event of a takeover offer being declared wholly unconditional, then the terms of delivery will be in accordance with a General Notice issued by the Exchange.

Stock suspension

A stock suspension happens when the London Stock Exchange suspends the dealing and settlement of shares in a particular security. During a stock suspension a buyer may still submit an exercise notice, via his broker, to the London Clearing House (LCH). If it is possible to deliver the underlying security through the London Stock Exchange settlement system the settlement of the exercised option will take place on settlement day as usual. If it is not possible to deliver the underlying security through the London Stock Exchange's settlement system, then settlement will take place as per instructions laid down by LCH. These terms and conditions will be issued by a General Notice by the Exchange (LIFFE).

In the event of any stock suspension it is important that an investor knows what effect the event has or could have on his holding and the exercise procedures associated with it. If the investor is in any doubt as to his position or holding, his broker will be able to advise him as to the bearing of the event on his holding.

Trading rules/guidelines

Due to their versatility, futures, and particularly traded options, can offer numerous investment opportunities to both private and professional investors alike. The amount of risk associated with any option's trade can be tailored to suit the user's circumstances, but in order to achieve this, the user must understand as much as possible about options and just as importantly have a clear idea of what he wishes to achieve.

Information

The greater the investor's understanding of derivatives, the greater will be his chance of trading profitably. Educational material is available from most good book shops as well as the exchanges themselves. In addition many stockbrokers will provide their own in-house publications.

Objectives

Before entering into any derivatives trade, investors must have a clear idea of what they are hoping to achieve, not just using the contracts for speculation, hedging or portfolio enhancement. Included in the investors' trading plan should be:

- Expectations for the market/share price. Is it going up, down or sideways? If it is going up or down, how far is it going?
- At what level will the investor take a profit?
- At what level should the stop-loss be placed?

A derivatives contract is a wasting asset, so if the position starts moving against you and breaks through the stop-loss level, it is better to close out the position and accept a small loss. There are a number of sayings in the investment world and two spring to mind here. First, a small profit is better than a large loss, and second, sometimes the bears win, sometimes the bulls win, but the pigs never win!

The trading plan, once devised, should be strictly followed.

Newcomers to the derivative markets should consider conducting a series of ghost or dummy trades before committing any real money to the market. This will allow them to gain a "feel" for the market and ensure that their expectations, and just as importantly, the reasons behind them, are correct.

Which option

Once the investor has made up his mind as to the market and share price expectations, he is faced with the choice of which option series to use. The choice is as important as having the correct expectation for the market/stock.

If a small move is expected in the underlying security, an in-the-money series, which is likely to move penny for penny with the stock price, should be selected.

If a larger move is expected, an at-the-money or possibly a slightly out-of-the-money option should be used.

An out-of-the-money option should only be used if a large movement, over a short period, is expected.

Money management

It is generally recommended that no more than 10 percent of an investor's total amount available for investment should be used for speculating in futures and/or options.

The amount available should be divided into ten units with no more than two units being invested in any one trade or position. When any profits are made, either the size of the units can be increased, or the profit can be withdrawn from the fund, or a combination of the two. If any losses are incurred the size of the units can be reduced.

Keeping up to date

The derivatives markets are so fast-moving that keeping up to date can be difficult and time consuming, but it is vital to do so.

Taxation of options for private investors

For UK resident private investors, options are subject to Capital Gains Tax rules. This section gives a brief description. However, an investor should always seek professional guidance.

Just as the underlying securities are treated as assets in their own rights, so are traded options on equities and indices.

1. **Buy an option and allow it to expire worthless:**
   A loss arises on the date of the option's expiry.
2. **Buy an option and make a closing sale:**
   A gain or loss arises on the date of the closing sale.
3. **Buy a call option and exercise it:**
   The shares are treated as being acquired on the business day that the exercise notice is delivered. The CGT base cost is the exercise price plus the premium.

4. **Buy a put option and exercise it:**
   The shares are effectively sold at the exercise price on the day the assignment notice is delivered. The cost of the option, i.e. the premium, is an allowable selling expense.
5. **Write an option which expires worthless:**
   The premium is treated as a gain arising on the date the option was written.
6. **Write an option and subsequently make a closing purchase:**
   The gain or loss arises on the day the option was written. The cost of the closing purchase is treated as a loss.
7. **Write a call option which is subsequently exercised:**
   The shares are effectively sold on the assignment date for the total of the exercise price and the option premium.
8. **Write a put option which is subsequently exercised:**
   The writer acquires the shares on the day of assignment for a consideration of the exercise price less the option premium received.

The regulation and taxation of futures and options in UK funds

1. PENSION FUNDS

Regulation

With the exception of local authority superannuation funds, there are no statutory regulations governing the use of futures and options by pension funds other than those imposed by general trust law. However, before dealing in them, pension fund managers, trustees and their advisors need to ensure that the trust deeds do not prohibit their use. In the case of local authority superannuation funds, responsibility for interpreting the current powers in the Local Government Superannuation Regulations 1986 (as amended) lies with the appropriate local authority.

Investment guidelines

In the absence of investment guidelines determined by legislation, before dealing in futures and options, it is essential that guidelines for their use are agreed between the fund managers and trustees of a pension fund. LIFFE, in association with the British Rail Pension

Trustee Co. Ltd, has produced recommendations for "Investment Guidelines for the Use of Financial Futures and Options" to help fund managers and trustees determine the principles on which futures and options should be used. These guidelines are published in full in LIFFE's publication, *Futures and Options: A Guide for UK Fund Managers*.

Reporting and performance measurements

LIFFE, in association with William M. Mercer Fraser Ltd, has produced standards for the reporting and performance measurement of financial futures and options in investment portfolios, and in association with Bacon and Woodrow has produced a guide to the standards for pension fund trustees. The standards have been endorsed by the Investment Committee of the National Association of Pension Funds (NAPF) and the two largest independent performance measurement organizations in the UK, Combined Actuarial Performance Services (CAPS) and The World Markets Company plc (WM).

Taxation

The 1990 Finance Act clarified the tax treatment of futures and options transactions carried out by approved UK pension funds. It exempted from tax all such transactions, thereby enabling the managers of these funds to use futures and options without the fear of incurring tax liabilities or an unfavorable tax status of the fund. This has resulted in a more favorable tax treatment for futures and options than for the underlying asset. Profits on assets held on trading account are liable for tax as trading profits, whereas futures and options are tax exempt under all circumstances subject to the provisions of the Taxes Act 1988 dealing with the reduction of pension fund surpluses.

2. AUTHORIZED UNIT TRUSTS – SECURITIES FUNDS

Introduction

All Authorized Unit Trusts (AUTs) are subject to the Financial Services (Regulated Schemes) Regulations 1991 (the Regulations). The Regulations permit:

- The use of futures and options by all AUTs for efficient portfolio management (EPM); and,
- The creation of AUTs which are Futures and Options Funds (FOFs) or Geared Futures and Options Funds (GFOFs).

Efficient portfolio management

In broad terms, the Regulations for EPM impose two fundamental constraints on the use of futures and options by AUTs:

- Each futures and options transaction must be "economically appropriate," and
- Each futures and options transaction must be fully covered by the correct amount of cash or other asset to meet any obligation or potential obligations to pay for or deliver securities that could arise.

Futures and options must not be used for speculative purposes.

It should be noted that the use of futures and options by AUTs is also subject to restrictions which may exist in the trust deed or the scheme particulars of a scheme.

"Economically appropriate" transactions

Futures and options transactions are deemed to be "economically appropriate" if they fulfill at least one of three aims:

- reduction of risk
- reduction of cost
- generation of additional capital or income

Reduction of risk

The reduction of risk includes hedging existing positions and anticipatory hedging for receipt or expenditure of money which is certain to take place at some time and is anticipated to take place within one month. Where index futures and options are used for hedging purposes, the relationship between fluctuations in the price of the index futures and options and fluctuations in the price of the underlying portfolio (or the part being hedged) should be such that it is reasonable to regard the futures and options contracts as appropriate to be used in order to reduce risk.

Reduction of cost

The implementation of an asset allocation switch is permitted by a combination of the two techniques above, hedging and anticipatory hedging, provided the intention is to switch into the underlying assets within one month.

Generation of additional capital or income

The enhancement of returns includes arbitrage and writing options. Written call options must be fully covered by appropriate underlying securities. The fund manager must be both willing and able to sell the underlying securities, should the buyer of the call options exercise them.

Written put options must be fully covered by cash. The manager must be both willing and able to buy the underlying securities, should the buyer of the put options exercise them.

Cover requirements

In providing cover for futures and options contracts, securities funds must have the correct amount of cash or other assets immediately available to enable the fund to comply with the obligations or potential obligations of the futures and options transactions. Each individual futures and options contract must be covered. A position in one futures or options contract cannot provide cover for another.

The implication for options positions is that both long and short options positions must be covered in full (e.g. one long ABC put option must be covered by a holding of 1,000 ABC shares), except where two options contracts combine to create one synthetic futures contract.

Synthetic futures

The regulations recognize that the combination of two options positions can create one synthetic futures contract. In these circumstances only the synthetic futures position needs to be covered, and not the two separate options positions.

Synthetic futures positions can be created as follows:

>   Purchase call option + write put option = Purchased future
>   Purchase put option + write call option = Sold future

The two positions must have the same exercise price and expiry date.

Taxation

The 1990 Finance Act clarified the tax treatment of futures and options transactions carried out by AUTs. It exempted from tax all such transactions enabling the managers of these funds to use futures and options without the fear of incurring tax liabilities. This has resulted in a more favorable tax treatment for futures and options than for the underlying assets. Profits on assets held on trading accounts are liable for tax as trading profits, whereas futures and options are tax exempt under all circumstances.

3. AUTHORIZED UNIT TRUSTS – FUTURES AND OPTIONS FUNDS

Introduction

The Regulations have established a framework enabling AUTs to invest in futures and options, not only for EPM purposes, but also as part of the investment management policy of the fund.

There are two categories of the latter type of AUT:

- Futures and Options Funds (FOFs), and,
- Geared Futures and Options Funds (GFOFs).

The types of assets permitted to be held are virtually the same for both FOFs and GFOFs. However, there are important differences between them in the degree to which gearing is permitted. In particular, a FOF can only invest on a fully covered (i.e. ungeared) basis, whereas a GFOF as this name suggests can enjoy a moderate degree of gearing.

Futures and options funds (FOFs) – permitted exposure

Investment in futures and options is constrained by the requirement that such transactions must be fully covered by:

- cash,
- securities, or,
- other futures and options contracts

except those purchase options contracts that are transacted within a specified 10 percent limit (see below).

10 percent limit
Up to 10 percent of the value of a FOF may be used to purchase options (less the value of the fund invested in warrants), without any cover. Due to the nature of purchased options (the maximum loss is the option premium), the level of gearing achieved through purchased options (and warrants) is limited.

Cash and borrowing
A FOF may borrow up to 10 percent of its value. There is no limit on the amount of cash that can be held by the fund.

Fund assets
Futures and options contracts which could lead to the delivery of securities are permitted only if the security could form part of the assets of the scheme or (in certain circumstances) if they are fully covered and may readily be closed out. This effectively rules out transactions in commodity futures and options.

Geared futures and options funds (GFOFs)

Permitted exposure
Investment in futures and options by a GFOF is not limited by the requirement that all such transactions must be fully covered. This gives a GFOF greater gearing powers than a FOF. The extent to which a GFOF can gear is limited by the 20 percent "initial outlay" limit (see below) and the 10 percent limit (see below) and not by a specified limit on gearing itself.

20 percent limit
A GFOF cannot retain more than 20 percent of the value of the fund in "initial outlay." "Initial outlay" effectively means the initial margin for bought and sold exchange-traded futures and options. In the case of options (and warrants), initial outlay means the premium, where option and warrant premiums are paid/received immediately. Variation margin is not included in the term "initial outlay."

10 percent limit
In addition, up to 10 percent of the value of the fund may be used to buy options (less the value of the fund invested in warrants) without cover, exclusive of the 20 percent initial outlay regulation.

Cash and borrowing

A GFOF is not permitted to borrow, unlike a FOF. However, there is no limit on the amount of cash that can be held by the fund.

Fund assets

Within the 20 percent limit, there is no limit on the value of the fund which may be devoted to the initial outlay with respect to futures and options on, or related to any one category of underlying security, commodity or other investment. However, no more than 5 percent of the value of the fund should be devoted to initial outlay for over-the-counter transactions with any one counterparty. GFOF managers have to ensure that their investments in futures and options are prudently diversified. This requirement can be met by investments in futures and options which are diversified in nature such as broadly based market indices (for example, the LIFFE FT-SE 100 Index futures and options contracts).

A GFOF is permitted to invest in the futures and options on products and instruments which it is not permitted to hold otherwise, provide the transactions are closed-out before delivery or, in the case of involuntary assignment, provided the underlying asset is sold as soon as is commercially possible.

Comparison of futures and options funds and securities funds

At present Securities Funds (SFs) represent the vast majority of UK AUTs. There are some interesting comparisons to be made between SFs and FOFs and GFOFs.

- FOFs and GFOFs are permitted to execute, and maintain on a long-term basis, strategies such as tactical asset allocation and synthetic index funds, which are unavailable to authorized SF funds under EPM regulations.
- Unlike SFs, there is no limit on the amount of cash FOFs and GFOFs are permitted to hold.
- Both FOFs and GFOFs can gear through the "uncovered" purchase of options, a GFOF having greater gearing powers than a FOF. (GFOFs, in addition, can gear through the use of futures.) This strategy is not permitted in SFs.
- Neither FOFs nor GFOFs are recognized as UCITS under the UCITS Directive and so cannot be sold elsewhere in Europe under the "single passport" authorization.

Taxation

Since authorized FOFs and GFOFs are AUTs, the 1990 Finance Act applies to them.

4. INSURANCE COMPANIES

Regulation

Insurance companies are subject to the Insurance Regulations 1981, and the Insurance Companies Act 1982. The regulations do not prevent the use of futures and options by life or general business insurers. However, futures and options cannot be used in "link funds."

The regulations stipulate rules for the valuation of investments for the purpose of the DTI returns, which all insurance companies must complete to demonstrate their solvency. The DTI specifies which assets insurance companies can count towards their solvency margins, and in what proportion. Futures and options are not included in the list of recognized assets, except purchased options up to 0.5 percent of the value of the fund.

Taxation

In general, financial futures and options transactions are treated in the same way as the equivalent securities transactions for tax purposes.

5. INVESTMENT TRUSTS

Regulation

Investment trust companies are regulated like any other company listed on the London Stock Exchange and face no specific regulatory limitations on their use of futures and options.

However, the "income test" imposed by the Taxes Act requires that a substantial proportion of an approved investment trust's income, normally taken to be 70 percent, must be derived from shares or securities. Therefore, if an investment trust uses futures and options, care must be taken not to breach the "income test" requirement.

Taxation

As with other types of transactions, income, profits and losses arising from futures and options transactions can be treated as either capital or trading in nature under tax rules, depending upon the relevant circumstances. (All capital transactions by an investment trust are exempt from capital gains tax.)

> **Income, profits and losses arising from futures and options transactions can be treated as either capital or trading in nature under tax rules.**

The Inland Revenue issued a Statement of Practice (SP 14/91) in November 1991, which can be found in the Appendices, and which clarified the type of futures and options transactions carried out by an investment trust that would be treated as capital in nature.

"In general, a financial futures and options transaction which is clearly ancillary to a transaction which is not a trading transaction on current account will be capital."

(Inland Revenue, SP14/91).

In general, futures and options transactions clearly relate to underlying assets, which are themselves capital in nature, and are treated as capital. In determining the tax treatment for futures and options transactions, the Inland Revenue would consider whether:

- there is an underlying asset to which a futures or options transaction relates, and
- the derivatives transaction is for the purpose of eliminating risk or transaction costs.

Barings

On Friday, 25 February, 1995 Peter Baring, the chairman of Barings Merchant Bank, one of the oldest merchant banks in the City of London, went to the Bank of England to see Rupert Pennant-Rea, the then deputy governor. Eddie George, the governor, was on holiday, skiing in France. To Rupert Pennant-Rea's, and later the financial world's, surprise, Peter Baring announced that due to a rogue derivative trader in Singapore, Barings had totally wiped out its capital base.

During the next two days, Saturday 26th and Sunday 27th, the Bank of England, together with a consortium of leading clearing and merchant banks, attempted to put together a rescue package. However, it soon became clear that the total losses faced by Barings could not be quantified. At that time (26/27 February) the losses were estimated at close to £400 million and, not only could the losses not be fully quantified and capped, they would increase by £100 million for every 1 percent fall in the Japanese Nikkei Index. No one was prepared to take on such a risk.

Once the news of the bank's collapse broke, the reason for the situation was put down to a "rogue" derivatives trader in Singapore. Yet again the derivatives monster story raised its ugly head. However, as more and more of the story emerged and parts of the Bank of England's report were leaked, it became clear that the problems stemmed from lack of internal control within Barings Bank rather than any inherent risk with derivatives.

So how were the losses made and what went wrong? The so-called rogue trader in Singapore was 28-year-old Nick Leeson. While not in the same league or with the same lifestyle as some rogue financial traders, who have used their position and clients' money to buy yachts and private jets, his basic salary of around £50,000 plus expatriate package would have made life rather sweet. In addition to his basic salary, it is reported that he was in line for a bonus of £450,000, after one of £100,000 the previous year. While it appears that Leeson did not gain materially out of his trading, so theft was not the motive, how and why did such losses occur that eventually brought down one of the oldest merchant banks in Britain?

Nick Leeson was first sent to Singapore as the head of settlement for Barings Futures Singapore (BFS) but, after sitting a number of Singapore International Money Exchange (SIMEX) exams, was allowed to trade on the SIMEX market floor. Originally his job on the market was to execute trades on behalf of clients of BFS. By mid-1993 he was allowed to use Barings' own money to trade on behalf of the company. This is known as "proprietary trading" and is one way that a relatively small merchant bank can, potentially, make a great deal of money.

As part of his proprietary trading, Leeson was allowed to trade not just in Singapore, but also in Osaka, and Tokyo Japan. The idea was to take advantage of price differentials, on the same products, on the different markets. This would involve Leeson, let us say, selling a futures or options contract in Osaka at one price and buying the same contract in possibly Tokyo at a lower price. Essentially, this type of trading is risk free and can be very profitable. Unfortunately Leeson did not take the equal, but opposite position in the second market. He was, in fact, going into the second market and taking the same position as in the first market. Effectively, he was doubling up on the position and, more importantly, the risk.

By 1994, Leeson was reporting profits of over £28 million on his proprietary trading, which amounted to the majority of the profits made by the financial products group. So why was Leeson trading in such a way and why was he allowed to get away with it for so long?

One of the first questions must be, was Leeson a "fit and proper person" to be a trader? It turns out that Leeson's application to be a trader in London was withdrawn by Barings after it came to light that he had not declared or cleared two outstanding county court judgements against him totalling £3,000. Barings were aware of this when he was sent to Singapore and when he became a trader on Singapore International Money Exchange (SIMEX), but they kept quiet and backed his application.

Secondly, Leeson had only been trading a relatively short time before he was made head of Barings' derivative trading in Singapore. This lack of experience and understanding of derivatives and their markets led him to sell vast numbers of futures and options contracts on the Nikkei Index on the different exchanges.

Not only had he amassed a short position of 28,000 contracts on SIMEX and 16,000 on the Japanese exchange of Osaka in Nikkei futures, he had also sold them when the volatility of the market was near its all-time low. This low volatility of 12 percent then jumped to 25 percent, following the Kobe earthquake.

If the first two errors were not bad enough, Leeson was not just head of dealing, but also head of settlement. This is contrary to all good practice financial guidelines. It enabled him to hide any trading errors for long periods without having to account for them to anyone else. All traders or firms run errors accounts for trades that have been misdealt and are awaiting closure as soon as possible. Leeson's errors account was called Errors Account 88888. Eight being the Chinese lucky number! However, Leeson's error account concealed losses of over £350 million. (Knowing this, it is questionable whether Leeson, and therefore Barings in Singapore, ever made a profit. On paper, he is reported to have made £8.8m profit in 1993, the largest in the bank.)

As if the absence of these management controls was not bad enough, Barings' internal lines of communication have been shown to be in utter disarray, with no one person being accountable for Leeson's activities. Barings also had a number of warnings from one source or another over the last eight to nine months before the collapse.

In June 1994 an internal memo raised concerns about the confusion and size of margin payments by London for Leeson's futures and options positions in Singapore. Money was transferred, not just from London, but also by Barings' Japan office. These funds were borrowed from Japanese banks!

In August 1994 an internal audit report voiced concern at the possible risks of having the same person (Leeson) in charge of both dealing and settlement.

In January 1995 SIMEX wrote to Barings about the shortfall in margin payments for Errors Account 88888.

And finally, again in January 1995, Leeson was advised not to increase his short position in Nikkei futures, which he ignored.

While we are still awaiting the final report from the Bank of England, it appears that the biggest banking collapse in recent British financial history was due to the lack of internal control and management expertise, rather than the use of derivatives.

■ ■ ■

'All traded options contracts are standardized to allow easy trading on a market floor.'

Appendices

1 Derivative instruments: risk disclosure statement

2 IMRO notice to members – the use of index derivatives for efficient portfolio management

3 The Inland Revenue Statement of Practice SP 14/91

4 LIFFE index and equity futures and options

5 Contract specifications

Appendix 1
Derivative instruments: risk disclosure statement

The following risk disclosure statement is designed to set out the risks associated with trading in futures and options and must be signed by private investors before a broker may deal on their behalf.

This notice draws attention to some of the main risks associated with derivative instruments, that is:

- *options;*
- *futures – a binding contract to buy or sell at a future date, but at a price agreed when the contract is entered into;*
- *"contract for differences" for example, instruments linked to stock indices.*

It is very much in your interest to read this notice carefully. It has been prepared in compliance with the rules of the Securities and Futures Authority, the self-regulating organization recognized under the Financial Services Act 1986 that regulates the way in which we conduct our business with you in these derivative instruments. However, this notice does no more than summarize some of the main risks involved and additional or higher risks are inherent in certain types of instrument. You should also make yourself aware of the tax implications.

You should not deal in any derivative instrument unless you fully understand the nature of the instrument and the transaction you are entering into and the true extent of your exposure. You should also be satisfied that the instrument is suitable for you in the light of your circumstances and financial position.

The main point is that the risks associated with derivative instruments are usually different and can be much greater than those associated with securities such as shares, loan stock and bonds. It is possible to lose, quickly, the whole amount that you have agreed to pay in premium to buy an option. Futures transactions and the selling (writing) of options involve a risk of becoming liable to pay an amount considerably greater than the margin originally paid. Rapidly moving markets, of course, accentuate these risks.

The following are further points to keep in mind:

OPTIONS

Buying options

Buying options normally involves less risk than selling (writing) options or transactions in futures. This is because if the price of the underlying asset moves against you, you can simply allow the option to lapse (i.e. abandon) and your loss should be limited to the premium you agreed to pay to buy the option plus transaction charges. However, if you buy a call option on a futures contract and you later exercise the option, you will acquire the underlying futures position/contract. This will expose you to the risks described under "Futures" and "Contingent Liability Transactions."

Selling options

By selling (or writing) an option, you accept a legal obligation to purchase or sell the underlying security if the option is exercised against you. Variations in the market price of the underlying security can lead to liabilities and losses considerably greater than the premium received when the bargain was entered into. Moreover, you may be required at short notice to deposit additional margin to maintain your position. Failure to do so may lead to your position being liquidated and your being liable for any resulting loss.

In the case of writing what are known as "covered call options," the risks may be reduced in that you already own the underlying security you have contracted to sell. In the same way, when you write a "covered put option," risks are reduced in that you already hold sufficient funds to purchase the security you have contracted to buy. If you do not own the underlying security (known as covered call options), the risks can be unlimited.

Only experienced persons should consider writing uncovered options, and then only after securing full details of the applicable conditions and potential risk exposure.

Traditional options

There is a distinct difference between traded and traditional options.

Traded options are standardized option contracts which can be bought or sold on a recognized investment exchange.

Traditional options are contracts effected in the UK between two parties and it is normally not possible to sell or transfer their liabilities.

Two-way prices are not usually quoted and there is no exchange on which to close out an open position or to effect an equal, but opposite, transaction, in order to reverse an open traditional option position. It may also be difficult to accurately assess the value of an existing traditional option position or for a seller (taker or writer) to accurately assess the risks involved.

Certain options markets operate on a margined basis, under which buyers do not pay the full premium on their option at the time of its purchase. In this situation you may subsequently be called upon to pay margin on the option up to the level of the premium. Failure to do so may result in your position being closed or liquidated in the same way as a futures position.

FUTURES

Dealing in futures

Transactions in futures involve the obligation to make or take delivery of the underlying security or asset at a future date, or in some cases to settle your position with cash. On entering into a futures transaction, you will normally be required to pay a deposit or initial margin.

Variations in the price of the underlying security can lead to liabilities considerably greater than the amount of margin deposited by you. You may be then required, at short notice, to deposit additional margin to maintain your position. Failure to do so may lead to your position being liquidated and subsequent liability for any resulting loss. There is no limit on the loss you may sustain.

Options on futures

If you buy an option on a future and you later exercise the option, your risk will normally increase because you will then own a future which is a more hazardous investment than an option.

CONTRACTS FOR DIFFERENCES

Futures and options contracts on the FT-SE 100 Index or any other index, as well as currency and interest rate swaps, are referred to as "Contracts for differences" and carry the same risks as investing in futures and/or options. However, unlike futures or options, these contracts can only be settled in cash. Transactions in contracts for differences may also have a contingent liability and you should be aware of the implications as described under "Contingent Liability Transactions."

CONTINGENT LIABILITY TRANSACTIONS

Contingent liability transactions, which are margined, require you to make a series of payments against the purchase price, instead of paying the whole purchase price immediately.

Even if a transaction is not margined, it may still carry an obligation to make further payments in certain circumstances, over and above any amount paid when you entered into the contract.

If you trade in futures, contract for differences or sell options, you may sustain a total loss of the margin you deposited with us to establish or maintain a position. If the market moves against you, you may be called upon to pay substantial additional margin at short notice to maintain the position. If you fail to do so within the time required, your position may be liquidated at a loss and you will be liable for any resulting deficit.

OFF-EXCHANGE TRANSACTIONS

It may not always be apparent whether or not a particular derivative is on or off-exchange. We will make it clear to you if you are entering into an off-exchange derivative transaction.

Under the rules of the Securities and Futures Authority, off-exchange transactions which have a contingent liability are only permitted for the purpose of protecting your assets against currency fluctuations. You should also be aware that transactions in off-exchange or "non-transferable" derivatives may involve greater risk than investing in on-exchange derivatives, because there is no exchange market on which to close out an open position.

SEGREGATION OF YOUR FUNDS

We are required to hold your money in segregated trust accounts in accordance with the regulations of the Securities and Futures Authority, but this may not give complete protection.

COLLATERAL

Any stock which you deposit with us as collateral to cover margin liabilities for derivative instrument business will be held by and registered into the name of (joint nominee company). This is the nominee company jointly owned by (name of broker) and (name of clearing agent), the member firm of LIFFE though whom we transact all our derivatives business.

Stock held in (name of joint nominee company) will be pledged to, and under the control of (name of clearing agent) in accordance with the terms of a collateral lodgement authority. (Name of broker) are responsible for the administration of the nominee and will account to the beneficial owner for all dividends and will contact you whenever there are any capital events effecting a stock.

Any stock deposited in the nominee is segregated by (name of clearing agent) in accordance with our instructions and enjoys Trust status by way of this segregation. However, deposited collateral may lose its identity as your property, once dealings on your behalf are undertaken, and you may not get back the same assets which you deposited and you may have to accept payment in cash.

You consent to the use by (name of broker) of any security you deposit as collateral to cover the margin liabilities of (name of broker) to (name of clearing agent). You must understand that in the event of default by (name of broker), (name of clearing agent) may liquidate the said securities.

SUSPENSIONS OF TRADING

Under certain conditions it may be difficult or impossible to liquidate a position. This may occur, for example, at times of rapid price movement if the price rises or falls in one trading session to such an extent that, under the rules of the relevant exchange, trading is suspended or restricted. Placing a stop-loss order will not necessarily limit your losses to the intended amounts, because market conditions may make it impossible to execute an order at the stipulated price.

COMMISSIONS

Before you begin to trade we will provide written details of all commissions and other transaction charges for which you will be liable. Should you be uncertain about any charges not expressed in money terms (but, for example, as a percentage of contract value) we will provide, upon request, a clear written explanation, including appropriate examples, to establish what such charges are likely to mean in specific money terms. You should realize that, in the case of futures, when commission is charged as a percentage, it will normally be as a percentage of the total contract value and not simply a percentage of your deposit.

CLEARING HOUSE GUARANTEES

On many exchanges the performance of a transaction undertaken by us (or a third party with whom we are dealing on your behalf) is "guaranteed" by the exchange or its clearing house. However, this guarantee is unlikely to cover you, the customer, and may not protect you if we or another party defaults on its obligations to you. On request we will explain any protection provided to you under any guarantee applicable to any on-exchange derivatives in which you are dealing.

There is no clearing house for traditional options, nor normally for off-exchange instruments which are not under the rules of a recognized or designated investment exchange.

YOUR BROKER'S INSOLVENCY

If we or any broker involved with your transaction should become insolvent or default, this might lead to your positions being closed out without your consent. We will not accept liability for any insolvency of, or default by, other brokers involved with your transactions.

EXECUTION-ONLY SERVICE

Any transactions undertaken when using the execution-only service takes no regard of your individual financial circumstances and you must be aware of, and accept the risks inherent in, traded options and their uses. Any guidance given will be on the merits of a specific option, without regard to your personal financial standing or circumstances of any description.

FOREIGN MARKETS

If you instruct us to deal on foreign markets, we may instruct a broker in the country concerned. Normally that broker will not be subject to the rules and regulations of the Securities and Futures Authority and the exchange on which he effects the transaction may not be subject to such strict regulations as a recognized or designated investment exchange in the UK. Consequently you will not have the benefit of rights designed to protect investors under the Financial Services Act 1986, and under the rules and regulations of the Securities and Investment Board (SIB) and the Securities and Futures Authority. On request, we will provide an explanation of the protections which will operate. However, you could lose all that you have invested or stand to gain if the foreign broker defaults. We will not accept liability for any default of the foreign broker.

The potential for profit or loss from transactions on foreign markets or in foreign-denominated contracts will be affected by fluctuations in foreign-exchange rates.

I have received from you, read and understood the Risk Disclosure Statement set out above.

Signature of client................................

Date..

Name of client......................................

Appendix 2
IMRO notice to members

THE USE OF INDEX DERIVATIVES FOR EFFICIENT PORTFOLIO MANAGEMENT

The following is a notice issued to IMRO (Investment Management Regulatory Organization) members covering the use of futures and options for the purpose of efficient portfolio management.

Introduction
1. SIB's Financial Services (Regulated Schemes) Regulations 1991 permit unit trust managers to use a number of techniques for efficient portfolio management (EPM).

2. This guidance is in response to questions from the unit trust industry on the use of index derivatives under those Regulations.

The regulatory requirements
3. Part 5 of SIB's Regulations permits the use of index derivatives for efficient portfolio management purposes. Where such derivatives are used the relationships between fluctuations in the price of the index derivative and fluctuations in the price of the underlying portfolio must be such that it is reasonable to regard the derivative instrument as "appropriate" to be used in order to reduce risk or cost or to generate extra income. Speculation must be avoided.

4. Where index derivatives are used cover may be provided by securities even if there is not complete congruence between the components of the index and the securities, provided that it is reasonable to regard the one as appropriate to cover for the other taking into account the closeness of the relationship between fluctuations in their prices

5. These requirements have given rise to questions in the industry concerning the relationship between the index and the trust property.

6. In considering the appropriateness of the instrument, management will need to be satisfied that it is economic, suitable and reasonably congruent. It is the matter of congruence which has resulted in this guidance.

What level of congruence?
7. Purposely, the Regulations do not attempt to determine whether there is any, and if so what, level of congruence necessary to satisfy the requirement that it is reasonable to regard the index derivative as

"appropriate." That can be determined only in the light of the individual circumstances of the case concerning a particular scheme.

8. For similar reasons it is not possible for IMRO to reach a view, in the abstract, on any particular level of congruence. Clearly the higher the level of congruence the less likely the manager would be open to any challenge that the index derivative chosen is not appropriate. Whilst it does not necessarily follow that a low level of congruence means the the index derivative chosen will be inappropriate, the derivative used in those circumstances is likely to require much higher justification. In certain types of funds it may be that no index derivative is appropriate.

9. It should be noted that it is not the intention of the Regulations to preclude the use of an appropriate index derivative that has a relationship with part of the property of the scheme. That is particularly so where the EPM technique is to be adopted in respect of part only of the scheme property, as will normally be the case.

10. Given, however, that it is not possible to be any more specific than this without reference to the individual circumstances of a particular scheme, SIB and IMRO consider that general guidance on the steps that might be taken to assist compliance with the regulations would be helpful.

Steps to take when using index derivatives

11. Consideration of these steps needs to reflect the respective responsibilities of managers and trustees under the Regulations. Broadly, the nature of managers' and trustees' responsibilities in respect of transactions in derivative instruments are no different to their respective responsibilities for securities transactions. The manager is responsible for deciding whether derivative transactions should be carried out, and if so, that they are entered into and remain in compliance with the Regulations. Managers must therefore be satisfied that an index derivative is "appropriate," based on their professional judgement. The trustee is required to review derivative transactions and determine whether he agrees with the view of the fund manager.

12. Whilst managers and trustee therefore have separate responsibilities for index derivative transactions, a degree of common understanding over what may be considered to be appropriate instruments to use in given circumstances, will assist in ensuring that managers are able to take advantage of the scope given by the Regulations to use index derivatives in a manner that is in accordance with the Regulations. In IMRO and SIB's view the following procedural steps may help to achieve that common understanding in situations where managers intend using index derivatives for EPM purposes:

(a) In determining the extent and manner in which index derivatives are used for EPM, the manager should set out why he considers the transaction to be appropriate. In-house "rules" should be prepared which identify, **on a fund by fund basis**, the instruments the manager is likely to use and the extent of such use.

(b) Managers should show these in-house "rules" to, and discuss them with, the trustee. Trustees are not obliged to endorse the "rules," although they may wish to give a view on whether they consider them as being reasonable in principle.

(c) Procedures should be established between the manager and the trustee that enable the trustee to monitor compliance with the Regulations. Such procedures will cover the details of any index derivative transactions entered into and the manager's justification that the transaction complies with the Regulations.

(d) If the matter is not covered by the in-house "rules" and the manager is in doubt over whether a particular transaction is appropriate, he should discuss it with the trustee before taking any action.

(e) Any remaining doubt should be discussed with IMRO.

13. The above is intended as a general guide on procedural steps that a manager might take when using index derivatives. It is not intended as a blue-print to be followed in all circumstances. Other approaches may well be appropriate in the light of the manager's own circumstances. Whatever approach is taken managers will need to review, as and when circumstances dictate, and in light of developments on indices, the instruments they regard as appropriate to be used in their funds.

14. This advice has been drawn up after consultation with UTA, TACT and LIFFE.

D J Leonard

Secretary   23 February 1993

Appendix 3

The Inland Revenue Statement of Practice SP 14/91

TAX TREATMENT OF TRANSACTIONS IN FINANCIAL FUTURES AND OPTIONS

Introduction

1. This statement sets out the Inland Revenue's views on the tax treatment of transactions in futures and options of the sort defined in Section 72, Financial Act 1985 and relating to shares, securities, foreign currency of other financial instruments. The principles set out are of relevance to:

- UK residents such as investment trusts, unauthorized unit trusts, charities and others (including companies) which either do not trade or whose principal trade is outside the financial area; and
- non-residents' collective investment vehicles (whether open- or closed-ended), pension funds and others (including companies) which either do not trade or whose principal trade is outside the financial area.

The statement does not apply to authorized unit trusts or approved pension schemes, whose profits from futures and options are generally exempt from tax.

2. "Financial futures" is a wide term. It covers:

- contracts for future delivery of shares, securities, foreign currency or other financial instruments;
- contracts that are settled by payment of cash differences determined by movements in the price of such instruments (including contracts where settlement is based on the application of an interest rate or a financial index to a notional principal amount), as well as contracts settled by delivery; and
- both exchange-traded and over-the-counter contracts.

3. "Options" include:

- both exchange-traded and over-the-counter options;
- options that are settled by a cash payment between parties, as well as those that provide for delivery; and
- warrants.

Relevance of trading

4. Section 128 Income and Corporation Taxes Act 1988 and Section 72 Finance Act 1985 provide, broadly, that transactions in financial futures and options will be treated as capital in nature unless they are regarded as profits or losses of a trade.

5. If, under normal statutory and case law principles, profits or losses fail to be treated as trading in nature the Sections 72 and 128 have no application to those profits or losses. It is therefore necessary first to determine whether or not the taxpayer's transactions in futures and options give rise to trading profits or losses.

6. Whether or not a taxpayer is trading is a question of fact and degree, to be determined by reference to all the facts and circumstances of the particular case. However, the Inland Revenue consider that an individual is unlikely to be regarded as trading as a result of purely speculative transactions in financial futures and options. Transactions in financial futures and options by a company may be either trading or capital in nature.

7. However, a financial futures or options transaction which is clearly ancillary to a trading transaction on current account will give rise to trading profits or losses. In contrast, a financial futures or options transaction which is clearly ancillary to a transaction which is not a trading transaction on current account will be capital.

8. A financial futures or options transaction that is not clearly ancillary to another transaction may be a trading transaction in its own right. Whether this is so will depend on all the facts and circumstances of the case. Consideration will be given to what are known as the "badges of trade." In such a case intention and frequency are important. The transaction will not necessarily be regarded as trading. It may well be regarded as capital in nature, depending on all the facts and circumstances.

Elimination or reduction of risk

9. In determining whether a financial futures or options transaction is ancillary to another transaction the following points are relevant:

- there must be another transaction;
- that other transaction must already have been undertaken, or there must be the intention to undertake it in the future;
- the financial futures or options transaction is ancillary to the other transaction if the intention is to eliminate or reduce risk, or to reduce transaction costs, in respect of that other transaction;

- the financial futures or options transaction must be economically appropriate to the elimination or reduction of risk, or to the reduction of transaction costs;
- the financial futures or options transaction may be ancillary to more than one other transaction, and more than one financial futures and options transaction may be ancillary to another transaction;
- it may be necessary to enter into new financial futures or options transactions or to terminate existing ones to reflect changes in the value of the assets or liabilities resulting from the other transaction.

These points apply to long and short positions and apply whether the futures are closed out or held to final maturity, or in the case of an options position, closed out, exercised or held to final expiry.

10. In considering whether the financial futures or options transaction is "economically appropriate" to the elimination or reduction of risk, the Inland Revenue take the view that:

- the transaction must be one which, by virtue of the relationship between fluctuations in the price and any fluctuations in the value of the other transaction, may reasonably be regarded as appropriate to be used in order to eliminate or reduce risk;
- the use of a financial futures or options transaction based on an index of some sort is not regarded as precluding the existence of such a reasonable expectation;
- it would not normally be expected that the amount of the principal on which the financial futures or options transaction is based should significantly exceed the principal of the other transaction.

11. A financial futures or options transaction may be entered into to eliminate or reduce risk, but the other transaction then falls away (or the intention to enter into the other transaction is abandoned). If the financial futures or options transaction is closed out within as short a period as is practicable after this happens the transaction will continue to be treated in accordance with the principles outlined above. If, however, the futures or options transaction is not closed out at that time it may be arguable that the profit or loss arising subsequently is of a trading nature. In practice, where the taxpayer is not otherwise trading, the Inland Revenue would not normally take this point in view of the taxpayer's original intention.

Base currency

12. The question may arise as to whether a financial futures transaction to buy or sell currency forward is ancillary to a capital transaction. In

Appendix 3

many cases the answer will be dependent on which currency is the taxpayer's base currency (that is the currency in which value is measured).

13. For UK resident taxpayers the base will normally (but not necessarily) be sterling. In determining whether there is a non-sterling base currency the Inland Revenue will have regard to factors such as:

- the currency in which accounts are prepared;
- the currency in which share capitals is denominated; and
- evidence of the taxpayer's intentions (for example in a published prospectus).

Examples

14. The following examples illustrate the above and are not intended to cover every situation that may arise. In the first eight, the assets concerned are held or will be acquired as investments and the financial futures or options transactions would normally be treated as capital (on the assumption that the condition in the first indent in paragraph 10 is fulfilled):

(1) A taxpayer which holds gilts sells gilt futures to protect the value of its capital in the event of a fall in the value of gilt-edged securities generally.

(2) A taxpayer which intends to purchase an asset does so in two stages, by (a) purchasing a foreign currency future in advance of an asset denominated in that currency, or (b) purchasing an option in respect of an underlying asset as a first step towards the acquisition of the asset itself.

(3) A taxpayer which holds a broadly based portfolio of UK equities sells FT-SE 100 Index futures or purchases FT-SE 100 Index put options to protect against the risk to the value of the portfolio from a fall in the market.

(4) A taxpayer holding foreign currency assets acquires a futures or options contract to reduce the risk of a fall in the value of the foreign currency assets (as measured in the taxpayer's base currency).

(5) A taxpayer which is intending to acquire a broad range of UK securities buys a call option on an FT-SE 100 Index to protect against a rise in the price of the securities in the period before they can be acquired.

(6) A taxpayer sells or buys options or futures as an incidental and temporary part of a change in investment strategy (e.g. changing the ratio of gilts and equities).

(7) A taxpayer either has existing liabilities (e.g. loans) denominated in a currency other than its base currency or expects to incur such liabilities

(e.g. as a result of an intention to borrow to acquire investments) and uses a futures or options contract to protect itself against a rise in the currency in which the liabilities are or will be denominated.

(8) A taxpayer whose base currency is the dollar holds yen-denominated securities and, in order to eliminate the perceived risk of a fall in their value, enters a forward contract to sell for dollars an amount of yen equivalent to the yen value of the securities. (This is because the forward contract may be regarded as ancillary to the transaction in securities.)

15. The next two examples involve financial futures or options transactions which would be treated as trading (because they would be ancillary to other trading transactions):

(9) A taxpayer's futures or options transactions are incidental to its trading activity, for example, a manufacturer entering into transactions to reduce risk of fluctuations in the price of raw materials. (The profits and losses from these transactions would be taken into account as part of the profits and losses of the trade.)

(10) A taxpayer has borrowed money at a floating rate of interest, for trade purposes, and enters into an interest rate future or option with a view to protecting itself against rises in interest rates. (Receipts or payments relating to the future or option would be taken into account as trading income or expenditure on current account. This is because the future or option is ancillary to a trading transaction, i.e. the payment of interest for trade purposes. Given this it does not matter whether or not the borrowing is on capital account.)

16. Finally, the examples below illustrate circumstances where a taxpayer's transactions in financial futures and options will not generally be regarded as ancillary to another transaction. It is therefore necessary to look at the transactions in their own right to see whether they are to be treated as capital or as trading transactions.

(11) A taxpayer uses futures and options in conjunction with a holding of cash, bonds etc. so as to create synthetic assets. (On the assumption that, in such circumstances, the financial futures or options transactions cannot all be shown to be ancillary to other transactions.)

(12) A taxpayer uses futures and options to take a position in a currency in which it does not have a portfolio and has no intention of acquiring a portfolio, so as to create an exposure to fluctuations in that currency, by reference to its base currency.

(13) A taxpayer whose base currency is sterling holds yen-denominated securities and, in order to eliminate the perceived risk of a fall in their

value, enters a financial futures transaction to sell for dollars an amount of yen equivalent to the yen value of the securities. There is no intention of selling the yen-denominated securities and using the proceeds to acquire dollar-denominated securities. (The effect of the financial futures transaction is to *increase* the taxpayer's dollar exposure as well as to *decrease* its yen exposure.)

Approval of an Investment Trust under Section 842 ICTA 1988

17. Section 842 (1) (a) Income and Corporation Taxes Act 1988 provides that the Board of Inland Revenue shall not approve any company as an investment trust unless the company's income is derived wholly or mainly from shares or securities (in practice taken as 70 percent or more). In the Revenue's view, any profit on a financial futures or options transaction which falls to be treated as a revenue nature would constitute income not derived from shares or securities.

18. The Inland Revenue will be prepared to review any case where an investment trust infringes the test in Section 842 (1) (a) in consequence only of a profit on a financial futures or options transaction being treated as of a revenue nature for tax purposes, and the infringement of the test is an isolated occurrence and the trust income derived from shares or securities for the accounting period does not fall below 70 percent. But the Revenue can give no categoric and universal assurance that, in such circumstances, a trust will never lose its approved status.

Appendix 4
LIFFE Index and Equity Futures and Options

Jan Apr Jul Oct	Feb May Aug Nov	Mar Jun Sep Dec
Allied Domecq	BAT Industries	Abbey National
Argyll Group	BTR	Amstrad
Asda	British Aerospace	Barclays
BAA	British Telecom	Blue Circle
Bass	Cadbury Sch	British Gas
BP	GEC	Dixons
SmKln Beecham	Grand Met	Fisons
Boots	Guinness	Forte
British Airways	Hanson	Glaxo
British Steel	Ladbroke	Hillsdown
Cable & Wireless	LASMO	Lonrho
Courtaulds	Lucas Inds	National Power
Commercial Union	P & O	Scottish Power
Glaxo	Pilkington	Sears
HSBC	Prudential	TSB
ICI	RTZ	Tarmac
Kingfisher	Redland	Thorn EMI
Land Securities	Rolls-Royce	Tomkins
Marks & Spencer	Royal Ins	Wellcome
NatWest Bank	Tesco	
PowerGen	Vodafone	
Reuters	Utd Biscuits	
Sainsbury J	Williams Hld	
Shell		
Std Chartered		
Storehouse		
Thames Water		
Traf House		
Zeneca		

Appendix 4

FT-SE 100 Futures

Mar, Jun, Sep and Dec

FT-SE 100 (American Exercise)

Four Closest Months + Jun Dec

FT-SE 100 (European Exercise)

Mar, Jun, Sep, Dec + Two Additional Near Months

Appendix 5
Contract specifications

All traded options contracts are standardized to allow easy trading on a market floor. This means there is no lengthy and time-consuming negotiation about what is being traded, the life of the option or its exercise price.

Type of Option	UK Equity Options	FT-SE 100 (American exercise)	FT-SE 100 (European exercise)
Based on	Ordinary shares of 72 leading UK companies	Financial Times – Stock Exchange 100 Index	Financial Times – Stock Exchange 100 Index
Normal contract size	1,000 shares	Index value x £10	Index value x £10
Expiry cycle	1. Jan, Apr, Jul, Oct. 2. Feb, May, Aug, Nov. 3. Mar, Jun, Sep, Dec.	Nearest four months plus June and Dec.	Mar, Jun, Sept, Dec plus two additional near months.
Maximum life	9 months	12 months	12 months
Exercise times	Until 17.20 on any business day. Extended to 18.00 on any last trading day.	16.31 on any business day. Extended to 18.00 on the last day of trading	18.00 only on expiry day
Expiry day & time	16.10. Normally the third Wednesday of the expiry month.	10.30. Third Friday of the expiry month	10.30 Third Friday of the expiry month.
Quotation	Pence per share	Index points	Index points
Trading hours	08.35 – 16.10	08.35 – 16.10	08.35 – 16.10

GLOSSARY

Abandon To allow an option to expire without exercising or trading it.

American Option An option that can be exercised at any time during its life.

Arbitrage The trading in two or more instruments to establishment of risk-free profit.

Ask Price The price at which market makers will sell. Also known as the "offer price."

Assignment A notice from the Clearing House notifying the writer of an option that he has been exercised against and deliver (calls) or take delivery of (puts) the underlying security.

At-The-Money An option whose exercise price is the same or almost the same as the underlying security price.

Bar Chart A chart plotting the daily high, low and closing prices of a security.

Bear Spread A spread designed to make a limited profit from a falling underlying security price.

Bear Market A market in which prices are falling.

Bid Price The price at which market makers will buy an asset.

Binomial Pricing Model A pricing model first designed by Cox, Ross and Rubinstein.

Black-Scholes Pricing Model An options pricing model designed by Fischer Black and Myron Scholes.

Bonus Issue See capitalization issue.

Bottom A low for a security or a market.

Break-Even Point The price at which an option position will neither make or lose money.

Broker An individual who transacts business on the options market on behalf of clients.

Bullspread A spread designed to make a limited profit from a rising underlying security price.

Bull Market A market in which the prices are rising.

Butterfly Spread A combination of a bull and bear spread using three different exercise prices.

Buyer An investor whose first trade is to purchase an option. Also known as a "holder" or "being long."

Cabinet Bid A bid of 1p for a whole contract which is deep out-of-the-money.

Calendar Spread A spread involving the simultaneous sale of a near-dated option with the purchase of a longer-dated option. Also known as "horizontal" or "time spread."

Call Option The right, but not the obligation, to buy an asset at an agreed price on or before a given date.

Capitalization Issue The issue of new shares, fully paid for out of company reserves, to existing shareholders.

Cash Market The market in the underlying security on which the futures or options contract is based.

Cash Settlement The process of settling an exercised future or options contract by the payment of receipt or cash.

Clearing House A company responsible for the registration, settlement and the exercise of traded options business.

Class All options of the same type pertaining to the same underlying security. Calls and puts from different classes.

Closing Purchase A transaction in which the writer of an option buys back an option identical to the one sold, thereby extinguishing any obligations.

Closing Sale A transaction in which a buyer sells an option identical to the one held, extinguishing his rights as a holder.

Combination A spread created by purchasing a call and a put on the same underlying security, but with different exercise prices.

Contract All traded options are bought and sold in contracts. Each contract, for UK equity-traded options, normally representing 1,000 shares. Fractions of contracts cannot be traded.

Convergence The process by which the futures price moves towards the price of the underlying security as the expiry of the futures contract approaches.

Covered Call Write The writing of a call option against a long position in the underlying security.

Glossary

Covered Put Write The writing of a put option against either the short sale of the underlying security or a cash holding sufficient to purchase the stock if assigned.

Cox Ross and Rubinstein Pricing Model A binomial pricing model designed by Cox, Ross and Rubinstein.

Crowd A group of market traders for one particular sector.

Cum A security that comes with all rights and payments.

Delta A measure of the amount an options fair price will change for a 1p change in the underlying security.

Delta Hedge A hedge in which the amount of contracts purchased is determined by the Delta of the option.

Diagonal Spread A spread in which the exercise price and expiry dates of the options differ.

Delivery The act of settlement for an exercised futures contract.

Discount The amount by which the futures or options contract is priced below the theoretical value of the contract.

Dividend A payment, from the company's post-tax profits, made by a company to its shareholders.

Dividend Cover The number of times that a dividend is covered by available profits.

Early Exercise The exercise of an option before its expiry date.

Earnings Per Share The amount of profit attributed to shareholders divided by the number of shares in issue.

Earnings Yield The earnings per share as a percentage of the current market price.

EDSP Exchange Delivery Settlement Price – the price set by the exchange for the settlement of the futures or options contract.

European Option An option that can be exercised only at expiry.

Exercise The act, by the holder of an option, to exercise his right and purchase (call) or sell (put) the underlying security.

Exercise Notice A formal notification by a stockbroker to the Clearing House that his client wishes to exercise his rights and purchase (call) or sell (put) the underlying security.

Exercise Price The price at which the holder may buy or sell the underlying security. Exercise prices are set by the exchange in accordance with their rules and regulations.

Expiry Cycle The three different cycles for expiry dates.

Expiry Date The last day on which an option may be exercised or traded.

Fair Value The theoretical price of an option derived from a pricing model.

Floor Broker An individual qualified to trade on the options marker floor on behalf of others.

Fungibility The ability to open and close contracts with different counter-parties.

Futures Contract A contract giving the holder the right to buy or sell the underlying security. Unlike an option, a holder of a futures contract is obliged to exercise the contract at expiry if the position has not been closed.

Gamma The amount by which the Delta of an option changes for 1p change in the underlying security.

Gearing The change in the value of an option when compared to the change in the underlying security.

Hedge An opposite position in options or the underlying security that increases in value to compensate for a fall in the value of the instrument being hedged.

Historic Volatility The standard deviation of an underlying security obtained from historic prices.

Holder An investor who opens or increases his position by buying an option.

Implied Volatility The standard deviation of an underlying security obtained from prices currently trading in the market.

Index Options Traded options based on the FT-SE 100 share index.

Initial Margin The initial payment made to the Clearing House by a writer of an option as part of the margin payment.

In-The-Money A call option whose exercise price is below the current market price of the underlying security or, a put option whose exercise price is above the current market price of the underlying security.

Intrinsic Value A call option has intrinsic value when its exercise price is below the current market price of the underlying security *or* a put option has intrinsic value when its exercise price is above the current market price of the underlying security. Any option that is in-the-money has intrinsic value.

LIFFE The London International Financial Futures and Options Market.

Line Chart A chart plotting the closing prices of a security connected by a line.

Glossary

Local A trader on the market floor who trades for his own account.

Long The position established by buying (holding) an option.

LTOM The London Traded Options Market set up by the London Stock Exchange to trade options. LTOM merged with LIFFE in 1992.

Margin Collateral required from a writer to guarantee he can meet his contractual obligations. A form of insurance in case of being exercised against.

Market Maker A trader who buys and sells securities on behalf of his firm's account.

Marking To Market The process whereby a futures or options contract is revalued daily for the purpose of risk management.

Mid-Price The price of an option or a security midway between the bid and offer price.

Moving Averages A method of smoothing out price fluctuations to obtain a clearer picture of price trends.

Naked Call Writing The writing of call options without holding the underlying security.

Naked Put Writing The writing of put options without either making a short sale of the underlying security or holding sufficient cash to purchase the stock if exercised against.

Net Asset Value The amount by which the assets of a company exceed liabilities.

Normal Distribution Curve A method of displaying the probability of different returns on an underlying security or portfolio.

Novation The process of replacing the counterparty of a trade with the clearing house.

OMLX The London Securities and Derivatives Exchange. Part of the Swedish OM Group.

Open Outcry The method of trading on LIFFE where all bids and offers are made verbally and are audible to all.

Opening Purchase An initial transaction in which an investor becomes the buyer and holder of an option.

Opening Sale An initial transaction in which an investor writes and sells an option.

Out-Of-The-Money A call option whose exercise price is above the current market price or a put option whose exercise price is below the current market price of the underlying security.

Over-The-Counter Options (OTC) An option, tailored to individual needs, not traded on a recognized exchange.

Pit An area of trading on a market floor.

Pit Observer A member of LIFFE exchange staff responsible for over-seeing trading on the market floor.

Portfolio The combined investments of an investor or fund.

Position The holding of an investor in a particular security. Either long or short.

Premium The price of an option, expressed in pence per share, paid by the buyer to the seller.

Price-Earnings Ratio The ratio of a security's price to the earnings per share.

Price Objective The level to which a security's price is expected to rise or fall.

Pricing Model A mathematical formula designed to generate a fair value of an option.

Public Limit Order A firm dealing instruction from a private investor that can not be executed immediately and is therefore left with the exchange official to execute when possible.

Put-Call Parity The relationship between put and call prices that implies the absence of arbitrage opportunities.

Put Option The right, but not the obligation, to sell an asset at an agreed price on or before a given date.

Ratio Spread A spread in which the purchase and sale of options is not equal.

Resistance A technical analysis term for a price level that the underlying security cannot break. The resistance level is always higher than the current price.

Rights Issue An offer to existing shareholders to subscribe to a new issue of shares.

INDEX

A shares 16
accounting procedures 188
accounts
  audited accounts 33
  broker accounts 186–7
  error accounts 32–3, 205–6
advisory services 25
American options 156–7
Amsterdam European Options
    Exchange 49, 85
Amsterdam Trade Centre 2
anticipatory hedging 180–1
APT (Automatic Pit Trading) 52–3, 58
arbitrage-free channel 163
arbitrageurs 10, 14, 78, 160–2
ask prices 48–9
asset allocation strategies 173–6
assigned market makers 44, 45
Association of Futures Brokers
    and Dealers 24
'at best' orders 48, 58
'at market' orders 48, 58
at-the-money options 112
audited accounts 33
authorization of investment firms
    37–8, 186
authorized unit trusts 196–202
  cover requirements 198
  economically appropriate trans-
    actions 197
  efficient portfolio management
    197
  enhancement of returns 198
  futures and options funds
    (FOFs) 199–200, 201–2
  geared futures and options
    funds (GFOFs) 200–2
  reduction of cost 198

  risk reduction 197
  securities funds 196–9, 201
  synthetic contracts 198–9
  taxation 199, 202
Automatic Pit Trading (APT)
    52–3, 58
Autoquote system 51

B shares 16
back offices 31, 186
Baltic coffee house 2
Barings Bank 31, 203–6
best execution rules 25
beta 168
bid prices 48–9
binomial option pricing model
    122–3
Black 76 model 74
Black-Scholes model 74, 119,
    121–2
Bobl 79
bonds *see* government bonds
bonus issues 189–90
Bretton Woods Agreement 3
broker accounts 186–7
broker dealers 31, 45–6
broker/client relationship 50
BTP 109
Bunds 79
buy write strategy 138–8, 181–2

C shares 17
Cabinet trading 47
call options 5, 103, 111, 119
  speculative trades 128–31
  strategies 126–8
  writing 133–40, 176–8
Capital Adequacy Directive 35
capital adequacy regulations 25

capitalization issues 189–90
cash and carry arbitrage 162
cash flow management 181–2
Chicago Board Options Exchange (CBOE) 3
Chicago Board of Trade (CBOT) 2, 52, 53
Chicago Mercantile Exchange (CME) 3, 52, 53
Chinese Walls 31–2
choice of options 129–30, 137–8, 149, 193–4
churning 25
Clearing Houses 61–5
  Financial Services Act requirements 65
  guarantee of performance 93
  information to customers 88
  Introducing Broker Agreement 89
  introduction of 3, 4
  and locals 90
  London Clearing House (LCH) 19, 50, 62–5
  margin requirements 65–9, 93–6
  membership 16, 65
  model A service 89
  model B service 89
  novation 64
  for OMLX trades 71–2
  registration of trades 64, 92
  regulatory environment 91–2
  relationship with brokers 89
  systems resources 90
Clearing Processing System (CPS) 62
CLICK trading system 8, 20, 21, 70–1
client money rules 27–8, 29, 91–2, 93
CME (Chicago Mercantile Exchange) 3, 52, 53
coffee house exchanges 2
collateral for margin 68–9
Complaints Bureau 39
Complaints Commissioner 39
Compliance and Audit teams 19
Compliance Officers 25, 28, 29, 30
compliance requirements 91
computerized random selection 64
conduct of business rules 27
contingent margin 68
contract specifications 228
corporate events 189–92
cost of carry 119
costs
  reducing 198
  of trading methods 55
  transaction costs 160, 163, 176
counterparty risk 4, 64, 152
covered call writing 135–6, 176–8
covered put writing 178–80
Cox-Ross-Rubinstein model 119, 122–3
CPS (Clearing Processing System) 62
crash of October 1987 5–6, 84
Credit Managers 33–4
Criminal Justice Act 30
cross-margining 74
Customer Documentation 91

D shares 17
dealing slips 59, 60, 61
delivery margin 68
delta 124–5
Designated Investment Exchanges (DIEs) 26–7
Direct Member Input (DMI) 61
discretionary services 25
diversification 167
dividend payments
  and futures pricing 159–60
  and option pricing 118–19, 133
Dojima Rice Market 2
downside protection strategies 139–40
DTB 78–9

E shares 17
EDSP (Exchange Delivery Settlement Price) 19, 156, 157–8, 161
electronic trading systems 42
  CLICK trading system 8, 20, 21, 70–1

Index

compared to open outcry trading 52–6
EMQS (exchange minimum quote size) 44–5
end users 78, 82–6
equity options *see* options
error accounts 32–3, 205–6
Eurodollar contracts 76
Euromark contracts 79
European Commission directives 35
European options 156–7
European Options Exchange (Amsterdam) 49, 85
European options markets 5
Exchange Delivery Settlement Price (EDSP) 19, 156, 157–8, 161
Exchange Members (EMs) 20, 21
exchange minimum quote size (EMQS) 44–5
exchanges 14
 Designated Investment Exchanges (DIEs) 26–7
 Recognized Investment Exchanges (RIE) 18, 23, 26–7
exercise prices 103–4, 120
exercise procedures 63–4, 133
expiry dates 104–5, 121, 157

Financial Intermediaries, Managers and Brokers Regulatory Association (FIMBRA) 23
Financial Services Act 18, 22, 25, 27, 29, 36
Financial Services (Regulated Schemes) Regulations (1991) 196–7
flexible exchange options 76, 152–6
FOFs (futures and options funds) 199–200, 201–2
Footsie (FT-SE 100 index) 5, 155, 158
foreign exchange 6
front offices 31
FT 30 index 5, 153
FT All Share index 5

FT-SE 100 index (Footsie) 5, 155, 158
Fulham local authority 34
futures contracts 106–10
 basis 158, 159, 162
 financial contracts 3, 76, 109
 index futures 82, 83, 110, 149–52
 and risk management 167
 margin requirements 65–9, 93–6, 108
 marking to market 93, 108
 order types 58–9
 order-driven system 57–8
 pork bellies 3
 pricing 158–63
 settlement 59–63
 size 110
 underlying asset 108–10
futures and options funds (FOFs) 199–200, 201–2

gamma 125
geared futures and options funds (GFOFs) 200–2
General Clearing Members (GCMs) 20, 21
generating additional income 148, 198
George, Eddie 203
German government bonds 79
Globex 52
government bonds
 German (Bobl) 79
 German (Bunds) 79
 Italian (BTP) 109
 Long Gilt Future 109
 long- and medium-term contracts 7
 market crash (1994) 54
Gower Report 22
guarantee of performance 93

'hair cut' 69
Hammersmith local authority 36
Hawes, Tony 84
hedgers 9, 14, 78
hedging 169–71
 anticipatory hedging 180–1

IMM (International Monetary Market) 3
implied volatility 74
IMRO (Investment Management Regulatory Organization) 23, 217–19
in-the-money options 112
independent traders 90
index futures 82, 83, 110, 149–52
  and risk management 167
index options 7, 75, 82, 83, 153–8
  expiry date 157
  and risk management 167
  settlement price 157–8, 161
information
  availability 86, 193
  from Clearing Houses 88
  systems 188
initial margin procedures 187
Inland Revenue Statement of Practice SP 14/91 220–5
institutional derivative use 83–4
insurance companies
  regulation 202
  taxation 202
insurance of portfolios 171–3, 174–5
interest rates
  Euromark contracts 79
  and option pricing 119, 121
  short-term contracts 7
internal controls 31, 188
International Monetary Market (IMM) 3
intrinsic value 111–13
Introducing Broker Agreement 89
investment advice 25–6
Investment Management Regulatory Organization (IMRO) 23, 217–19
Investment Services Directive 35
investment trusts
  regulation 202
  taxation 203
investments, definition 27
Investor Compensation Scheme 29
IPE (London International Petroleum Exchange) 9
Italian government bonds 109

Jerusalem coffee house 2
Jonathans coffee house 2
Jones, David 36

LAUTRO (Life Assurance and Unit Trust Regulation Organization) 23
LCE (London Commodity Exchange) 2, 9
LCH *see* London Clearing House
LEAPS (Long-Term Equity Anticipation Securities) 76
Leeson, Nick 31, 204–6
legal risk 34
Life Assurance and Unit Trust Regulation Organization (LAUTRO) 23
LIFFE *see* London International Financial Futures Exchange
limit orders 58
liquidity 77, 106
LME (London Metal Exchange) 2, 9, 33–4
local authority superannuation funds 195
Local Government Superannuation Regulations (1986) 195
local traders 57, 90
Locals Agreement 90
locking in a purchase price 132–3, 148
locking in a sale price 146
London Clearing House (LCH) 19, 50, 62–6
  see also Clearing Houses
London Commodity Exchange (LCE) 2, 9
London International Financial Futures Exchange (LIFFE)
  board of directors 17
  broker dealers 45–6
  broker/client relationship 50
  committees 17–18
  flex contracts 153, 154
  futures trading 57–9

Index

market makers 44–5
membership 15, 92
merger with LTOM 6–7, 92
open outcry trading 14, 42–4, 52–6
regulation and supervision 18–19
'seat' system 15–16
trading halts 50
trading jackets/badges 43
trading permits 16–17
see also option trading
London International Petroleum Exchange (IPE) 9
London Metal Exchange (LME) 2, 9, 33–4
London Securities and Derivatives Exchange see OMLX
London Stock Exchange 2
London Traded Options Market (LTOM) 4–6
merger with LIFFE 6–7, 92
Long Gilt Future 109

margin requirements 65–9, 72–4, 93–6, 108, 140–1
and capitalization issues 190
initial margin procedures 187
Market Advisory Board 21
market indices 5, 153–6
see also index options
market makers 44–5
market risk 166–7
Market Supervision Department (MSD) 18–19
Market Surveillance units 19
marketing derivatives 82–7
markets see exchanges
marking to market 93, 108
membership
of Clearing Houses 65
of LIFFE 15, 92
of OMLX 20–1
model A service 89
model B service 89
money management 194
MSD (Market Supervision Department) 18–19

Nagioff, Roger 32
Net Liquidation Value (NLV) 66
nominated market makers 44, 45
non-specific risk 166–7
novation 64

objectives of option trading 193
offer prices 48–9
OM CLICK 8, 20, 21, 70–1
OM Group 20
OM London (OML) 8
OM Stockholm (OMS) 8, 20, 71
OMLX (London Securities and Derivatives Exchange) 7–9, 20–2, 70–4
CLICK trading system 8, 20, 21, 70–1
cross-margining 74
dealing process 71–2
flex contracts 153, 154
futures trading 73
management structure 21–2
margin requirements 72–4
membership 20–1
options trading 74
regulation 22
OMS II margin system 72–4
open outcry trading 14, 42–4
compared to screen trading 52–6
opening rotation 46
option pricing 110–27
binomial model 122–3
Black 76 model 74
Black-Scholes model 74, 119, 121–2
Cox-Ross-Rubinstein model 119, 122–3
and dividend payments 118–19, 133
and interest rates 119, 121
intrinsic value 111–13
sensitivity measures 124–6
and share price movement 120
time decay 116–17
time value 113–16
volatility 117–18, 120
see also traded options

option trading
  choice of options 129–30, 137–8, 149, 193–4
  end users 82, 83
  exchange minimum quote size (EMQS) 44–5
  exercise procedures 63–4, 133
  flexible exchange options 76, 152–6
  margin requirements 65–9, 93–6, 140–1
  money management 194
  objectives 193
  order processing 46–7
  position limits 106
  price spreads 48–9
  settlement procedure 59–63, 108
  trading at Cabinet 47
  see also strategies; traded options
order-driven systems 57–8
out-of-the-money options 112
Over the Counter (OTC) market 152–3

Pennant-Rea, Rupert 203
pension funds
  investment guidelines 195–6
  performance measurement 196
  regulation 195
  taxation 196
performance enhancement strategies 136–8, 176–80, 198
performance measurement 188
  pension funds 196
Perrins, Julian 75
Personal Investment Authority (PIA) 23
pit observers 18
pits 43
pork bellies 3
portfolio protection 139–40, 168–73
  anticipatory hedging 180–1
  hedging 169–71
  insurance 171–3, 174–5
position limits 106
premiums 105, 108
price spreads 48–9

private investors' derivative use 84–6
Proctor and Gamble 34
product development 55, 75–81
  end users 78, 82–6
  feasibility studies 80–1
  general business development 86–7
  launching 79–80
  success criteria 76–7
  trends 76
profit/loss graphs 127
Project A 52
prosecutions 38
Public Limit Order Board 48–50, 59
put options 5, 103, 112, 119, 141–3
  hedging stock positions 144–6
  speculative trades 143–4
  writing 146–8, 178–80

quote vendor services 59, 188

Recognized Investment Exchanges (RIE) 18, 23, 26–7
Recognized Professional Bodies (RPB) 26
Registered Options Traders 46
registration of trades 64, 92
regulation
  authorization of firms 37–8, 186
  client money rules 27–8, 29, 91–2, 93
  Complaints Commissioner 39
  Customer Documentation 91
  framework 29
  insurance companies 202
  internal controls 31
  investment trusts 202
  key staff 31, 33–4
  of LIFFE 18–19
  monitoring process 38
  of OMLX 22
  pension funds 195
  prosecutions 38
regulatory bodies 14–15, 22–6, 29–30, 36–7
Reierson, Andrew 52

Index

reporting structures 187
Reuters 52
reverse cash and carry arbitrage 162
rho 126
RIE (Recognized Investment Exchanges) 18, 23, 26–7
rights issues 190–1
risk
  counterparty risk 4, 64, 152
  internal risk control 188
  legal risk 34
  management 95–6, 166–8, 176–8, 188
  reducing 197
risk disclosure statements 28, 211–16
Risk Managers 33
risk reward profiles 167, 168
Royal Exchange 2
RPB (Recognized Professional Bodies) 26

S&P 100 Index contract 75
Satterthwaite, Mark 28
screen-based trading *see* electronic trading systems
scrip issues 189–90
SEAQ (Stock Exchange Automated Quotation) 50
'seat' system 15–16
secondary market 4, 152
securing a selling price 139
Securities Association 24
Securities and Futures Authority (SFA) 15, 23, 24–6, 30, 36–9
Securities and Investment Board (SIB) 14–15, 22–4, 29–30
Self Regulatory Organizations (SROs) 23, 24, 30
  exemptions 26
selling options *see* writing
sensitivity measures 124–6
settlement periods 34
settlement procedure 59–63, 108
share price movements 120
size of futures contracts 110
sole traders 57
SPAN (Standard Portfolio Analysis of Risk) 66–7, 94–6

specific risk 166–7
speculators 10, 14, 78
spreads 48–9
SROs *see* Self Regulatory Organizations
staff
  and internal controls 31, 33–4
  trading for personal gain 32
Stock Market Crash 5–6, 84
stock suspensions 192
stop loss orders 58
strategic asset allocation 173
strategies 126–49
  asset allocation 173–6
  buy write strategy 138–8, 181–2
  call options 126–8
    speculative trades 128–31
    writing 133–40, 176–8
  downside protection 139–40
  generating additional income 148
  locking in a purchase price 132–3, 148
  locking in a sale price 146
  maintaining exposure 131–2
  performance enhancement 136–8, 176–80, 198
  portfolio protection 139–40, 168–73, 180–1
  put options 141–3
    hedging stock positions 144–6
    speculative trades 143–4
    writing 146–8, 178–80
  risk management 166–8
  securing a selling price 139
  walking up 131, 144
swaps 34
Swedish option market 8–9
synthetic contracts 198–9

tactical asset allocation 173, 176
takeovers 192
taxation 194–5
  authorized unit trusts 199, 202
  Inland Revenue Statement of Practice SP 14/91 220–5
  insurance companies 202
  investment trusts 203
  pension funds 196

theta 125–6
time decay 116–17
time value 113–16
'to-arrive' contracts 3
Totley, Jacqueline 88
Trade Registration System (TRS) 59–61
traded options 100–6, 226–7
  American options 156–7
  call options 5, 103, 111, 119
    strategies 126–31
    writing 133–40, 176–8
  contract specifications 228
  definition 102
  European options 156–7
  exercise prices 103–4, 120
  expiry dates 104–5, 121, 157
  index options 7, 75, 82, 83, 153–8
    expiry date 157
    and risk management 167
    settlement price 157–8, 161
  premiums 105, 108
  put options 5, 103, 112, 119
    strategies 141–6
    writing 146–8, 178–80
  underlying security relationship 106
  see also option pricing; option trading; strategies
traders 14
trading at Cabinet 47

trading halts 50
trading jackets/badges 43
trading permits 16–17
Trading Surveillance team 19
transaction costs 160, 163, 176
TRS (Trade Registration System) 59–61
Turnover Tax 8–9

UCITS Directive 201
uncovered writing of options 135–6
unit trusts *see* authorized unit trusts

valuation procedures 188
variation margin 108
vega 126
Virginian coffee house 2
volatility
  in foreign exchange 6
  implied volatility 74
  and option pricing 117–18, 120
  and product development 77
  and SPAN (Standard Portfolio Analysis of Risk) 66, 95

walking up 131, 144
writing
  call options 133–40, 176–8
  put options 146–8, 178–80